AN
OFFICER
and
HIS
HOLINESS

PRAISE FOR THE BOOK

'His Holiness the Fourteenth Dalai Lama and his entourage arrived at the Indian border tired, anxious and uncertain, after the Tibetan uprising against the Chinese occupation of their land, the bombing of His Holiness's palace and other major sites in the city of Lhasa. Mr. Har Mander Singh was then a Political Officer in North East India, and he welcomed His Holiness and his entourage. Mr. Singh's niece, Rani Singh, has written a book with detailed information. It is an account of a critical period for Tibet. It is a very special book with personal anecdotes and very important insights into His Holiness and her uncle. It is very readable and this will be a new addition to modern Tibetan history.'

Namgyal Lhamo Taklha, author and sister-in-law of
His Holiness the Dalai Lama

'In *An Officer and His Holiness*, author Rani Singh chronicles the fascinating and previously untold political intrigues around the escape of a young Dalai Lama from Tibet and the negotiations for his eventual welcome in India. Set within the political drama of India-China relations in the time of Mao and Nehru, Singh's interviews with the Dalai Lama and Har Mander Singh—the Indian official who greeted him at the border—read like an adventure novel, gripping the reader in a story that is both a moving personal testimony and an important historical record.'

Thubten Samdup, former Representative of
His Holiness the Dalai Lama for Northern Europe

AN OFFICER
and
HIS HOLINESS

How the Dalai Lama Crossed into India

RANI SINGH

EBURY
PRESS

An imprint of Penguin Random House

EBURY PRESS

USA | Canada | UK | Ireland | Australia
New Zealand | India | South Africa | China

Ebury Press is part of the Penguin Random House group of companies
whose addresses can be found at global.penguinrandomhouse.com

Published by Penguin Random House India Pvt. Ltd
4th Floor, Capital Tower 1, MG Road,
Gurugram 122 002, Haryana, India

Penguin
Random House
India

First published in Ebury Press by Penguin Random House India 2020

ISBN 9780670089192

Typeset in Adobe Caslon Pro by Manipal Technologies Limited, Manipal
Printed at Replika Press Pvt. Ltd, India

www.penguin.co.in

For Sukh and Jai

CONTENTS

Preamble: How and Why I Wrote this Book   ix

Prologue: Giants' Dance   xxi

1. Looking Back   1

2. The Early Years   7

3. In the Land of the Dawn-lit Mountains   24

4. The Warriors   35

5. Inside Potala Palace   43

6. Tension in Lhasa   54

7. The Escape   65

8. Mission Command   77

9. The Execution Phase   85

10. The Set Up   92

11. Getting Closer   100

12. Tawang to Lumla   108

13. Meeting Tenzin Choegyal, and the Chase   114

14. Dream Warriors and the Old Town   123

15. The Miracles   133

16. Across the Border   141

17. The Encounter   151

18. Lumla to Tawang   159

19. Tawang Impressions   170

20. The Orchid   180

21. Air Drops   192

22. Sela Pass   199

23. The Bomdila Club   211

24. Tibetans in Dehradun   227

25. The Dalai Lama and the Singh Family   236

26. To Tezpur   245

27. Reasons for War   257

28. Tibetan Trail   272

29. The Tibetan State   287

30. Influences   298

Notes   309

Acknowledgements   335

PREAMBLE: HOW AND WHY
I WROTE THIS BOOK

It had long been a part of my family's history that my late mother's only brother, Har Mander Singh and his team had played a small part in the Dalai Lama's arrival and first weeks in India in 1959. Of course, there were many more important people who supported the Dalai Lama and ensured that he escaped with his life from his home in the capital, Lhasa, in March 1959. Whole teams and governments across the world were involved in this dramatic story. This book is not designed to inflate Har Mander Singh's role in any way, and I know he does not want this. It is simply a reveal, a lifting of a curtain.

In any event, the young spiritual leader, the Dalai Lama himself, inspired the dedicated rescue effort that resulted in him being among us today.

This book is simply an attempt to record a moment in time when my uncle and his family were brought close to one of the most significant figures of the twentieth and twenty-first centuries.

I first heard about it when I was growing up. My mother, Parsan, would occasionally thread episodes about what had happened into conversations. She seemed to dimly recall, maybe not always accurately, how perhaps Har Mander and his men did not sleep throughout the journey to meet the Dalai Lama near the border and bring him back through Kameng, and how perhaps they oversaw the tasting of the food that the Dalai Lama ate during those weeks to check for suspicious ingredients. The anecdotes were part of family lore and took on a mythological aura. I felt that behind the anecdotes there was a mystery waiting to be unravelled.

These oral memories formed a hinterland whenever I met Har Mander Singh in India.

When I was young, my father Harbans took my siblings and me out of public school in the United Kingdom to go on an extended tour of India and Sri Lanka. At the time, my uncle was posted to Sikkim on behalf of the Indian government and worked closely with the Sikkimese monarch (the country was then a kingdom, independent of India). I remember staying with Har Mander and his family; my aunt Neena, cousins, Raj Mander and Harsh Mander, in Gangtok. I still have wonderful memories of wild, hilly, grassy, terrain, being fitted for and wearing the Sikkimese national dress (*bhaku*), and visiting the kingdom's informal, affable royal family.

I vividly recall a toddler prince running around in the long grass during a lunch with the royals and being asked to watch out for leeches that might attach themselves to our legs, only to find that later, when I went back to my room, they had done just that. I remember my uncle's large wooden home in Gangtok, with its veranda looking out over the hills. Fresh, green forests and crisp alpine air still stand out in my memory.

I also think back to visiting Har Mander Singh when he was Chief Commissioner of the Andaman and Nicobar Islands. We flew in a rickety airplane to land at Port Blair, ate exotic fruits at a big, round wooden table, and cruised the islands overnight in the chief commissioner's ship, *Tarmugli*. My sister and I appeared on the local All India Radio station. For our appearance we played and sang Punjabi Sikh hymns live on air.

At the chief commissioner's residence, the wooden rooms were huge, with big windows and shutters. Every day, as Har Mander would leave for work, smart, white-uniformed soldiers would snap into action and to attention, parading and saluting. We youngsters would run out to watch the spectacle.

But no one overtly spoke of the Dalai Lama episode; it just hung around quietly in the background.

When I was commissioned to write a children's book with stories from the Sikh World for MacDonald publishers, I put in a version of this book's narrative as the publisher wanted a story featuring an adventurous and modern Sikh.

I knew that it was important to have Har Mander's permission to work on the story someday. He doesn't like to talk about his work too much, so I got my mother to ask him. He agreed to talk to me for publication and to start going on the record. In 2005, I began to interview him.

One night, in January 2005, at the India International Centre (IIC), he sat with his late wife Neena and he talked to my two sons and me, allowing me to record him on a minidisc in our room there. I listened as he explained what happened during those eventful weeks in March and April 1959.

He had brought with him a beige folder labelled 'SECRET' that he read from.

That was the first time I saw the diary he wrote in 1959. The pages that had yellowed with time were magical to behold; they spoke of the history and adventure that lay hidden between the lines. I knew those pages were priceless, and that they were a true and special record of those times. I had no idea until a decade later just how valuable a journal this was. Har Mander allowed me to photocopy the diary at the IIC library along with newspaper reports his office had compiled of the journey.

I decided to start investigating the subject of Tibetans in South Asia and obtained a commission to examine the situation in Nepal for the BBC's World Tonight programme from its enlightened editor, Alistair Burnett. It meant making inroads into Tibetan-focussed organizations in the United Kingdom (UK) and Nepal, talking to the Nepalese government on the topic, and travelling to the Nepal–Tibetan border. It was one of my hardest assignments. The subject is sensitive there and few talk about it in public.

In 2013, I got the opportunity to ask former President Jimmy Carter about the situation regarding Tibetans while he was visiting his Carter Centre in Kathmandu. He gave me a full and honest answer—saying that Tibetans in Nepal needed more protection from the government as they are subject to persecution.

I was admonished by an official at the Carter Centre for my question after a Chinese official in Kathmandu lodged a complaint with him. When Jimmy Carter's quote to me made national headlines the next day, I knew that this was a story that needed further scrutiny. However, I got caught up with other BBC projects and put it on the list of things I would one day get around to.

Time went by.

In 2014, Har Mander suffered a severe stroke that left him debilitated. When I spoke to my cousins, Rajan and Harsh, I was told that his memory might be gone and that he was bedridden, severely weakened.

This motivated me into suspending most of my other work—particularly the reporting with the BBC that excites me and nourishes me the most—to focus on telling his story. I needed to gain an interview with His Holiness the Dalai Lama, so I put in a formal request through the very helpful and supportive London representative of His Holiness, Thubten Samdup. The Dalai Lama's UK office is his liaison for northern Europe and looks after the UK, Ireland, Sweden, Iceland, Norway, Denmark (including autonomous Greenland), Finland, Lithuania, Latvia, Estonia and Poland.

I was told that there might be a delay. Thubten loyally and persistently stayed on the case. Months passed but there was no news. Thubten concluded his London posting and left for his native Canada.

I turned to another well-placed contact in India who used his own network to leverage access, and I was asked to resend my letters to the Office of the Dalai Lama. I immediately received an apology for the delay in processing my request, and within just three weeks, I was granted an interview that was to take place in Dharamsala.

I spent a few weeks in India in May 2015, during which I interviewed the Dalai Lama and his youngest brother Rinpoche Tenzin Choegyal in Dharamsala.

On my second day with the spiritual leader of the Buddhist Himalaya belt, he allowed me into his private garden where, to the best of my knowledge, few journalists have been.

I also gathered material in and around the McLeod Ganj temple where the Dalai Lama was teaching a session.

Fortunately, with good care and twenty-four-hour staff, Har Mander Singh made a full recovery both in mind and body. If anything, he was sharper than before.

So, I was able to record Har Mander and his sons, Raj Mander and Harsh Mander, in his home with an audio machine in May 2015. Har Mander read from his diary and I got a visual recording of it for the very first time. He showed us his personal photo album, virtually the only full photographic record of those precious weeks after the Dalai Lama crossed into India. Har Mander had shared his photo album with the Dalai Lama whose office has distributed some of the contents to concerned parties. Many of the photos are reproduced in this book, some, perhaps, for the first time.

In the third week of May 2015, I spent three mornings with Har Mander drilling down into the story's details. Detail was important, as I didn't know when I would be able to meet or talk with my uncle again. I needed to understand the military-style abbreviations in the diary and the specific meanings of the seemingly obscure language he used, for my own accuracy.

So, in addition to my first recording and telephone conversations with my uncle, I now had primary interviews with the Dalai Lama and his youngest brother. I also had a good insight into the Tibetan community around the Dalai Lama in his hometown in India. The three critical interviews formed the narrative and substance of my work. It was enough for now but researching in the location of the actual journey, Arunachal Pradesh, was going to be necessary later.

I waited a year. I started to make inroads, and then learnt that the Dalai Lama was going to visit Arunachal Pradesh in March 2017. I had to go. Once again, I requested an interview with His Holiness from his office, and to my surprise, got turned down. A contact in the Indian government explained that the sensitivity of the Indo–Chinese border area dictated caution regarding formal interviews.

I trusted that something would turn out for me and set about finding support for the trip. Gradually, it all came together as contacts of mine plugged into their networks to help. I relied on them to find my accommodation. A team of guardians and allies came together to support me. It reminded me of 1959, when Har Mander Singh had gathered a team of his staff and village chiefs to help him during his important mission.

My idea was to follow the Dalai Lama for much of his trip through Arunachal Pradesh.

I arrived in the north-east to find Har Mander's photograph in several places, like Circuit House—a central building used for hospitality and meetings—in Tawang. Har Mander's name was well known in the state and there was a lot of respect for him. This reassured me and validated my work. Har Mander Singh's name seemed to be a touchstone in places like Tawang and Bomdila, and that slightly eased my path because locals realized the importance of my story. Suddenly, I could stop the lengthy backgrounders I had been narrating when explaining the project to people.

Visiting places in which the Dalai Lama and Har Mander Singh had been to together and listening to researchers who knew about Har Mander's role in 1959 was nourishing. It brought the story alive. One of my guardians in Arunachal, Koncho Gyatso, showed his sensitivity to the project. He conveyed to me the importance of investigating on the ground to find people who remembered what had happened in 1959.

The people on the ground and the key protagonists connected with this story are mostly in their eighties and nineties. So, recording the material in print is now necessary.

In November 2017, I was invited to India with my sons, Jairaj and Sukhraj, to speak about this book at the Valley of Words Literature Festival in Dehradun. Here I was introduced to the Dalai Lama's sister-in-law, Mrs Namgyal Taklha. Former Indian Ambassador Ranjit Gupta chaired our session. Mrs Taklha was very warm. She allowed me into the historic library she looks after and to interview her in her own room.

Two days later, the recording continued in Delhi with an emotional reunion between the Dalai Lama and Har Mander, held in secret to avoid a media frenzy (they have met from time to time since 1959 but not quite in this way).

It was the climax to several years of hard labour on this project. The bond between them was palpable, and from the moment that he met him, the Dalai Lama held his friend close. The Tibetan leader is tactile and playful, and this felt to me like a very intimate and personal gesture. During our interview, he also made a joke and, creasing up with mirth, tapped me on the head with a fair amount of strength to emphasize his point.

Much of the material for this work was gathered in interviews, with the subjects agreeing to talk on audio or on film for complete record taking and for the avoidance of error. This audio or footage was then transcribed, sometimes by others, but all checked by me for accuracy. I had all my chapters checked by experts in Tibetan matters, so I hope I will be forgiven for the remaining odd mistake as I am neither a historian nor an expert in Indo-Sino relations.

Though the facts in my book centre on the activities of the Dalai Lama and of Har Mander Singh, weaving it all into a narrative is something I did alone. There is no other writer or co-writer on this story. For its creation, I have kindly been given cooperation by certain members of the Dalai Lama's family and his office, as well as that of Har Mander Singh and his family.

As I release fairly intimate and private details to the world, I ask the public to fully respect the ages, dignity and privacy of the protagonists as they are of tender years.

Further, the Dalai Lama, Har Mander Singh and all protagonists gave me the gift of access in good faith and I hold that trust close to my heart with a closed fist. This story may one day develop further through different media, but in order to respect the sanctity of the relationships I have built I will supervise any representations be they visual or aural, so representatives for and the people in this story need deal only with me and need not entertain any other parties. No other party would have the authenticity that arises from a blood relationship and from a bond of history. I have a duty of care to all the relationships arising from this story and I will protect that bond.

All the interviews involved in the telling of this story, in whatever format, came about because of the work I did to create and develop critical relationships in India and the rest of the world. I registered my ownership of this story decades ago through official channels.

After my manuscript was completed, in 2019, I was granted a highly valuable interview with Sikyong Lobsang Sangay, President of the Central Tibetan Administration. I am privileged to have that relationship now and learnt much about the future of the CTA from Sikyong Lobsang Sangay. His office kindly enabled the witnessing of a session of parliament.

I add here some contingency clauses.

To the best of my knowledge, India did not grant the Dalai Lama and his family asylum in the strictly legal sense.

Also, since Peking and Beijing are old and new names for the same city—the capital of China—I have tended to use Peking when talking about old times, and only used Beijing in the present or future. The exception is if either name appears in a quote.

One of my fact checkers, Thubten Samphel, asked me to refer to the Dalai Lama as the 'Spiritual leader of the Buddhist Himalayan belt'.

Har Mander Singh provided permission for his diary to be reproduced in chronologically interspersed sections through my book and provided me with explanations in various separate interviews. His elder son Raj Mander was mostly present throughout our sessions. I have reproduced the diary exactly as it was written, with the spelling, grammar and punctuation as it was recorded in the pressurised heat of the moment. These may differ from modern day usage for obvious reasons.

One of my reference books, *The Crossing of the Frontier*, by the Losel Nyinje Charitable Society and the Monyul Social Welfare Association, has no page numbers.

This lesser-known part of the Dalai Lama's story is set in India but involves both China and the USA. By the time of the 1962 Indo–Sino war, other countries like Canada and the UK were involved as well.

French historian and Tibetologist, Claude Arpi, painstakingly compiled letters and documents and placed them on the Internet and in articles. They are authoritative and, together with other published works, form a helpful source for the narrative.

Why was I doing this work? Why should anyone, particularly young people, care about this story?

The Dalai Lama is revered by six million Tibetan Buddhists who look to him for religious guidance. He is also the leader of about 150,000 Tibetans who live in exile in India. The Tibetan spiritual leader is the most famous political refugee on the planet. His message of non-violence and his charisma attract global attention. His plea for peace earned him a Nobel Peace Prize in 1989. Being the spiritual leader of the Buddhist Himalaya belt and bearing such a religious aura makes the Dalai Lama a figure that it is important to write about. Also, the story demonstrates, above all, an act of kindness that needs reflecting in our conflict-ridden world today.

The line that the Dalai Lama treads is chosen carefully. He maintains his Buddhist philosophies, but has advocated a 'Middle Way' for his people. It does not mean, he indicates, that Tibet should seek independence from China, but simply autonomy within that country.

In the past, he has told western Buddhists, 'To be interested in religion you have to be involved in politics.'[1] With his own Tibetan Buddhists, however, he guides them and directs their behaviour.

With Buddhism being the fastest growing eastern religion in the west and with the Dalai Lama's Hollywood-style popularity, China, a powerful economy, is concerned. Since the Dalai Lama speaks freely to whomsoever he likes, China cannot control him, no matter what it decides to do in Tibet. And since the Dalai Lama is not only a unifying, but also a rallying figure, China cannot control his tremendous influence, whatever it may say about him inside China.

China refers to those who follow him as the 'Dalai Lama clique' and the spiritual leader himself as a 'splittist' or a 'separatist'.

But it is what China does internationally that makes the Dalai Lama such a critical figure. Even with a recent slowdown in growth, China is still the biggest contributing country to world growth since 2008, according to the World Bank.[2]

By shrewd and generous investment across the world, China has created a climate of dependency on it on every continent. Trade with China has been critical to Western countries damaged by economic crises. And despite a slight slowdown, the country has maintained a growth rate that far outshines other nations. With the dragon spreading its wings from Africa to the US, from India's neighbours to Australia, there are few countries that would not prioritize trade with China above anything else.

This creates a growing power base for China. It also creates a socio-political context that makes this book relevant today, with China and the Dalai Lama seeming to operate like players on the world's chessboard.

If the Dalai Lama is invited to visit a country and chooses to go, China rounds up its arsenal of economic links to apply pressure on that nation to rescind or reduce the importance it might give to him.[3]

This book comes at a critical moment that is tied to the Dalai Lama succession. It has been at least sixty years since he escaped Tibet. He has announced that the next Dalai Lama—if there is a next

Dalai Lama—will neither appear in China nor in any country that is not free by his terms.

China wants to find a way to control its six million Tibetans and has probably set up its own potential leaders-in-waiting. But Tibetans will always follow what their own leader says, for he was anointed in their lifetimes. They trust him.

This places the Dalai Lama's position on a knife's edge.

This is why this story is relevant today.

This is not a definitive work of high history and should not be viewed as such. I have written this book to provide a personal insight into the lesser-known part that Har Mander Singh and his team played in the larger narrative of the Dalai Lama's escape from Tibet into India. In doing so, I have also included reflection and comment from the protagonists involved.

However timeless a story, current events will necessarily overtake what is stated in this book. I hope readers will understand.

This book is designed to provide an impression of my attempt to gain insight into a small but critical part of one of the most important escape stories of all time.

I chose to write this story because often there is limited material on this part of the Dalai Lama's escape in mainstream published books. As I could not do much of my other professional work due to the intense research and writing needed for the book there was a heavy financial toll on me. Books like this often end up as an investment by the author and though I had no idea it would take so long or require so much work, I do not regret having volunteered five years of my life in service to this story.

In order to write this book, I arranged for a visual record to be made during much of the research period. That way, there was a collection of material recorded with a camera to help me recall exactly what was said, how it was said and where. Given the significance of the research, little audio and visual clips, together with my written notes and observations, are perhaps a modern version of Har Mander Singh's diary.

By the end of my project, I had collected a set of short visual and audio clips to use for reference that could perhaps be compiled by me one day.

This work comes from my very heart. I share it now with you. Please look after it carefully.

PROLOGUE: GIANTS' DANCE

The greater part of India was under the rule of the British throughout the nineteenth century. At first, it was ruled by the British East India Company, then by the Crown.

In 1876, Victoria was accorded the title 'Empress of India'. Around the same time, the British established and expanded a military presence in the country. As an imperial power, the focus was on creating and maintaining centres of domination where it counted— among the heartlands of the Indian people. It was where the rulers felt comfortable and were able to command and control.

Delhi, Mumbai, Kolkata and Bengaluru[1] all still bear the hallmarks of colonialism. These are apparent in historic clubs and buildings, inhabited now by the Indian upper class as they were, previously, by a British one.

The British did not bother much with outlying areas that would make for uncomfortable living and hard effort. Among such regions, the Himalayas were too cold and too wild for them. Higher altitudes, involving treks and sparse road access, were better ignored. Only tribal and local people lived there anyway, and the British had little interest in them.

Foothill retreats like Mussoorie and Simla, however, were fine to escape to from the summer heat. Families and retinues could be transported there fairly easily. For their occasional visits the Raj built solid, and by the standards of that time, luxurious buildings for themselves in these accessible hill stations. Many of these homes are still used by local governments and are now known as circuit houses. The bungalows also functioned as accommodation for British officers who travelled across India on authorized visits. These structures are particularly noticeable in remote regions like Arunachal Pradesh and are now used by local governments for visiting officials and town meetings. One example is the Tawang Circuit House in the Kameng district of Arunachal Pradesh.

By August 1947, the British imperial rule had ended. India and Pakistan had become independent nations. The Indian Independence Bill was hailed by the activist leader Mohandas Gandhi as the 'Noblest act of the British nation'.[2]

In the new world order, the then Prime Minister Jawaharlal Nehru had to tread a fine diplomatic line. From 1945, the country had been a founding member of the United Nations (UN) and its prime minister had great ambitions for it.

Gandhi's focus was on the common man; therefore, his post-Independence emphasis was to create a traditional, homespun India for Indians. In contrast, Nehru's focus was to drive the nation towards becoming the leader of the third world.

Nehru envisioned India becoming more like the European nations. He emulated the five-year plans of the USSR. During his seventeen years in office, a domestic planning policy was created, with a whole planning department formulating ambitious, five-year development programmes. Under this scheme factories, highways and railroads were built.

To some degree, India's foreign policy after the Second World War was influenced by the wider trends in international development, the reduced strength of the forces of imperialism and a rise in the power of democracy and progress.

Nehru's foreign policy was something he had been formulating long before Independence. It was based on the strict principle of non-alignment. He wanted no truck with any imperialist bloc, any global wars or any fascist tendencies.

This policy was laid down in an accord known as the Panch Shila Agreement in 1954. It established policies of non-interference in the military matters of others, non-aggression and mutual respect for each other's sovereignty.[3] As part of this agreement, India recognized Tibet as an autonomous part of China.[4]

Non-alignment was intended to help the countries follow their own policies while refraining from interfering in the internal affairs of other nations. The guiding principle was also to remain independent of the two major US and Soviet blocs. This would, Nehru's theory posited, allow India to build democratic strength. It did not mean, however, that the country could not accept much-needed foreign economic support; so, aid from the USSR (current day Russia), USA, Japan, Germany, and the UK was readily received. India was looking east, as well as west, for economic support, an idea that had begun a while before non-alignment kicked in.

The policy of non-alignment that Nehru espoused was new to the arena of international relations, but he found support for the idea from Egypt, Indonesia and Yugoslavia. Non-alignment meant that officials in Delhi felt empowered enough to begin drafting independent policies. It also meant that India and others in the non-aligned movement neither allied with ideological or hegemonic groups, nor did it offer any assurances that might involve itself in the wars of other nations.

India decided to side neither with the West, nor with the East, even though it was close to the communist bloc on certain issues. India sympathized with the communists on topics such as disarmament, but it also was occasionally critical of North Korean aggression.

In 1947, India convened an Asian Relations Conference in Delhi, which was attended by twenty-nine nations. Tibet was invited, despite a protest by China.

India was laying down the foundation for a mightier version of itself—its ambition to become leader of the then third world was by now clear. Key conferences such as the Asian Relations one brought country leaders together and helped build a support network.

An Afro-Asian Conference on non-alignment, where Nehru was also present, took place in 1955 in Bandung, Indonesia. It allowed further dissemination of the idea. The newly independent nations of Ghana, Indonesia and India were the prominent leaders of the Third World Movement and Nehru assumed the role of *primus inter pares*. India was still an integral part of the UN and the Commonwealth. This allowed it to be independent, but at the same time to cooperate with other countries after due consideration.

The need of the hour for India was self-preservation and self-protection. The non-alignment policy never precluded self-defence but it did hinder seeking military assistance from other states. In particular, it prevented taking help from those who took a side in the Cold War struggle.

*

Across the border, China's territorial ambition meant that all physical communication routes were open so that it could extend its presence in the world.

In the land mass that they had ready access to, the ancient Silk Route (or Road) assumed importance as one that must be revived and strengthened to achieve the spheres of influence that China sought. It achieved it over the next few decades.

From the time of the Han Dynasty (206 BC–220 AD), the Silk Road had been a trade route that crossed from China right through to Eastern Europe. It traversed the northern borders of China, India and Persia until it met Eastern Europe near what is now Turkey and the Mediterranean Sea. There are several routes that comprise this network, starting in north-west China, extending to Pakistan, India and eventually, Rome.

In ancient times, Chinese silk was one of the most important products for trade. Asia and Europe valued this luxuriously soft material. Silk had been sold in China for thousands of years, dating back to Roman times, when the country was dubbed the 'land of silk'. So naturally, reviving the Silk Route was integral to China's territorial ambition and featured prominently in its implementation plan.

Part of China's strategy was to stake a claim on an ice desert plateau in India, known as Aksai Chin, because it straddled a highway from Xinjiang to Tibet. Aksai Chin was probably occupied in 1953, though the occupation became official in 1958.[5]

Chinese pilgrims had been visiting India for centuries. At the same time, trade and diplomatic relations were also in place between the two countries. These had been set up by India after China's communist revolutionary victory over its nationalist government in 1949.

Both nations found common ground on many issues, such as a distancing of themselves from European imperialism. It helped that India had sympathized with China during the Sino–Japanese War (1894–95).

However, there was another side to this relationship. There was the ideological clash between the supposed democratic socialism of India and the revolutionary Marxism–Leninism of China. Each, in the context of the Third World, sought to prove its supremacy, and China certainly wanted to overtake India as the perceived leading nation of the Third World at the time.

*

Neighbours often rile each other, and in this case the cause for irritation between the two countries happened to be Tibet. In 1947, the Government of India had asserted what it deemed certain territorial rights over the region. China was already laying claim to Tibet, which hitherto had enjoyed a degree of autonomy.

Delhi asked Peking to sort out growing tension over the matter through peaceful discussion, but in 1950, China invaded Tibet. It claimed that the eastern plateau had always been an integral part of mainland China and that Tibet had paid tributes to its emperors. China also claimed that Tibet had signed agreements that proved its desire to be looked after by the 'Motherland'. The larger power declared that as the Tibetans had not fought for autonomy, it followed that they could never have wanted it. Ostensibly, China announced that it was important that Tibet's religious leaders should partner with Peking, though all due respect needed to be shown to the head of the Tibetan Buddhist faith. China said it was a tolerant nation. Thereafter, a department called Chinese Internal Affairs took over jurisdiction of Tibetan matters.

The key reason for the disagreement between India and China was that contrary to India's perception of matters, the Chinese saw themselves as leaders of the new world order. They therefore expected— indeed demanded—the prestige, respect and servitude that went along with it.

When China overran Tibet, partly as a way of securing its western flank, India did not react. Instead, elephant-like Delhi sat and waited patiently for the aggression to abate.

It did not. Instead, it grew in intensity.

During the 1950s, Chinese premier Zhou Enlai had been on two 'goodwill' visits to India. But Zhou Enlai's polite gestures at diplomatic meetings had not stopped him from laying claim to India's vulnerable northern flanks outside of these discussions: Ladakh and territories in the NEFA, now known as Arunachal Pradesh. Moreover, China was eyeing Barahoti in Uttar Pradesh, just south of Tibet. Indian troops were based there, and when Chinese soldiers tried to cross the southern border into India, the elephant finally protested. But the dragon did not blink.

In the late 1950s, China denounced the McMahon Line, challenging its international validity. At the end of that year, Zhou Enlai visited Nehru in India with soothing words, assuring him that the border issue with Tibet would be resolved peacefully. In that same meeting, China also recognized the Indian boundary with Burma.

By that time, Chinese soldiers were actually in Barahoti and had marched ten miles into Indian territory. The latter had taken too passive a role and now sat helpless as the dragon advanced, fired up.

The following year, talks took place between the two countries. China was persuaded to withdraw its military but left its civilians in the territory.

In January 1959, Zhou Enlai formally claimed Ladakh and NEFA for his country, giving orders for his command to be reflected in Chinese maps.

Just four years earlier, India had formally handed over control of communication services in Tibet to China. When the Tibetan Buddhist leader, the Dalai Lama, asked Nehru for refuge in India because of increasing Chinese pressure on him and the Tibetan people, Nehru who was balanced precariously on a political tightrope, chose to side with Peking and refused the request.

By March 1959, the eyes of the world were on the highly charged power plays. Following a crackdown on the Tibetan capital of Lhasa by the People's Liberation Army (PLA), the Dalai Lama managed to escape possible capture and containment. He again sought refuge in India.

Aside from the loyalty of his own Tibetan followers, the gentle young Buddhist leader was popular in India, with much of the country sympathetic to his plight after China's invasion of Tibet.

The Indian prime minister was in a fix. He did not want to antagonize China, which was building a formidable military might.

On 30 March 1959, Nehru told the Lok Sabha, the lower house of parliament, that a large group of Tibetans would not be allowed to cross the border into India should they apply for permission. It was a sop to the Chinese regime.

But among Indians there was a groundswell of opinion in favour of the Tibetans. There were many Buddhists, too, among India's diverse population, and their sympathies lay with the spiritual leader.

Nehru's dilemma was clear. Indian opinion and the media overwhelmingly condemned China's invasion of Tibet. The Indian government was caught between not antagonizing China and taking account of Indian sentiment and opinion.

While Jawaharlal Nehru was mulling over this dilemma, a message, in the form of a directive, arrived from Washington.

The US, specifically the Central Intelligence Agency (CIA), had for some time been closely involved with a Tibetan rebellion against the Chinese. They saw it as a way of hindering the advance of communism and had been training Tibetan guerrillas in the US. Several of these rebels had been dropped back into Tibet, and two of them were tasked with liaising with the Dalai Lama. They were instructed with ascertaining his movements, his plans for escape and to report to Washington on these matters. Most importantly, they were asked to find out if the Dalai Lama had a country to escape to, i.e., India. These two Tibetans liaised with the official in charge of the Dalai Lama's household, and it was he who told them, during the last dramatic days of March 1959, that no official permission had arrived for the Dalai Lama to enter India.

The CIA-trained Tibetan rebels relayed this information to Washington, and the CIA took immediate action. One of its former senior officers told author Mikel Dunham, 'Specifically, it [a correspondence] went quickly from the Agency, to the State Department, to the White House, and finally to Prime Minister Nehru.'[6]

How the Dalai Lama escaped from Lhasa with the help of the Tibetans and the CIA, how he crossed the Indian border and travelled through still—dangerous Himalayan territory protected by a minimum number of soldiers—forms much of the content of this book.

Nehru's decisions led to a high point of tension between China and India. These decisions were: to give shelter to the Tibetans fleeing the Chinese takeover of Tibet, to give the Dalai Lama sanctuary and to recognize him as the spiritual leader of the Tibetans. China never forgave India for what it saw as a betrayal of trust and a lack of respect for Chinese sovereignty. The tension simmered until it soon boiled over into all-out conflict.

1

LOOKING BACK

From the tactical headquarters at Bomdila in Kameng Frontier Division, puffs of cloud were visible in the sky between the roofs of houses, as if a giant smoker had exhaled into the cold alpine air 8000 feet above sea level.

Climbing up towards this shanty town that was the main settlement of the region afforded a good view of the thick, verdant forests all around, covering swathes of the peaks of steep mountains. The dense forests came about because of the large amount of rainfall the region received each year. With lush vegetation everywhere, the near vertical slopes looked almost uninhabited and untouched by humans.[1]

This area forms the youngest part of the Himalayas. Since these mountains are still forming, they are subject to the shifting of tectonic plates and frequent turmoil. These topographical problems translate into landslides, earthquakes, tremors and hurricanes, causing uncertainty and insecurity. For the native people who dare to live in this terrain, the changes in the landscape can mean death and destruction.

The earliest inhabitants here date back to before the Bronze Age; to the Indus Valley civilization.

Other ethnic groups from Tibet and China are relative newcomers, arriving some 2000 years ago.

Here live the Monpa tribes. Most of the Monpas from this region were part of the Monpa Kingdom of Monyal, which was at its peak between 500 and 600 AD. The Monpas or Miji tribes are gentle, religious, hard-working, sturdy, remarkably stoic people of the mountains.

There was a strong Tibetan influence here that was properly established later in the seventeenth century. By that time cultural and religious ties to the Tibetan capital, Lhasa, were very strong.

The Monpas are devoted Buddhists. While some of the Mijis have Buddhist influences, celebrating Tibetan New Year, Losar, for instance, in the main they are Animists. This means that the Mijis find God in nature—in trees, in water tributaries, even in natural rocks. They tend to wear silver ornaments, glass or brass necklaces, and they make indigenous cosmetics from pine, resin and coal. Both Mijis and Monpas breed yak hybrids like the Dzo, a cross between a yak and a highland cow, that produces butter and cheese for them. Their indigenous weapons were swords, spears or sticks: lathis.

An ethnic Monpa, Tsangyang Gyatso, was the sixth Dalai Lama. He lived from 1683 to 1706.

The Monpa Monyal kingdom encompassed eastern Bhutan, Tawang, Kameng and south Tibet. Today, most Monpas follow Gelugpa Buddhism, the largest and most influential tradition of the religion.[2] The Fourteenth Dalai Lama, too, belongs to the Gelugpa tradition.

In the nineteenth century, representatives of the British Raj began to take an interest in this area, finding that it could be of strategic importance. One, an Indian called Nain Singh Rawat, noted at the time that the Monpas, although quite isolated, were developing trade with Tibet.[3]

In 1914, the British haphazardly drew a line through the large area in which the Monpas lived. This famous line, McMahon, named after the man who created it, caused many Monpa tribespeople to suddenly become geopolitically divided.

British India gradually claimed control of much of the former Monyal kingdom south of the McMahon Line.

As mentioned earlier, China did not accept the McMahon Line, preferring instead to use the pre-McMahon border as the contour between Tibet and India.

The discussion between China and India on this issue remains active.

The British called this remote corner of India the North East Frontier Agency (NEFA).

Few outsiders ventured here.

NEFA jutted out from the north east corner of India, abutting Tibet and China in the north. To the west was Bhutan, and to the east, Burma. Kameng Frontier Division was the westernmost segment of the six divisions of the NEFA. Each of the six divisions was headed by a political officer. These officers were part of the Indian Frontier Administrative Service (IFAS), which formally replaced the old Indian Political Service (it was created informally in 1953).

In these steep mountains, there were few roads. In the places that did have dirt tracks, there was barely room for a horse and one person to walk side by side.[4]

This was one of the most remote and dangerous parts of India, just south of the Chinese border. With the two giants jostling for control of the region, a stray word or a stray bullet could trigger conflict.

Both the elephant and the dragon seemed constantly on the edge of war in the late 1950s. China, then and now, refuses to recognize India's claims to sovereignty over the area and includes much of Arunachal Pradesh in its maps.

In 1959, the official team responsible for and in charge of the Kameng Frontier Division was run at ground level by political officer Har Mander Singh and his team.

*

On 26 March 1959, Har Mander received a crackly message over the ancient and unreliable wireless set in his communications room.

His office was not far down the hill from his bungalow—a solid, black and white structure set apart from other buildings with a guest house for visitors. It was one of the most prominent buildings in this remote outpost. Behind the political officer's home, a hill had been cleared. Such solitary dwellings looked incongruous amid the thatched structures, fields and rolling hills, for the place was desolate and lonely. It was not surprising that junior officials posted here faced a challenging time, for there was little company and no entertainment outside office duties.

'The communications were terrible at that point of time. People carried huge wireless sets on their back weighing 20 kilograms or more,' Har Mander Singh told me, nearly sixty years later.

He's still a tall, handsome man, with a bald pate and a frame that fairly quivers with the intelligence that seems to inhabit every cell of his body. He is ninety-three, but alert like a coiled spring. Not much given to description, emotion or explanation, he speaks slowly and thoughtfully, as if every word has been turned over at least three times in his mind.

There are long pauses when he speaks. These add a certain amount of tension to our interview, which takes place at his dining table by an open window in his comfortable home in south Delhi. We can hear typical city street noises on a hot, dusty summer's day. Singh uses his body language to add emphasis, demonstrate or mime the meaning of his words.

'It was very difficult to communicate at that time, and even more difficult to communicate in code. To first convert the message into code, transmit it and then get the other party to decode it used to be a tremendous process.'

'Did you do this yourself?' I asked him.

'No, we had staff to do that. One person was dedicated to the coding and decoding, and an extra person was designated to carry the wireless set on which the messages were received. The communication channel was between Delhi and Shillong. The latter was our headquarters. From here, it was sent to Bomdila, which was the next station, one rung lower in order and rank.'

'How did you receive that critical instruction in 1959?' I queried.

'Passing on these messages was very difficult, so two or three people from Shillong came and told me that they were expecting the important person on the border, and everything was left to me to handle after that,' he replied.

'Did they tell you who the important person was?'

'Yes.'

'Was he given a code name? Did you give him a code name?'

'I think between them they used a code name, but I didn't use one.'

The important person in question was the Fourteenth Dalai Lama. I asked Har Mander what his official assignment had been.

'My job was to go and receive him and bring him back to the plains of India safely.'[5]

*

Har Mander Singh and his team only had news that the Tibetan leader had escaped. They had no other details about the Dalai Lama's flight to freedom, least of all the route he was expected to take. The challenge for them was to figure out the exact point at which the young God-king would enter India, so that they could meet him on time and prevent him from being intercepted or captured by anyone else.

Har Mander showed me a map, pointing out various routes. One of the possible ways the Dalai Lama could have used to escape was through Bhutan, to the south of Tibet and west of the NEFA.

'Actually, we had a rough idea,' he drew a diagram for me, indicating the area. 'There was another route here, to a place called Along in NEFA, but this route had been totally destroyed by an earthquake in 1950, which had caused massive landslides in the area.' He pointed to the right of the map, east of Kameng to indicate the location of Along.

'So this was not much of a possibility. The only other entry points were through here [he pointed to the area next to Kameng Division], which was in Bhutan. The local authority in Bhutan, a chap equivalent to me and a head of that area, made contact with me and said, 'You know, it's very difficult to go through Bhutan. The route is difficult and he won't be able to reach the destination. So, please don't take him through Bhutan.' I assured him, despite this not going through the chain of authorities, that there was no possibility of the Dalai Lama being taken through his country. I said to him, 'I know your fears; you are a very small country and China could play havoc with you if the Dalai Lama went through your country.' He did not acknowledge the reason outright, but it was apparent that that was what was playing on his mind. He also made some other excuses like, 'we have a chickenpox epidemic and it will not be proper.'[6]

*

Looking back on these dramatic events, Tenzin Gyatso, the Fourteenth Dalai Lama, sitting in his brightly decorated reception room at his home in Dharamsala, told me about the anxiety he felt as his representatives approached both Bhutan and India seeking refuge.

'You see . . . I received a message from the Indian side. They were facing some kind of dilemma as to whether the Government of India would allow us or not. We had already tried to contact the Bhutanese government, so if one side did not feel able, then we would have tried to go to Bhutan. So, we sent two delegations, official delegations, one each to Bhutan's border and India's border.'

*

In the coming pages, I will explain in broad terms how the Dalai Lama escaped from Lhasa and made the journey across hazardous peaks to southern Tibet.

In detail for the first time, Har Mander Singh will reveal how he prepared to receive the Dalai Lama and conduct him across the equally hazardous peaks of north-east India.

2

THE EARLY YEARS

From the early years right through the 1950s, in old Tibet, tradition dictated that elder sons were married and made the head of the family and one younger son would join the monasteries. Often when they were as young as six or seven. For Buddhists, both then and now, monasteries provided an education that peasant families could not otherwise afford.

In feudal Tibet, the clergy was the centre of power and politics. There was no more dominant influence in the land. Clans and warlords asserted their might locally, but apparently, such was the way of the Buddhist regime then that a strong national army was not always considered an area of necessary focus and development.

The Tibetan leadership was relaxed, focussing on formality and the observance of religious festivals. Monks held the highest place in Tibetan society and those running the country did not devote much thought to external threats. The monks ruled, and the monks would protect, so the people thought.

To get a glimpse of what was going on all those years ago, I spoke to seventy-five-year-old Namgyal Lhamo Taklha, a relative of the Sikkimese royal family and a sister-in-law of the current Dalai Lama.

Her grandfather, Dasung Dadul Tsarong, was a senior officer in the Tibetan army in the early 1900s. Namgyal's description of him gives an idea of the atmosphere in the Tibet in the first part of the twentieth century, the Tibet that I described above.

'The Thirteenth Dalai Lama fled to Mongolia. My grandfather, Dasang Dadul Tsarong, accompanied the group. Later, when they came back to Tibet, the Chinese sent their army. This was in 1912. When the Thirteenth Dalai Lama was fleeing to India as a refugee, my grandfather fought the Chinese army with a small group of men and stopped them from following. He became very famous.

'Later he became a commander-in-chief of the army, a minister, and opened his house to everybody. Therefore, any foreigners who came from different parts of the world always came to Tsarong's house. That's why from a very young age I had exposure to many different people.

'My grandfather was very modern. He wanted Tibet to be opened up to the international world, but the country was not ready for it. Tibetans were very conservative; traditionalists. And they said, "Oh if we have foreigners coming into Tibet, we will lose Buddhism and if Tibetans go out, they will lose Buddhism." I think that's how we lost the country, because we were not educated.'[1]

*

Since Tibetans depended on the clergy for everything, the most revered and important person in the country was the spiritual leader of the Buddhist Himalaya belt. The Dalai Lama was the ultimate temporal and spiritual authority for his people. He was a powerful and symbolic figure. They united around him.

Two years after the Thirteenth Dalai Lama died in 1935, the search for his successor began.

There had been signs indicating where the next Dalai Lama might be found. When the Great Thirteenth died, monks dressing his body to lie in state placed his head facing south, the direction said to be the right one for prolonging life. Over two consecutive mornings, they found that his head had turned towards the east despite the priests turning his head back towards the south each night. So, the senior monks took it as a sign that his successor, the Fourteenth Dalai Lama, would be found in east Tibet.

The Regent, Reting Rinpoche, was Tibet's interim political head while the quest for the next Dalai Lama was ongoing. Escorted by a search party, he travelled to a mountain top next to a mystical lake known as Lhamoi Latso. There, he performed prayers, accompanied by ritual music, to gain some clarity. After completing his prayers, the regent looked into the lake. While several of those with him claimed to see nothing but blue water, he saw the images of three Tibetan letters rising from the water and then sinking back into the lake. Reting Rinpoche saw the image of a monastery with three storeys and a green and gold roof, he saw a road going eastwards. He saw a little rural home with rare green-blue eaves, and a brown and white dog in the garden. The three letters that Regent Reting Rinpoche had seen were the Tibetan 'Ah', 'Ka' and 'Ma'. The letters were interpreted as indicating the location at which the next Dalai Lama would be found.

The following year the regent told the National Assembly what he had witnessed. The National Assembly sought the counsel of the state's most important spiritualist agency—the Nechung Oracle.

The members of the National Assembly decided to send out three search parties from Lhasa heading east. One party, led by Kewtsang Rinpoche, the abbot of Lhasa's Sera Monastery, moved towards the large north-east region of Amdo. A second group went to Kham in the east, and the third group moved towards the south-east to the Takpo and Kongpo regions.[2]

Given the signs, the regent and his teams felt that the most likely place for the Great Fourteenth's location would be somewhere in the vast tracts of Amdo, to the north east of Lhasa. For two months, the Amdo team led by Kewtsang Rinpoche travelled a thousand miles, battling through snow and blizzards with temperatures plunging to minus 10 degrees. Eventually, the search party arrived at a monastery which—just as Regent Reting Rinpoche had seen in his vision—had a green and gold jade roof and was three storeys high.

The team from Lhasa had received a list of three boys who had been recommended either because of their behaviour or by powerful backers. The first child proved to be too shy to be a brave incarnation and was dropped from consideration. The second boy died before the search party arrived. Lhamo Thondup was the last boy on the list.

*

Lhamo Thondup was born on 6 July 1935 into a peasant family that lived in a village called Taktser. He was the fifth of sixteen siblings. Only seven of these children survived. Lhamo Thondup's father was a farmer and horse trader called Choekyong Tsering, and his mother was Diki Tsering. The eldest of his brothers, Thubten Jigme Norbu, had already been recognized as the reincarnation of a senior lama, Takster Rinpoche. Then there were Gyalo Thondup and Lobsang Samden. The youngest brother was Tenzin Choegyal and he too had already been recognized as a reincarnation of a high lama, Ngari Rinpoche. Lhamo Thondup had two sisters—Jetsun Pema and Tsering Dolma. Lhamo Thondup was very close to his mother. In his village of roughly twenty families, the boy played happily among the animals and serene surroundings.[3]

The search team found that Lhamo Thondup's family home had unusual turquoise eaves, just as Regent Reting Rinpoche had seen in the lake.

So, disguised as a servant, Abbot Kewtsang Rinpoche, with two other religious functionaries and a government official, arrived at Lhamo Thondup's family home wearing an item belonging to the Thirteenth Dalai Lama. When the two-and-a-half-year-old Lhamo saw it, he took it in his hands and is said to have exclaimed, 'I want that.' Without being told, the child correctly guessed the abbot's true identity as a lama from Sera Monastery. He also knew the identities of the others in the visiting group.

The search party found all the indicators promising and returned sometime later with a complement of forty devotees. Kewtsang Rinpoche presented the child with a series of tests, giving him pairs of items, such as rosaries and walking sticks, of which one in each pair had belonged to the Thirteenth Dalai Lama. The boy chose the holiest item each time. Finally, he was examined for physical signs that are associated with being a Dalai Lama—signs like curling eyebrows, tiger stripes on the legs and large ears. The team found three of these signs on the child, enough to reassure them that he was the enlightened being they sought.[4]

When he was four years old, the new Dalai Lama ceremoniously left his village for Lhasa. With him was his six-year-old elder brother, Lobsang, an uncle, the child's parents, bodyguards, and a retinue—a group of fifty in all.

Amdo's governor and warlord, General Ma Bufang, sensed a chance to make money. He claimed an enormous ransom in order to allow the newly discovered religious incarnate to pass. A group of merchants who formed part of the procession was asked to lend the Dalai Lama's office this sum to give to the warlord.

The new Dalai Lama was duly granted egress after a long, long wait.

Once allowed passage, the party set off for Lhasa. About 350 mules, camels and yaks were needed to carry the party's baggage for the three-and-a-half-month journey (in contrast to Kewtsang Rinpoche's two-month sojourn to Amdo with only three companions).

As they neared the Tibetan capital, Lhamo Thondup was helped to shed his peasant's clothes forever. He was then formally dressed in the maroon and gold monk's robes the world now associates him with.

It is a Tibetan tradition that travellers are escorted on arrival and departure. When the new religious royals were two miles from Lhasa, Tibetan officials, soldiers, monastery heads—all the most significant people in Lhasa—came out to greet and accompany the arrivals with due pomp and ceremony. Among the items they ferried was a special wooden throne used solely for greeting and welcoming the Fourteenth

Dalai Lama into Lhasa. The throne was called the 'Great Peacock'. There was also an ordinary monk amid all these dignitaries named 'Ponpo', which means 'boss' in Tibetan. Ponpo would be in charge of the young incarnate's kitchen.

The Great Peacock was later replaced by the Lion Throne, the high ceremonial seat in the Dalai Lama's winter palace, Potala, in Lhasa.

The little boy who up to this point had only known long days spent playing with his siblings and enjoying nature, was now leaving behind temporal freedom forever.

The Fourteenth Dalai Lama's brother Lobsang was allowed to stay at Potala Palace but his parents lived separately with only periodic access to their son. Ponpo was kind and gentle, reminding the Dalai Lama of his mother, but the young boy was mostly surrounded by serious-minded elderly monks. Potala Palace was big and cavernous, ancient and musty, and the old religious tapestries that had gathered layers of dust behind them sat forlorn and silent. With over a thousand rooms and miles of corridors, it was a strange and giant home for a peasant child to get used to.

He often sat, staring around him at the bewildering surroundings of his new abode.

*

Across the border in India, little did a young Har Mander Singh know that the events and memories of his childhood were to be a precursor to the political atmosphere he would later face in life.

From his boyhood into his early twenties, with the outbreak of war and conflict, Har Mander Singh experienced turbulence and trauma first-hand. Incidentally, he grew up to live and work in a region that was sensitive and occasionally erupted into armed hostility. The first part of his active career was at India's northern borders.

His father had had a responsible position as a police officer. His work also involved building relations between communities, chiefly between the Indian government and its dominions. This work would influence the young Har Mander.

Har Mander Singh was born on 10 June, 1926 in Tanganyika, now called Tanzania. The family lived in the capital, Dar es Salaam. His early childhood was spent in different towns all over Tanganyika because his father, Piara Singh, was often transferred to different postings. The family variously lived in Mombasa, Tanga and Morogoro.

Piara Singh had been in the army cavalry. He had fought in World War I in France and in Iraq between 1914 and 1917. After the War, he was demobilized and discharged. He began to look for employment and joined the Colonial Police in Tanganyika. Three of his children, Har Mander Singh, Updesh and Parsan, were born in Africa.

While working in Africa, Har Mander's father would take his family by ship to their ancestral home in Kahota in undivided India every four years for four months. Har Mander Singh's late youngest sister Parsan, my mother, recalled a childhood of boat trips and picnics. She also remembered dinners at home where fresh lamb or goat's meat was the main dish.

In Tanzania, the Indian population was made up mainly of people from the Punjab, Uttar Pradesh and Gujarat.

Har Mander was keen to tell me about his birth. As with much of his career, the story was understated.

'Just before I was born, my father was transferred to the capital city, Dar es Salaam, from a suburban town. My birth took place on the journey, in a train. When the Governor of Tanganyika heard the news, he was so worried that he came personally, got the compartment detached from the train, wished my mother and father good luck, and then left. That's how I was born; in a running train.'[5]

Back then, the country was still, in the minds of many, sentimentally attached to Germany, having been colonized by it during World War I. The plantations remained under German ownership. Har Mander remembers that though the currency was British, the people of Tanganyika called one of their coins—valued at around a hundredth of a rupee—a *heller*, the German equivalent of an older coin in British

East Africa. Such was the local people's affection and nostalgia for their former colonizers.

As Har Mander studied in Indian schools, the languages he was exposed to were Gujarati and Urdu. He remembers his childhood as being 'very happy'.

Even as a five-year-old, he showed the discipline that would be a fixture of his life. Har Mander did not allow himself to have temper tantrums or express much jubilation. 'I didn't bother very much about emotion, I was too caught up in my studies,' he said.

The inscrutable temperament and character that would withstand tense situations was already fashioned during these early years. This does not mean that Har Mander Singh wasn't an adventurous child. He recalls one incident of being disciplined. 'I remember one late evening I went with my friends and dived into the sea. My parents were worried. They drove me home and thrashed me.'[6]

Har Mander had a sister, Iqbal, who was two years older than him. She was protective of her brother. The next sibling, Updesh, is four years younger than Har Mander. Then came Parsan, who was two years younger than Updesh. Like Har Mander, Parsan remembered their childhoods as happy and joyous.

The children were familiar with Swahili as it was the language of everyday use in that country. Parsan could still remember the Swahili for 'stop!' (*Banukaba!*) into her late seventies.

Parsan remembered that her brother was 'carefully watched' as he was the son, and that her eldest sister Iqbal was tutored at home. However, when Piara Singh moved the family to India, all three sisters received the finest formal education available.

In Africa, Har Mander's father, Piara Singh, would go to the pub occasionally for a drink. He sometimes took Har Mander with him, particularly on public occasions. This is how and where Piara Singh's son remembered hearing about Hitler's advance and actions in Europe. 'It was a harbinger of World War II,' he reminisced.[7]

'There were huge radios at that time,' he said, indicating the shape of a giant radio stretching from his waist to above his head with his hands. 'The radio voices would only talk about the impending World War II.'[8]

Before war broke out, Piara Singh, who was the chief of police, was given the delicate task of rounding up German plantation owners—seen as potential enemy sympathizers—and taking them into custody.

The days and weeks of the late 1930s soon turned into a period of major international conflict. Parsan remembered Churchill's voice booming out from their radio. Living in a region that was tense and febrile probably provided the subconscious mental makeup for Har Mander to work in other volatile regions later in life.

Around the same time, Har Mander also met the girl who would become his wife.

According to him, when she, Neena, was five years old, she sat on his mother's lap and declared a liking for him. 'I was seven. My grandmother expressed a wish that Neena would be my bride when we grew up, and so that is exactly what happened,' he remembered.

At the outbreak of war, Piara Singh sent the family to live in Kahota. The family then moved to Rawal Pindi. 'We rented a home next to my future father-in-law's house. My future father-in-law was very strict. So Neena and I would communicate through one of my friends who had agreed to act as a messenger.' Neena was sixteen and Har Mander seventeen.

One day, the friend got caught sending messages between the two young neighbours and got a thrashing from Neena's father.

Piara Singh went to Rawal Pindi in undivided India at the beginning of World War II in 1939. He got a job in the Intelligence Bureau, then moved from Rawal Pindi to Calcutta by early 1940.

Around 1946, Har Mander, his mother, Tej Kaur, and his sisters moved to Calcutta (now Kolkata) from Africa. The girls studied in convent schools where Urdu was the main teaching language, and the family had a community of well-settled neighbours and friends. Among them were the racehorse owners, the Balas, and businesspeople, the Sharmas. The family mingled well with the community, and it was a time of carefree fun and socializing.

Between 1939 and 1945, India was anticipating a Japanese invasion. As an intelligence chief, Piara Singh's task was to build a resistance movement across Bihar, Orissa and Bengal from Calcutta. 'So if the Japanese walked into India, there would be underground people keeping the British informed,' Har Mander Singh explained.[9]

While Piara Singh was creating a secret information network in Calcutta, Har Mander went to school in Kahota and Rawal Pindi in what was then western India. His mother was with him to care for him.

Har Mander and his mother joined the family in Calcutta just after he completed Class 12. 'I was studious; I studied subjects like English, Punjabi, Maths and Science. I didn't like Science too much but wanted to become a doctor. So, for high schooling my mother and I moved to Rawal Pindi. I took up English, Urdu, Chemistry and Physics. I enjoyed non-science subjects like English and Urdu. I applied for medical college under the Punjab quota and was accepted.'[10] However, due to a lack of funds he couldn't pursue his dream, so he too, moved to Calcutta.

Har Mander was and is popular, but like all families in the services, it was hard to make lasting friends as they moved around so much. 'In Africa, I made casual friends; and in Rawal Pindi, I had friends I played cricket with,' he noted.[11]

As for his career, there was a path of inevitability. 'My great grand-parents came from an army lineage, and I knew I too would get into the same field,' he told me.[12]

After school, Har Mander Singh had a couple of civilian jobs, each lasting a few months. The first was in security, censoring letters; the second was working for the US Information Service.

In 1945, after World War II, he joined the officer training school at the Indian Military Academy in Bangalore. His entrance examinations consisted of rigorous psychological tests. The training he subsequently undertook was part academic, part military. 'We were twenty-five to thirty in number. Our training included lectures and talks. The Bangalore training was purely for the army,' he recalled.[13]

Due to the War, officer training at the time had been condensed into a year. After his term finished, Singh joined the Jat regiment, becoming an infantryman. This meant a stint at the Regimental Centre, the home of Jat soldiers, where all officers go first to 'fit' with their team.

His first substantial posting was to Calcutta, just before the Great Calcutta Killings took place. He witnessed a bloody day of riot and manslaughter between Hindus and Muslims in which between 40,000 to 50,000 people were killed that occurred on 16 August 1946. Singh had a role in relief and rehabilitation in the aftermath of that massacre. He never forgot what he witnessed that day.

'My battalion, 5 Jat, was at Calcutta on internal security duty when the Great Calcutta Killing took place. The Muslim League under Premier Suhrawardy[14] was in power. Thousands of poor Hindus from Bihar, Orissa and other states were massacred by the ruling party's armed mobs, known as Razakars. One of the relief camps was set up by a voluntary organization in Ashutosh Mukherji college. The company commanded by me was responsible for the security of that relief camp,' he remembered.[15]

Traditionally, the armour and infantry wings that Singh was part of have been the most sought-after combat arms of the Indian army. There has never been a shortage of gentlemen cadets graduating from the military academies opting for these sections. Infantry has generally been known as the 'queen' of the battlefield.

By reputation, an officer in the infantry has the highest form of raw courage. He needs it as he must lead his men from the front. He also closes with the enemy. In the last 200 metres of a skirmish there is nothing between him and a foe's machine gun or bayonet. Apart from leading his men, an officer also shows them 'how to die, when the time comes'.[16]

Cadets joining the Indian armed forces had certain qualities. The development of these qualities is highlighted right through the selection and training process and then when the cadets finally join individual units. These traits are integrity, loyalty, physical and moral courage, initiative, decisiveness, selflessness, adaptability, perseverance, determination, team playing, esprit de corps, having a soldierly bearing, and the ability to remain cool under stress. One former senior military officer said, 'The degree to which a gentlemen cadet may possess these qualities will have a lot of bearing on his place in the order of merit when passing out from an academy. The arms and services are allocated according to an individual's choice and his place in the order of merit.'[17]

Officers were men who could rapidly think of solutions to situations on the ground, in peace as well as in the most dangerous of circumstances. Indian infantry officers were often sent to work in sensitive locations.

Har Mander Singh was selected as an aide de camp to a distinguished Indian army commander, Major General S.P.P. Thorat. Thorat was not only a military genius, but also an intellectual. He had commanded battalions against the Japanese during World War II and in NEFA, and developed security forces designed to fight insurgents. To counter the advantage that indigenous tribal militants hold when battling the Indian military, Thorat's men attacked mountainside villages on dark nights or in pouring rain, when they were least expected. Har Mander Singh absorbed the general's tactics.

Thorat had a reputation for being an upright, meticulous soldier, correct in his dealings with those above him as well as those lower in rank. His impeccable manners also made an impact on young Singh.[18]

Soon after 1947, when east Punjab became a part of India, Major General Thorat was put in charge of east Punjab and the border areas. These included the critical fringe region of Punjab.

His protégée, Singh, rose steadily in the army to the rank of captain. His last posting with the military was in Nepal in 1950. He was sent there with a group of Indian advisers to help Nepal run its administration because the regime there, dominated by the Rana Dynasty, was wrestling with a big transfer to democratic rule.

Across the border, in the mid-1950s, the Indian government was facing challenges in the administration of NEFA. It stemmed from the fact that the British had neglected to set up any kind of effective administrative body there, preferring to stay in the relative comfort of Assam, further south.

India called for applications from various services—the armed forces, police and forestry divisions to form a new Indian Frontier Administrative Service (IFAS). These men would handle intelligence and security matters but shy away from being called spies. According to one former military source, political officers did send reports about Chinese activity across the border in tribal areas. Their reports, says the source, contained 'strategic perceptions'.[19]

Ostensibly a civilian division of the Indian government, the new IFAS was a special cadre of men skilled enough to operate in frontier regions bordering NEFA—Tibet, Sikkim and Bhutan. It was also introduced to inculcate a softer, more respectful approach towards the indigenous locals. In 1952, Nehru wrote to his foreign secretary that the local tribal people needed to be handled 'With care and friendliness and require expert knowledge which our average administrator does not possess. Hence the necessity for a specially trained cadre.'[20]

Interviews were held in Delhi with candidates that included Har Mander Singh.

French-born historian and author Claude Arpi, who has spent many years closely scrutinizing the NEFA, is an expert on the Indo–Tibetan border zone. 'The initial recruitment to the Indian Frontier Administrative Service (IFAS) was made by the Central Government through a Special Selection Board with representatives from the Ministry of External Affairs [MEA], the Ministry of Home Affairs [MHA] and the Ministry of Defence [MoD], along with an expert in tribal affairs (often Verrier Elwin*),' Arpi wrote about the selection process.[21]

Applicants were likely to have been quizzed about their motives for leaving a steady job, their familiarity with NEFA and the tribal peoples of that area.[22] Over four to five days, the candidates were made to go through individual and collective interviews. Officer-like qualities alluded to above were sought during the hiring process. These included a certain level of selflessness, as well as the ability to lead and react quickly.

Prime Minister Nehru wanted his new border officers to be popular with the tribes. The interlocutors also needed their men to be able to deal with the issues of being in a frontier territory, and to be able to handle volatile relationships with neighbours like China.

China and India have always had territorial aspirations, with China seeing the advantage of gaining control over the mainly Buddhist corridor of land that forms north east India. Command of that entry point through the perilously high Himalayas would give the dragon a vice-like grip on a key corner of India. It would only have to send its army across for a successful invasion to inflict pain on its neighbour.

Given the difference in military strengths, there is little argument when it comes to a battle between the two nations.

*

Against this background, Har Mander was selected as a member of the IFAS. Thus, in 1954, he crossed over from the army to the Indian Civil Service (ICS). He was sent to Shillong, the capital of undivided Assam (now of Meghalaya), for two months of training.

Of the briefings he received, he recalled, 'There were lectures on anthropology. We were going to interact with tribal people, and a lot of us did not know anything about them. Some of these areas were opening up for the first time. A soldier doesn't know anthropology. We needed to learn about tribal culture, the way of life, the way of dealing with people who die.'[23]

In addition to learning about administrating in the eastern Himalayas, he remembers studying the works of the aforementioned anthropologist, Verrier Elwin.

As part of the new distinct and separate civilian service, Har Mander Singh was posted to Nagaland, living and working on bases and taking supplies to NEFA areas.

The British had not concerned themselves with establishing an infrastructure in the North East Kameng division. Consequently, there was much to be done for the local tribes.

Large parts of the north east region are populated by the Monpa people, who are further divided by various sects. They are god-fearing Buddhists and hold the Dalai Lama in great reverence. As stated earlier, the Monpa Sixth Dalai Lama was born and brought up here. When he left for Tibet, he predicted that he would return one day—and so he did, in the form of the current Fourteenth Dalai Lama as their followers believe.

Monpas are straightforward, Mongoloid people whose physiology is suited to the cold, unfriendly terrain. The men are compact even when tall, and the women are usually short. It is nature's way of adjusting to the environment as creatures of small stature conserve energy more effectively.

Everywhere, even today, the Monpa women can be seen wearing their striped aprons (called *chubas*) over long dark skirts. Their jewellery consists of large colourful necklaces and matching dangling earrings. Babies are strapped to backs with wide pieces of cloth. The men sport yak hats, short half-jackets made of hide and tuck their trousers into their boots. On special occasions, such as festivals, the men don silver-bordered black or red jackets with a diagonal front fastening.

The inhospitable environment breeds toughness and a hard-working mentality among the tribe. Whether or not their homes have a metal heat-giving *bhukari* (chimney) or electricity, the Monpas are stoic and uncomplaining. They are honest people. Attached to the land, they respect its produce and its power.

Among the unique flora and fauna of this region is the yellow *jana* flower.

There is a legend that the flower stands for an old Tibetan monarch who was so magnificent that he could talk to the sun. His palace had four open walls so that the sun could sit within it. The king, it was said, aged a lifetime from sunrise to sunset and was born anew each morning. When he finally left this planet, the *jana* flower appeared where his palace and kingdom had been.

There are many flora and fauna species indigenous to Arunachal Pradesh that the world outside has not yet discovered. It is well known, however, that orchids proliferate in the Kameng area. There are over 500 varieties here, in almost every colour imaginable.

Not far from the Arunachal border check point on the way to the monastery town of Tawang is a famous orchid sanctuary. The region is full of lakes too, contributing to the calm, peaceful atmosphere.

The Monpas now use the land to feed themselves, unlike in 1959 when many of life-giving provisions had to be air-dropped. Back then, they depended on millet, wheat and potatoes, but now the area is nearly self-sufficient.

Har Mander was posted in this area. Bomdila was his base and division headquarters.

Raj Mander recalls travelling home over summer vacations. He journeyed from St Edmund's boarding school in Shillong during the late fifties through to January 1960, the years of his father's Bomdila posting. On his first trip, Raj Mander travelled by pony. His father was having the road from Rupa to Bomdila built and it was nearly ready.

'I remember I used to travel by pony to Bomdila even before the jeep road was constructed. There was a road between Shillong and Tezpur and then further up to Foot Hills, but from there to Rupa we travelled by pony.

'The road journey took the better part of a day. And then from Rupa to Bomdila, I used a pony. On my second visit the jeep road was ready, so we went by jeep from Rupa to Bomdila, uphill. Downhill from Rupa to Foot Hills, the road was under construction. By the time of my third visit, the whole road was ready.

'We used to leave in the morning and arrive at Rupa in the late afternoon. It would take one day up to Foot Hills, where we would stop to rest for the day. We would then travel up to Bomdila in one day. So, two days in all.'[24]

At the time, the paths and tracks were just about visible through the undergrowth and rocks, and the roads were rudimentary compared to other Indian ones. Now, the roads are developed enough for buses, trucks, jeeps and cars to drive along at a steady pace. However, the national highway does not have many of the sharp corner safety barriers and danger signs that is the norm in Uttarakhand, for instance.

Bomdila is hidden by juniper and pine trees. In 1959, Bomdila was a sparse settlement, and even now it is not highly developed. The market's main feature is a big room with a tin roof. In the market, women sell kiwi fruit and apples, dried yak cheese, and homemade cloth bags with the striped patterns familiar in Kameng. Then, as now, there was a threat of landslides due to the heavy rainfall and shifting topography of the mountains.

Bomdila in Kameng was once part of the trade route between India and Tibet, so there is a history of ware-selling in this settlement. In the present day, there is a white-walled monastery in Bomdila, housing trainee child monks as well as their more sober elders.

As part of his responsibilities for the whole region, Har Mander Singh travelled to what were called 'Forward' areas, i.e., places near the border—in this case, the border with Tibet.

Tawang, a subdivision under Bomdila, housed west Kameng's district headquarters. The administrative settlement by the border was also home to what is India's biggest and Asia's second-largest Buddhist monastery, the place where the Sixth Dalai Lama was born. The Tawang complex dates from the seventh century.

Being on the route crossing the Kameng Division was like riding an elongated perilous mountain rollercoaster, descending then ascending again and again from Bomdila to Tawang, then further to the border and into Tibet. It was mostly just a narrow pony path carved into the mountainside. At best this path was created for one pony and a rider to be crossing on odd occasions. Back then, anyone traversing this narrow craggy ridge, lonely yet majestic, probably would have never imagined that it would one day be the rugged, worn-out, slippery path taken by an aristocrat upon whose shoulders rested the future of an entire people.

3

IN THE LAND OF
THE DAWN-LIT MOUNTAINS

Between 1955 and 1956, Har Mander Singh became the administrator of the frontier areas known as NEFA. Initially, he was the assistant political officer and then the additional political officer in the Tuensang Frontier Division. In all, he would spend fourteen years on different postings in these inhospitable mountain ranges, which closely resemble the Tibetan landscape just across the border.

After Har Mander's 1954 selection for NEFA, his first posting was as an assistant political officer (APO) in Tezu in the Lohit Division. At that time, Singh recalled, the adviser to the governor visited Lohit and asked the APO if he was experiencing any problems. When the young Har Mander answered 'No', the adviser sent him as an APO to the secretariat headquarters (HQ) in Shillong.

From 1956–57 Har Mander was the secretary, supply and transport at NEFA HQ. In this post, Singh was the senior officer in the NEFA secretariat, responsible for overseeing all aspects of supplies for the region.[1] In 1970, he was appointed security commissioner for the north-east.

The 1962 Indo-Chinese War caused India to create more administrative posts in Arunachal Pradesh. This was an Indian bid to protect itself from another Chinese invasion. The idea was to strengthen security in the region.

At the time when Har Mander Singh joined Kameng, NEFA consisted of six divisions. From 1957 to February 1960, when Har Mander was political officer of Kameng Division, his team included his personal staff, administration officers and all the workers in the area. This included doctors, teachers and villagers.

Since he was responsible for the welfare of his people, Singh and his team took care of deprived local tribal folk who needed support with education and healthcare.

When Har Mander arrived in Bomdila in August 1957, there was little more there than a few cabins. Bomdila was just a shanty town with bamboo shacks, some of which had been plastered with mud. The area had recently been settled by the first political officer, Major R. Khathing. Har Mander says, 'We had taken on the developmental part of the administration. We worked on educational facilities and health, handled marketing for handicrafts and took care of the security of citizens. In introducing these, we were pioneers.'[2] Development, he explains, was an ongoing process, and he needed staff to assist him.

A divisional medical officer would help with health-related concerns. He would advise the political officer on policy, but the health practitioner would take decisions in technical matters, such as medicine and communication with staff.

Singh and his team needed to make sure that the locals had a means of livelihood, and that there was some sort of industry in each settlement. To this end, in rural areas, they encouraged knitting and bag-making. Har Mander's staff also sought to develop agriculture and build roads wherever possible, all with a view to empowering the tribes.

Around the time of Indian Independence, the literacy rate of Arunachal Pradesh was one per cent. Through the fifties, it rose as educational programmes were implemented by the political officers. Even now in Arunachal, it sometimes appears as though it is considered less important to educate girls than boys, and certain remote areas are still without schools. Previously, the few Monpas and tribespeople who managed to study, did so through monasteries with a view to becoming monks.

But monasteries were few and far between. Though Monpas have their own script, the tribal culture was mainly oral. This oral culture still pervades Arunachal Pradesh, with mythology and folklore making up a major part of the region's philosophy and thinking.

When the Indian administration started to come into the area, elementary and secondary schools were set up. Tuition, books and uniforms were all paid for by the government. Today, virtually all the schools in the area are still government funded. Though children are seen working everywhere, little ones in uniform can also be spotted in conurbations.

*

French scholar on Tibet, Claude Arpi, explains in one of his articles, 'The NEFA was administered by the Ministry of External Affairs with the Governor of Assam acting as agent to the President of India, seconded by a senior officer (often from the ICS [Indian Civil Service]), designated as Advisor to the Governor.'[3]

The post of political officer, the one that Har Mander Singh held in 1959, along with the significant responsibilities and challenges it represented, was later given other titles: governor, head of district or district commissioner.

The advisor was based in Shillong. In the mid-1950s, it was K.L. Mehta from the ICS. The ICS was the organization that would later become the Indian Administrative Service (IAS). K.L. Mehta reported to the Governor of Assam, who was also based in Shillong. At that time, it was Fazl Ali, who occupied the post from 1956 to1959. He, in turn, reported to Jawaharlal Nehru, the prime minister, thus making Nehru Singh's senior most reporting authority.

The Indian Army did not have a strong presence in the region during the 1950s. Instead, there was an Assam Rifles force in NEFA under an inspector general. He took his orders from the governor and his advisor.

By 1959, Har Mander had spent five years in NEFA, accumulating knowledge and experience in the process. Having been on numerous local assignments, he knew the geography well and the logistics of travel in this uninviting area. He was aware of the dangers and hazards. It was not just the mountainous terrain that had to be navigated, but also the landslides which were a constant threat.

The infrastructure at the time was minimal.

Singh and his team built their own offices, hospitals and homes. There was no power or even running water, so they had rudimentary bamboo pipes fitted to bring water down to their houses. Electricity came to the township long after Har Mander Singh had finished his posting there. During his tenure, kerosene lamps were used to read by at night.

There was a supply and transport department of the NEFA administration that was situated in Shillong. A NEFA director of supplies controlled the distribution of food, kerosene oil and essential items all over the region. Har Mander Singh would keep in touch with this director through the wireless transmitter and thus managed deliveries in his division. The director was based at Tezpur, a little lower down the mountains.

Har Mander reminisced, 'There was no food available, so we had to have air drops. *Bakra*, goat, dropped to us. We called it "meat on the hoof".'[4]

For air drops, they would use Dakota planes stationed at Tezpur.

The living animal was dropped from a height by parachute in a way that it was not injured. Apart from food, the administration also coordinated supplies such as petrol, which were delivered through various routes. These included the air drops already mentioned; land transport, and in very remote areas, by people carrying loads on their heads or backs.[5]

'There was a lot of hardship, but this service stood up to those challenges. We went into already functioning places or created functioning places,' Har Mander said.[6]

Raj Mander Singh was around eleven years old when his father became a political officer. He has distinct memories of their house in Bomdila.

'On a hill there were bamboo shacks. The centre of the town had a flattened area called the Dropping Zone where the pilots used to aim their air drops. Further up the hill from that, right at the tallest point on Bomdila, was the political officer's bungalow called Kameng Sadan. "Sadan" means house. So it was Kameng House, reserved for the head of the local administration. It was a long, one-storeyed bamboo structure of three or four rooms, each next to each other. Adjacent to it and some distance away was the guest house. Behind the political officer's bungalow was another small shack that had a kitchen. It had a room to heat water, and a storeroom. Some distance down the hill from the house was the political officer's office, which was also a bamboo shack. I remember it had Papa's office at one end and two rooms for his staff, files and other things. Below, next to the Dropping Zone, was the Club, which Papa had had constructed.'[7]

It was lonely in Bomdila, as there was little light at night, and everybody was by themselves in their own shacks. The Club House that Har Mander had constructed was where all the officers of the station would gather in the evening. Each person would bring one pot of food, and this would be distributed among everyone. The team would then sit and share the meal together. They would sing songs and play games like Bingo.

Behind the Club was the Treasury which Raj Mander remembered as the only *pukka* (concrete) structure in Bomdila. Since it contained all the cash for salaries and ration money it had to be fortified and safe, which is why it was constructed with bricks and mud. This solid hut, the primitive equivalent of a vault, was where all the money that came from the Government of India was stored. This cash was sent to Bomdila by the governor and his advisor in Shillong and Assam.

Raj Mander Singh says, 'I didn't actually see it coming, but it must have come in army jeeps protected by armed Assam Rifles. There were no dacoits or anything at that time, it was already peaceful, so I think carrying it in sealed boxes in a jeep with *jawans* [police or soldiers] in front and jawans behind would have been enough to ensure its safe passage.'[8]

Food also arrived at Bomdila by pony. The air drops would happen several times a day, once or twice a week, or just once a month in the outposts. The more outlying the area, the higher the altitude, the more likely it was to receive air drops rather than by pony delivery, however infrequent. Tawang, for instance, mostly received air drops.

Just as in Tawang, most other deliveries into Kameng were by air; there were dropping zones at or near each settlement. The terrain was perilous, with craggy mountain ridges, crevasses and tiny open spaces. The aircraft would aim for these, but air currents would often take them off course or to the fringes of the target. The drops would miss their marked spots and crash into jagged rocks, which would cause the contents to spill out.

At Bomdila, Har Mander Singh had most of his family with him, including his wife Neena, all the time. Only Raj Mander was away at school. Raj's brother, Harsh Mander, was a happy toddler.

Raj Mander still has vivid memories of the time he would spend at Bomdila during the holidays. He remembers that the local townships, Shillong and Guwahati, were quite developed, compared with the Frontier area.

'I would imagine myself as a pioneer, a Frontiersman, an explorer. I was influenced by the Hollywood movies I would watch in those days. They were shown to us on Wednesday nights in school. So, I had a vision of myself as a cowboy,' he said, laughing at the memory.[9]

Raj Mander would find air drops very exciting. He explained that the open area near Bomdila called the Dropping Zone was designated for the Dakota aircraft to fly low over and drop gunny sacks of food grains. They would drop kerosene and even goats by air parachute.

'It was very exciting to see. At the same time, it was also quite dangerous, and a few aircraft even crashed over the years.'[10]

The planes were flown by skilled pilots, who would come in very low so that the packages would land gently. The planes would fly through a valley, up a hill and then over the Dropping Zone, where the sacks would be lowered. As far as the 'meat on hoof' was concerned, the goats were dropped from a slightly more elevated height by parachute, ensuring that the animals landed safely. A special semi-government force of labourers was recruited solely for the purpose of retrieving the food and animals.[11] The people at the station would then take the animals to the bazaar where all kinds of tradespeople convened, including butchers and meat sellers.

*

When Singh embarked on his mission to meet the Dalai Lama, he and his small entourage carried their food on ponies. 'When I set off from Bomdila, I was largely on my own. My personal secretary or assistant, and an interpreter would accompany me. Maybe four to five people in all. They were essential for me.'[12]

There were not too many Assam Riflemen available then because they were mostly deployed elsewhere. The total strength of Assam Rifles personnel available to him at the time would have been about thirty, some of whom would later take on protection roles.

Numbers were kept down as: 'The aim was to reach as quickly as possible. We would change horses along the way.'[13]

They would stop at villages, where they received hospitality. The settlements were far apart.

When Har Mander travelled through the region, he would be received by the head of the village and would interact with residents. But it was going to be a different case when the head of the Tibetan Buddhist world would be among them. For the Dalai Lama and his retinue of eighty, the available accommodation suitable for visiting dignitaries would be stretched to a maximum. By the time Singh returned with the Dalai Lama and his party, the number of people had increased to 100, as local Buddhist leaders and abbots had also joined the group.

By that time, some supplies could get to Bomdila by jeep from Tezpur. But managing the return journey was still going to be logistically challenging.

But nothing can take away from the primeval and breath-taking splendour of the area.

Kameng Division, indeed the entire Arunachal Pradesh, witnesses dawn before the rest of India due to its extreme north-east location. This is why it is called 'The land of the dawn-lit mountains.' The region's rugged terrain has also impacted the administration's approach to governance over the years.

It is one of the least populated regions of India. The average number of locals per square mile in the 1950s was no more than ten. Since then, there has not been a population explosion. The average person per square mile has only risen to twelve.

Har Mander Singh recalled how he and his staff managed the territory.

'Our policy, that is the Government of India's policy, was very different from the British policy. As far as the NEFA was concerned, the British had just three to five political officers posted in the foothills. The British policy was to protect the foothills where they had tea gardens and so on, so they wanted to prevent the tribal people from coming down from the hills and causing degradation.'[14]

In order to protect the tea gardens, their owners formulated a strategy.

Once a year, under the British, a column of Assam Rifles, the paramilitary force they had raised for the wider area would march to the tribal areas. The tribals who had not come down to the tea gardens and made themselves visible were presented with gifts of rock salt, tea leaves and trinkets. Those who had interfered with the plantations had their villages unceremoniously burnt.

Later officers in the region used their military personnel in very different ways to the British.

When Har Mander Singh first became political officer, he had a battalion of around 1200 men in his division. During his tenure, this number rose to seven battalions. In fact, as India increased its penetration and development of the region, the deployment of the Assam Rifles was expanded outside NEFA to Nagaland and Manipur.

A battalion was commanded by an army brigadier on deputation who was known as an inspector general. Later, commanding officers were of an even higher rank; a major general or someone more senior.

The inspector general reported to the governor of Assam.

The battalion was based at Lokra. At Bomdila barracks, there was a company of around 120 men.

Travelling to Lokra from Bomdila was quite difficult. Half the distance could be covered by jeep in four to five hours, but the rest of the journey had to be travelled by foot.

From around 1954 to 1960, when Har Mander was posted to NEFA as political officer, he and his team built and paved the entire route from Bomdila to Assam. After that, this entire journey from Lokra to Bomdila took a whole day by jeep.

Small groups of about ten to twelve Assam Rifles were posted to remote forward areas closer to the border. About forty to fifty in total were sent to such outposts. Har Mander could ask the brigadier in charge, or the Assam Rifles, for men as and when he needed them. The Indian strategy was to protect the land as well as help its people.

'If we did not occupy these areas, the Chinese would have taken them over,' he commented.[15]

The actual border drawn by the British—the McMahon Line—was so ill-defined in places that both countries adopted territory they considered as belonging to them, simply due to the passage of time.[16]

Har Mander also implemented a policy to take administration to the local people 'in small measures so that they could progress'. He said, 'And the proof of that progress is that today, after so many years, you have a government in Arunachal which is run by its own people.

You have people who have gone on to higher studies, people who are doctors, teachers, writers.'[17]

He continued, 'The administration established district, subdivisional and circle headquarters, to help develop and support the area. Gradually, medical and educational staff were brought to Kameng, NEFA.'[18]

Where tribals practised head-hunting, slavery and dowry-demand, the Indian official in charge gently discouraged such habits. With the arrival of more and more bureaucrats, technocrats, doctors and teachers over the years, and through common development and intensive agricultural programmes, the former NEFA now has over 140 educational institutions, and literacy has grown.

Har Mander would tour villages and, where possible, set up small administration centres right up to the border. The emphasis was on education and encouragement. In 1947, there were between two to four primary schools in the whole area.

There were just two roads. One was the route to Burma, the other was wiped out in an earthquake. Mainly, there were only foot tracks between villages. To cross a river, locals would either have to wade or use a cane hanging bridge.

The IFAS was meant to serve the border areas in the east and the west, such as the Khyber Pass. Compared with the commercially driven attitude of the British, the officials of the Indian government had a very different attitude towards this patch. Har Mander explained, 'After Independence, India's interest in these hills was because they are our people, because they are one of us. The idea was to develop them, to bring things that are already in the plains to them; like medical services, education services, agriculture services, craft services and so on.'[19]

Claude Arpi found that IFAS officers would undertake long tours, walking long distances, sometimes lasting several weeks, to visit remote villages by the Indo-Tibetan border. He praised these 'intrepid' officers and wrote, 'The fact remains that these officers who decided to sacrifice their careers to join the IFAS were all remarkable personalities, and even though the cadre does not exist anymore, these individuals should be role models for young IAS/IPS officers.'[20]

What was Har Mander's reaction when he received orders to escort the Dalai Lama into India? He said that he felt a surge of national pride.

'I didn't really feel at any time that I was not up to it. I was young, and I had a lot of ambition, so I never felt that I would not be able to do it. Somehow I felt that I was the right person for it.'[21]

But there must have been some concern? What difficulties did he anticipate?

'My only fear was that there might be sabotage and the Dalai Lama's life may be endangered. Fear of a fifth columnist. Fear that someone would harm him.'

'The prominent thought was that this is an important mission that has fallen to my lot,' he looked straight at me. 'I should carry it out well so that my career gets a further boost, and also somewhere I felt that nationally it was important. It was a question of India's prestige, and this matter has fallen to me just because of circumstances, because of communication difficulties, etc. Otherwise a much higher level of officer would have handled it. Those were the main feelings. The burden of responsibility.'[22]

4

THE WARRIORS

By 1954, Mao Zedong's education and reform programmes were taking hold in Tibet.

It started in the east, where Chinese culture and education were gradually imposed. Earlier policies in 1951 had used gentle persuasion, but now the strategy laid down by Peking was more direct and brutal.

Often the method applied was seen by the Tibetans and their sympathisers as particularly harsh, since the Han and Tibetan cultures were so different. Mao felt that in areas where communism and collective accountability was alien or resisted, it needed a push to become embedded into the population's psyche.

Tibet had mostly been a feudal society; whether under the sway of warlords, chieftains or monasteries. The poor were always beholden to their masters for their education and livelihoods.

So, the Chinese and the Tibetans tended to view each other with distrust and distaste. While the Chinese had clear aims—to secure the country's western flank and ensure that Tibet was under its control— the Tibetans were dismayed by the mostly violent attacks on their countrymen. Their Buddhist masters, the Dalai Lamas most of all, preached compassion and peace. It was, however, hard to reconcile an attitude of non-violence when villages were overrun and burned. It was hard for the Tibetans to adopt an attitude of compassion when monasteries were being pillaged and destroyed by the PLA.

The Buddhists were conflicted about how to handle the Chinese newcomers. Should they have compassion and look for humanity in the representatives of the new culture? Should they ignore them and carry on? Or should they try to find meaning in what was happening? Whatever the answer, armed resistance was not in the majority's lexicon. They were confused and helpless.

In 1954, the Tibetans did not appear to have an effective army or an adequate police force or any recourse to legal action. So, general pacifist monks in robes and sandals across the land had no protection. They, and the rural communities, were sitting targets.

However, there was a group of Tibetan warriors known as the Khampas. These men were skilled marksmen and were seldom seen without guns. Over time, they had developed a reputation for banditry. When the clash against the Chinese began to turn violent, they were the ones who picked up arms. Often, they were the only protectors of the Tibetans.

Around 1956–57, the important Sampheling monastery at Changtreng came under attack.

The locals revolted, and the Khampas blocked the water supply to the Chinese camp. In the grounds of Sampheling were 3000 monks and families who had either been left without homes because of new land reforms imposed by Peking or had been targets of the PLA. The Chinese circulated leaflets warning the rebels to give up, but the Khampas did not surrender. The Chinese deployed bombs resulting in mass civilian and Khampa casualties.[1]

Fortunately for Tibet, America was taking a strong and concerned interest in the advance of communism. According to Bruce Riedel, in 1950, Washington had been closely monitoring the situation.[2] President Eisenhower decided that his government must get involved. Thus, a Tibetan Task Force (TTF) was created with the aim of working with the Khampas to resist the Chinese advance wherever possible.

In Washington, John Greaney was made the deputy director of the TTF, which was led by director Desmond Fitzgerald. A former military intelligence officer who was fluent in Chinese, Ken Knaus, was also part of the team.

John Reagan was the first CIA agent to be part of the Tibetan team in Washington, later to be replaced by Frank Holober, who designed the actual plan for the TTF.

In 1955, President Eisenhower signed a presidential order, the National Security Directive 5412/2, which ordered the CIA to contain and control international communism.[3] This meant that America committed to supporting the Tibetan cause.

Financially, the Americans knew that the Dalai Lama and his family needed support and were already paying out $180,000 a year to Gyalo Thondup in Kalimpong. Gyalo Thondup had even created an account for this purpose.[4] The Dalai Lama was not involved, and some analysts feel he did not know what was going on.

The Dalai Lama's youngest brother, Tenzin Chogyal, now over seventy, told me his theory about why the Americans assisted the Tibetans.

'I think American help was to contain communism, not really to help the Tibetans, but the Tibetans became an instrument for that purpose. So, Americans, through the CIA, encouraged our freedom fighters by giving them arms, just enough to fight but not enough to make a difference. I think this started as early as 1955, when Tibetans in Kham and Amdo started to revolt because the Chinese were carrying out reforms. At that time American policy was spearheaded by John Foster Dulles, the Secretary of State, and the directive was to contain communism at any cost. This went on until Kissinger went to Peking and Nixon followed. I think the CIA help to the Tibetan freedom fighters did contribute towards His Holiness's escape, because they helped reduce Chinese presence in south Tibet.'[5]

On this issue, America had already been in close contact with the Dalai Lama's two eldest brothers, Thubten Jigme Norbu and Gyalo Thondup, who had settled in America and India respectively. Both

men kept up communication with the CIA. The brothers organized
for six Khampa rebels to be selected and taken to America in February
1957 for instruction. The two famous Tibetan men I mentioned
earlier trained by the CIA were called Athar and Lhotse. The others
were Wangdu, Tsewang, Dedrup and Dreshe. These men were tough
Khampa freedom fighters whose families and friends had suffered
torture, abuse and murder in the conflict. They were the ringleaders
of the Khampa soldiers who would mobilize to help the Dalai Lama.

The freedom fighters were taken from Tibet to America via a
circuitous route. First, they went to India, West Bengal; from here they
were smuggled into East Pakistan (now Bangladesh) and then taken by
the Americans.

'I think they were taken to Saipan first, an island in the Pacific,
then Okinawa, and later to Camp Hale in Colorado,' Tenzin said.

The training on Saipan Island was intense and took some getting
used to. The location was only a little above sea level, whereas much
of Tibet sits at 14,000 feet. But the Tibetans learnt fast, spending five
months on the training ground in total. Their chief instructor was
Roger McCarthy, who had been with the CIA for five years.

The Americans wanted the Tibetans to be a self-contained unit
when they went back to their country. The first batch was trained in
insurgency tactics and clandestine operations. In the autumn of 1957,
after the group had been prepared, they were sent back to Tibet. The
six men then split into two different teams. One team was to send
messages back and forth from Tibet to command headquarters in the
US, using an old Morse Code system dating from World War II with a
radio transmitter and a generator that was fired up by hand. The Dalai
Lama's older brother, Thubten Jigme Norbu, and a former manservant
of his, Jentzen, were with the group to translate the messages since
none of the Khampas spoke English.

The plan was to parachute one of the teams into Kham, near its
own home, to reinforce rebels fighting there. All six wanted to be
in this team, but only Wangdu, Dedrup, Dreshe and Tsewang were
selected. Athar and Lhotse were to form a team on their own and were

going to be dropped near Lhasa. Their mission was to make contact with high-ranking Tibetan officials here. These two Khampas had the communication skills needed for their task and they also knew Lhasa better than the others.

When the larger of the two teams, led by Wangdu, was dropped back into Tibet, it was not easy to mobilize resistance. The Tibetans had always believed in large numbers for their battlefield tactics; what McCarthy and the other Americans tried to teach them was the value of small unit strategy. While the team understood this, their counterparts back in Tibet still preferred larger groups that often stretched to fifty. Big numbers had worked in Kham and Amdo in 1956–57 and the Tibetans found it hard to be persuaded by their CIA-trained counterparts.

On the island of Okinawa, the Khampas received training in parachute dives. They were then taken to Camp Hale, which was at a height of 9200 feet, and the closest the Americans could get to simulating a Tibetan plateau.

Though the freedom fighters were taken to America for technical training in combat, according to Tenzin Choegyal, it was their expertise with guns, their bravery and the idea that they were defending Tibetan Buddhism that really kept them going. 'As it was the time of World War II, our chaps were trained to send Morse Code. People like Lhotse and Athar were trained to send messages and in reading maps. I think it's quite an achievement,' Tenzin recalled. 'The Tibetan code was formulated by a Mongol monk[6] who taught in New Jersey, America. You know, the roles people play, it's such a jigsaw puzzle, but they come together.'[7]

One author says that the Khampas also learnt how to use 60-mm and 57-mm rifles, explosives and grenades.[8] The Tibetan tele code Tenzin Choegyal refers to was created during this training.

· They also learnt:

'Fragmentation and incendiary grenades, fire and movement tactics, . . . offensive and defensive ambushes, an array of simple sabotage techniques, use of demolitions, Molotov cocktails, booby traps, unarmed and hand to hand combat, cross–country and night movement, observation, casing, authentication, elicitation, information collection, reports writing, tradecraft techniques, resistance organizations, sketching, preparation of drop zones, parachute ground training, simple psychological warfare techniques, first aid, simple disguise techniques, and physical fitness.'[9]

Athar and Lhotse were to be dropped near Lhasa to work directly with the Lord Chamberlain, Phala, the official in charge of the Dalai Lama's household and other senior Tibetans. They were also tasked with finding out what was needed by the Tibetan rebels with regard to equipment, their source of funding, and how many rebel troops could be relied on.

The pair was asked to find out if the Dalai Lama and his Cabinet, the *Kashag*, were being pressurized by the PLA and how he felt about the communist regime. They were to find out who the reliable people in the Kashag were and those that were not.

Athar and Lhotse were also asked to gauge the strength of common Tibetans and assess if they would engage in armed resistance. Another task involved gathering intelligence on the PLA troops that were in Lhasa—everything from numbers of troops to details of bridges, airports and roads built by the army. They were to trust no one except the two Tibetan officials they were going to meet in Lhasa, and Gyalo Thondup.

The other group was to be dropped in Kham where most of the Chinese-Tibetan conflicts were happening. Just before the re-infiltration, Tsewang accidentally shot his foot during training and was unable to recover in time to make the jump. This dampened the spirits of the remaining members of the group.

Both Khampa groups were brave and fearsome. Over the coming months and years, many Khampas were smuggled into the US and re-infiltrated into Tibet. Two members of the first team played a critical role in the Dalai Lama's escape, ensuring that he reached the Tibetan border safely. The rest also performed at such a level that they soon became targets for the PLA.

The Indians, as well as the Chinese, knew of the CIA-trained Tibetan rebels through intercepted messages. The PLA was able to track and kill most of the Khampas who had been through the CIA training, so that in the end, only twelve of the forty-nine Tibetan warriors survived. That is why, when I asked Tenzin Choegyal how the US-trained Khampas re-entered Tibet, he shook his head seriously, and said, 'By parachute, and most of them died.' He said that some did cross into Tibet by land.[10]

The ones who survived were tasked with gathering intelligence on the PLA and assessing the threats to the Dalai Lama's life. The two seniors, Athar and Lhotse, travelled with their revered leader, communicating with CIA headquarters, providing intelligence and taking advice.

Athar and Lhotse kept in touch with Washington and were tasked with receiving and distributing weapons—Lee Enfield .303 rifles, 60-mm mortars, 57-mm recoilless rifles, 2.36 bazookas, big grenade caches, .30 calibre light machine guns.[11] They were also given rifles of World War I vintage and later some M1 rifles. The Khampas had anti-tank guns, Sten guns, explosives, grenades and landmines, but in very limited numbers because it was difficult to drop these arms from a height of about 14,000 feet over a drop zone. The warriors were also given cyanide capsules to swallow in case of capture by the Chinese or in case of critical injury.

According to Tenzin, 'I think Athar and Lhotse were already dropped in Tibet in 1958 and they were hiding in the mountains. Later on, they joined the freedom fighter recruits in Southern Tibet, and became the leaders there. During that time, one Chinese military officer deserted his regiment and joined the freedom fighters. He also played a part in our freedom struggle, and later on he came to India, where he settled in one of our settlements in Bylakuppe, I think in Karnataka. He lived to a ripe old age.'[12]

*

Back in Tibet, in 1959, the Red Army continued to attack monasteries and villages, punishing anyone accused of harbouring the rebels.

They humiliated and tortured monks and nuns, wrapping monks in wool and dousing them in kerosene before setting them on fire. The Tibetan defence forces were disorganized and chaotic, and there was no effective chain of command.

As they had planned for many years, finally under Mao, the Chinese seized control of the water source of the whole region[13] and some of the most mineral-rich, strategically valuable parts of central Asia.

5

INSIDE POTALA PALACE

Aged four, the young Dalai Lama was installed in the dark, cavernous Potala Palace at Lhasa, a place where doors opened to more doors, leading to rooms, which opened out to more rooms; more than a thousand of them. There were chapels and huge chambers for large assemblies. It was like a vast, ossifying city within a palace. Located atop a hill, the palace was multiple stories high, towering at nearly 400 feet, and naturally it was overwhelming for a small child.

The Dalai Lama missed home. He needed affection and care. He found solace in his cook and caretaker, Ponpo, who had the same soothing, patient and affectionate manner as his own mother, Diki.

His younger brother, Tenzin Choegyal was placed in the Drepung Monastery, a few miles away from Potala Palace.

They had been taken prematurely from their home. Being so young, it was hard for them to articulate their feelings.

Speaking about his mother much later, Choegyal reminisced about being sent 'homemade cookies, lollipops, chewing gum . . . all wrapped up in a scarf'. He would 'sniff the scarf, desperately trying to recapture the smell of her'.[1]

Meanwhile, his brother was coming to terms with the bewildering, controlled, isolated, artificial world that cocooned the seniormost Tibetan Buddhist lama incarnate. His bedroom, on the seventh and highest floor of the building, was 'pitifully cold and ill-lit,' with 'decrepit'[2] wall hangings, hiding layers of dust. Breakfast would be at 7 a.m., after which he would have lessons. He and his older brother, Lobsang, a restrained and mild boy, studied the Tibetan Buddhist texts together.

As he sat on shiny stone floors of the cold palace, the boy Dalai Lama was soberly immersed in the history and the lives of his predecessors as they loftily stared down at him from ancient wall paintings.

The Dalai Lama was taught two scripts—one exclusively for writing personal and official documents, the other for writing manuscripts. His sharp memory and mind were honed partly in learning the classic scriptures by heart. After lessons, he would meditate—a practice he routinely follows to this day—for at least four hours each morning before sunrise and breakfast.

The next part of his day was spent in debating contests, a technique that is common to all trainee Buddhist monks and nuns. Whatever is learnt is debated with older monks, teachers and instructors. This tradition dates back centuries. One or two students, the Defenders, sit on the floor cross-legged while the Challenger—usually an older student—recites prayer chants before stating his or her question, looking the opponent straight in the eye. The Challenger may hold a rosary in their right hand. Before finishing the question, the Challenger pulls the rosary up to his or her left shoulder and leaves it there. If the Challenger does not have a rosary, he or she raises their right hand slowly until it is level with the top of their head. The Challenger then brings it down hard into the palm of his or her left hand while stamping a bent left leg on the ground to emphasize their point. The Challenger keeps their left hand pointing towards the Defender in a gesture that invites an answer from the seated student. If the Challenger has a rosary, it falls across the arm to the left hand by now.

The idea behind debating is to train the younger monk or nun to focus and concentrate on his or her thought processes. Subjects may vary from the deeply philosophical to seemingly random topics like the meaning of the colour grey, and each hand gesture has deeper meanings to do with rebirth, compassion and wisdom. This Buddhist ritual is enthralling, beautiful and poetic to observe. I am hypnotized every time I watch it in a monastery or a nunnery. For me, it remains one of the most absorbing experiences of Tibetan Buddhism.

Debating aside, after lessons, the young Dalai Lama would have to attend to affairs of state. Regent Reting Rimpoche would chair the session, with the child Dalai Lama instructed to remain silent throughout.

The boy found his studies—and the politics—boring, preferring the excitement of action and playing games of war. He was not allowed to play with other children, so he inveigled the adults around him into mock battles.

When he was eight years old, Lobsang was moved from Lhasa to a private school, severing another link that the Dalai Lama had with his childhood and family. Surrounded by pomp and pageantry, but living a sterile life, the boy's early years were far from normal, something he often refers to.

Though at that stage he had little interest in his studies, he enjoyed living at the Norbulingka summer palace in the warmer seasons. He and his entire retinue would decamp there each year.

Surrounded by greenery in Norbulingka, the teenage Dalai Lama felt a greater sense of freedom and would take Choegyal out in a little boat on a small lake. His attendants would keep pace with the boat, walking or running along the shore.[3]

From his studies, the Dalai Lama discovered the history of Tibet, but not too much about the outside world. So, he was endlessly curious, and always had questions for visitors, particularly Westerners such as the Austrian mountaineer Heinrich Harrer who later wrote *Seven Years in Tibet*.[4]

The young Dalai Lama, ensconced in a vast mountain palace surrounded by 16,000-feet high mountain ranges on three sides, was both physically and psychologically removed from the rest of the world.

The main knowledge he gained of World War II was through a seven-volume set of books that he transcribed into Tibetan, and through dated issues of *Life* magazine. The stories of power and leadership he had access to were histories of his disparate Dalai Lama predecessors who were a motley set of leaders. Some were more practically effective than others and each had different qualities; some more political, others more religious.

Tibet had once been ruled by religious kings, but by the ninth century the line ended, and the territory was dominated by groups loyal to various clan chiefs and warlords. Tibet's relationship with China was consolidated around the time of the Fifth Dalai Lama, known as the Great Fifth.

The Great Fifth was leading his branch of Buddhism at a time of competition with other emerging disciplines, so he reached out to Gusri Khan, the chieftain of Qoshot Mongols from Mongolia. Gusri Khan reunified the whole of Tibet and offered it to the Fifth Dalai Lama who became Tibet's spiritual and temporal leader.

Khan did battle with the Great Fifth's warlord enemies and placed him safely under his protection. One author wrote that the Great Fifth, and subsequent Dalai Lamas, owed their positions to Gusri Khan.[5] He was not from the Qing dynasty but rather, he was a Mongol.

The Qing dynasty was founded by the Manchus who later conquered the whole of China, and being Buddhist, the Manchu emperors developed a priest-patron relationship with the Dalai Lamas of Tibet.[6] Sometimes, the Manchu representative to Lhasa was ineffective, and Potala kept the power unto itself. At other times, Peking held full sway over the Tibetans.

Tibet's relationship with Peking would see-saw. The Tibetans were relaxed even when the Chinese capital exerted muscle, but they were always beholden in some sense to Peking and this may have crippled them when it came to reaching out to the world for help.

The Qing dynasty was overthrown in the 1911–12 Chinese revolution. At the time, the Thirteenth Dalai Lama was in exile in India. He returned to Tibet in 1913 and made a declaration that amounted to Tibet's independence from China.

Back then Tibet had the opportunity to petition the UN for international acknowledgement of its being a sovereign state. This was its one chance for autonomy, but it refused to take it. That inaction was to later be used as evidence by the Chinese that Tibet supposedly had no interest in its own independence.

By 1949, the People's Republic of China (PRC) had been created, unifying the country and ushering it into a communist era of stability. It was too late for any action on the part of the Tibetans, for as chairman of his huge nation, Mao Zedong would brook no argument.

The task for the new Chinese leadership was to capture outlying territories like Tibet, Mongolia and Xinjiang, home to the Uyghurs. The first was to secure its perimeters in the new world order. Though 5000 years old and one of the world's four ancient civilizations, China now felt that the growing might of Russia, Great Britain and America indicated a stronger need to protect itself.

The border also needed to be strengthened, especially on the western flank.[7] China felt that there were unresolved border issues with neighbouring India, such as a historic link to Tawang Monastery at the border. Tawang Monastery, for as long as Buddhists could remember, had always paid dues to the Buddhist monastery at Tsona. If it was always part of China's Buddhist empire, the Chinese argued, how could India justify its claim?

The second issue was the tricky situation of the Dalai Lama holding such sway over the entire Tibetan Buddhist community within Tibet and outside. Chinese communism did not allow for what it called breakaway factions and separatist movements, so while China professed full respect for the office of the religious head, it felt it needed to contain the leader and his people.

It had been to China's advantage that so far the prime minister of its big neighbour, India, respected its strength. Until now, Nehru had handled relations between them with cautious diplomacy. Nehru had a policy of outreach and friendship towards his neighbour. He recognized which of the two nations was mightier and more powerful, and which had better defence capabilities. He could be relied on to be careful and avoid rash decisions. There was no reason for him not to maintain the status quo.

In 1950, the PLA of China marched into Lhasa. About 80,000 of its troops faced a motley collection of around 8500 soldiers and officers. Tibet now had to face the consequences of the fact that its religious heads had devoted meagre resources to building a strong defence capability.

The Dalai Lama was fifteen years old and still a leader-in-training. Government ministers, after consulting two state ministers, decided that even if the teenager wasn't quite ready, the Tibetans needed to have a figurehead around whom to coalesce. The pressure mounted. The Dalai Lama remembers that he felt an urgency from the people, the cabinet, and even from his regent, the elder monk who was also his guide. The message he heard from all quarters was that it was now time for 'the Dalai Lama to take temporal responsibility'.[8]

With subjugation to the PRC likely to become fact, the young Dalai Lama was required to take command of affairs of state. He would be a figurehead and leader that disillusioned Tibetans could rally around. He would be a person of significance for the Chinese to negotiate with and might be something of a bulwark.

But he didn't feel ready. He fell back on his religious lineage, hoping that historic events would provide him with protection. The young monk cited the fact that his predecessor had not taken on the so-called temporary responsibility until he was eighteen.

'I told them, "Previous Dalai Lama, at eighteen years age he took [sic] ... So, let me, for at least about two years, let me take more study." That time, that period, I think is the prime time for study.'[9]

While the Dalai Lama did not feel ready to take on the burdens of state, he was only too aware that Chinese forces had already penetrated his rural childhood homeland, Amdo, as well as Kham.

The clamour from all those close to him, and his people, was so loud and intense that the Dalai Lama gave in.

The young Tibetan ruler did not disappoint, much to the relief of his regent and cabinet.

When the PLA attacked and captured Chamdo in 1950 the Dalai Lama sought protection in Dromo, in south Tibet across the border with Sikkim. While there, he deputed two Tibetan officials to negotiate with the Chinese.[10]

The Tibetan representatives arrived in Peking where they were presented with a proposal. On the basis of this, a document was prepared that came to be called the Seventeen-Point Agreement.

Though the officials stated that they could not act on the Dalai Lama's behalf and were only there in their personal capacities, they were made to sign what the Chinese would later declare to be an agreement for them to peacefully 'liberate' the entire region of Tibet and allow the Chinese to take control. The Tibetans did not want to but were told in no uncertain terms that there would be a takeover of Tibet one way or another, peaceful or otherwise. The Tibetan delegation was intimidated, and in 1951, the signing took place.[11]

The Dalai Lama recalled the sequence of events after he was handed full responsibility for the Tibetan people. The first time he heard that the Seventeen-Point Agreement had been signed was on India's national broadcaster, All India Radio, while he was in Dromo. 'Then, eventually, Chinese representative Mr Zhang Jingwu, reached Dromo through India. Then I, for the first time, received a copy of the Seventeen-Point Agreement.'[12]

He told me that he considers his then chief official representative, Ngapoi Ngawang Jigme, a virtual and literal 'prisoner of war' at the negotiating table. The Dalai Lama said that though representative Jigme was the head of the Tibetan delegation, he was forced to sign under duress.

However, it was done. The Chinese now had their symbolic trophy Agreement, and the Dalai Lama returned with the Chinese representative to Lhasa.

He had severe misgivings about the Chinese act, he recalled. He and his team were full of 'distrust and doubt'.[13]

At the start of this marriage of convenience, Mao Zedong adopted a soft approach towards Tibet, to see if the Tibetan leadership could be won over without coercion.

In 1954, he invited the Dalai Lama to China. The young man, who had barely travelled outside his native territory, was impressed with the country. He observed with delight a growing economy, an industriousness in the people and high productivity. A shiny new future was being presented, which might one day also be possible for his own beloved kingdom. He began to believe in a way to improve the conditions of his own people and reduce the lazy corruption that had taken hold of the Tibetan feudal system. He spent nearly a year in China.

'1954 autumn I received an invitation from the Chinese government to participate in Chinese National Congress, and I went. And about five to six months I spent in Peking itself. During that period, I met [on] occasion Chairman Mao Zedong and also many high officials. We became very close friends, particularly Chairman Mao Zedong. Then I developed full confidence; now we can work.'[14]

Excited by the modern, well organized environment, the Dalai Lama said that he was 'very much attracted' to Marxist socialism. On one occasion, he even told a Chinese official, 'I want to join the Chinese Communist Party.' But he was told, 'Wait, wait. Better to wait.' He says that as far as social economic theory goes, 'I'm Buddhist-Marxist.' He rejects Leninism as being 'ruthless, totalitarian, with too much emphasis on power'.[15]

The first of October is the National Day of the PRC. That year, the Indian prime minister and the Chinese premier were the chief guests at a dinner that was being held in honour of Chinese premier Zhou Enlai. It was a revealing encounter. The Dalai Lama remembers the rituals, saying, 'A strange sort of experience. We were waiting for Pandit Nehru. Zhou Enlai was there, very smart.'[16]

While saying this, he sat up straight in imitation of the Chinese leader.

Nehru was leading the Indian delegation. After introducing the Chinese dignitaries, Zhou Enlai introduced the Dalai Lama. The latter recounted, 'Nehru looked almost frozen, not moving.'[17] The Dalai Lama added that the Indian leader did not even make eye contact, let alone speak to him. 'Speechless. At least [sic] twenty, thirty seconds. I was a little bit embarrassed. Then Zhou Enlai—very smart—immediately introduced the next person, Panchen Lama.'[18] The Tibetan leader said that the idea to better watch and protect the Sino-Indian border may have occurred to Nehru around then, since the Indian prime minister realized how big a problem Tibet, abutting his country, was for the Chinese. He didn't want it to become a problem for India too. Here, the Dalai Lama referred to a letter that Nehru's home minister Sardar Patel had written to him in 1950, stating that Tibet was a big issue and that the undefined McMahon Line border needed much stronger defences. About Nehru, the Dalai Lama said, 'I think he reflected on these things in that shocked moment. So, that's our first experience of meeting with Nehru.'[19]

The Dalai Lama returned to Lhasa, but an armed resistance erupted in eastern Tibet in 1956 as the Khampa rebels and the Amdo nomads fought with the Chinese who were forcibly redistributing the land. This area was outside the jurisdiction of the Tibetan administration, which was almost impotent in this crisis.

The armed resistance would eventually lead to the explosive assault on Lhasa.

With the Tibetans powerless, the rebels turned to Washington for help, specifically the CIA, with whom Gyalo Thondup had been working since 1951.

Talk of cooperation between China and Tibet did not translate into action. In fact, in eastern Tibet, a programme of re-education had begun, since China could not carry out a system of reform unless all its people were under one school programme.

Since the Chinese leadership saw America as its principal foe, it felt that a united China was vital to make the country stronger.

This no longer left time for gentle seduction. Stronger persuasion, it felt, was now needed.

Kham and Amdo were the first areas to feel the effect.

The Dalai Lama was troubled by this move.

Between November 1956 and March 1957, the Dalai Lama was invited by the Indian government to celebrate a landmark Buddha Jayanti. The festival commemorates the day of Gautama Buddha's birth, enlightenment and death. Before getting onto a specially commissioned train with his family to visit various Buddhist shrines around the country, the Dalai Lama talked to Nehru about staying on in India and not returning to his troubled nation.

Nehru was stunned and said that peace in Asia depended on good relations between India and China. Further, by signing the Seventeen-Point Agreement with China, the Indian prime minister told his guest, Tibet had removed itself from interventions by international powers as it was now more or less a part of China.

The Dalai Lama was sorely disappointed.

As for what was going on in Tibet at the time, the Dalai Lama lamented at the manner in which the Chinese communists wished to carry out their reforms and cited it as the cause of the troubles. He said that the method applied by the Chinese could not adapt to an ancient landlord-peasant set up.

The Dalai Lama told me that after being handed the leadership, he set up his own Reform Committee. He wished to bring Tibet into the twentieth century by abolishing inheritable debt, by introducing a high-quality education programme, by establishing a judicial system and by creating roads capable of carrying wheeled transport.

These changes were not welcomed by the Chinese since they wanted to change the landscape with their own Communist systems. The Tibetan spiritual leader described the 1955–56 Chinese reform movement as 'ruthless'.[20]

The Dalai Lama spoke of the increasing numbers of Chinese troops entering eastern Tibet to combat the Tibetan resistance. He noted that though his country's rebels captured Chinese officials and killed their soldiers, the PLA onslaught was merciless, and the Red Army just kept arriving in steady waves. 'We already developed some sort of contact with Chinese government, we had the opportunity to send some fact-finding delegations,' he recalled.[21]

This 'contact' refers to the fact-finding delegation the Dalai Lama sent to Tibet from exile during 1979–85. These delegations were not sent in the 1950s because the Tibetan leadership was in constant, daily contact with the Chinese authorities and in touch with the conditions of ordinary Tibetans.[22]

Tibetan researchers based in Kameng found that entire villages were devoid of men because males above childhood age had either been killed or had escaped. The Dalai Lama told me: 'So International Jurists Commission,[23] finally they made one report. They called it genocide. Then, 1959, things become [sic] worse and worse and worse. Very difficult, in spite of our efforts to cool things down.'[24]

Notwithstanding his youth, the Dalai Lama had to negotiate two key relationships with global powers: one with India, the other with China. This meant communication and contact with Nehru, Mao and Zhou Enlai.

The story of the Chinese invasion of Tibet is easy to paint in black and white, but the fact is that Tibet had been disorganized and, in many places, corrupt. Just because the majority of the country was Buddhist did not mean that the clergy always ruled wisely or cleanly. On the contrary, there were instances of exploitation, sexual or otherwise.

The Tibetans had not planned for the future. They had not built an adequate defence infrastructure. The old leadership had simply buried its head in the sand and expected the raw young leader would somehow sort everything out.

It was an unfair and unrealistic expectation.

6

TENSION IN LHASA

The 10th and 17th of March are indelibly marked in every Tibetan's mind. Young and old, whether they lived through that time or whether they are millennials, these dates matter in the Tibetan calendar. The days are a reminder of the dramatic events that unfolded over one week in 1959.

While it is important to note these dates, the context will be made clearer by looking at what had been happening in Tibet some years before. In this chapter, I will also examine the childhood of the Dalai Lama and that of some of his siblings.

Tibet's traditional way of life had been in decline for several years. Through the early fifties, the Chinese had successfully won over key Tibetans from the monastic leadership, the merchant-trading community and the aristocracy. They had used wile rather than force. For instance, they gave monasteries sophisticated bribes in the form of donations.

As part of his reforms, Chairman Mao had created a new education system, setting up civilian schools. This masterstroke weakened the hold that the monasteries had over the common man. Suddenly, the children of ordinary families were learning Han culture in place of the traditional Tibetan syllabus and script. It also meant that the curriculum could be diversified. Language, religion and other topics were no longer decided and taught by Buddhist monks. One of the most important planks of power, education, was now held by the Chinese.

I'd like to illustrate what was happening in Tibet at that time with what a Tibetan noblewoman told me. Mrs Namgyal Lhamo Taklha, mentioned earlier in this book, was married to the Dalai Lama's older brother, Lobsang Samden Taklha, who passed away in 1985. As a young Tibetan at school in India, Namgyal experienced the power of the Chinese, even on upper class families like hers.

'I was in Darjeeling then, in 1954. The Chinese had really come into central Tibet and Lhasa, and they had been well established. They more or less pressured all the families who had children in schools in India to bring them back to Tibet. There was so much pressure that my parents took us back, to Tibet, where we joined a Chinese school for two years.'

As the unrest in Tibet escalated and clashes with the PLA increased, Namgyal recalls that a big family decision was made. 'Then my mother sort of more or less kidnapped us from school and told the principals that we were coming back. We were leaving for pilgrimage during Buddha Jayanti. We had to leave all our bedding, eating utensils and everything in school. We remained in Darjeeling from 1956 till 2005, when I made a one-month trip. I didn't go back to Tibet at all.'[1]

Namgyal's parents, mostly her mother, would come to visit her in India, making the perilous journey across Tibet just to see her daughter. 'But of course, in winter my parents came, especially my mother. It was not easy coming on a horse for maybe twenty, twenty-one days and then spending about three months with us before she could go back.'[2]

Namgyal, in her lifetime, remembers very open borders between India and Tibet. She said, '. . . really, everywhere, it was open. The whole India–Tibet border, there weren't really any restrictions. If anybody wanted to come they could easily come.'[3] She told me that things started tightening up 'after the Chinese entered, definitely after 1959'.[4]

The Chinese influence on Tibetans was rapidly increasing across the classes and most aspects of society and generations.

The next step on the Chinese agenda was to control whatever defence structure the Tibetans had built. So a new Tibetan army, led by ten command leaders, was established. Just two of these command leaders were Tibetan, and one was a close friend of the Chinese, a collaborator who even wore a Chinese officer's uniform at the inauguration ceremony.[5]

By early 1952, PLA generals were demanding that the Tibetan political leadership hand over control of the Tibetan army. The Kashag turned to two prime ministers who had been appointed to run Lhasa while the Dalai Lama had been away the year before. The popular, loyal prime ministers decided that instead of turning their troops over to the Chinese, they would shrink the whole of the Tibetan army to just three regiments. This enraged the Chinese, who sent 3000 more troops to Lhasa in response.

The Tibetan capital now reluctantly hosted roughly 20,000 foreign soldiers.

The PRC pressurized the Dalai Lama and his Kashag to dismiss the prime ministers or else risk a violent showdown. Left with little choice, the young Dalai Lama sacked his prime ministers.

The Tibetans were saddened. Their loss of confidence was exacerbated by the fact that the PLA was taking away any extra food that the people had, and as a result, famine was affecting swathes of the population. There had not been such a debilitating shortage of food in Tibetan memory. Rising food prices and outbreaks of disease were weakening the people. Ordinary Tibetans started to feel resentful towards the Kashag for not standing up to the PRC.

The Chinese, meanwhile, had thought of a way to solve the crisis and consolidate their hold on Tibet at the same time. They decided to import grains and other food from India to bring an end to the famine in its western region. So, the two nations created the trade compact, the Panch Shila Agreement, by which all trade negotiations concerning Tibet would go through Peking. Tibetan authorities were sidelined to such an extent that the first meeting between India and China on this topic took place without the knowledge of the Kashag or the Dalai Lama. A clause in the Panch Shila Agreement now referred to Tibet as 'a region of China'.[6]

As a result of what had been happening, the international perception of Tibet started to change.

Back in the region that was resisting subjugation, the Chinese began to introduce small technological developments and printed Lhasa newspapers in the Tibetan language with selected news items every ten days. This kind of tactic found favour among the people, although later actions by the Chinese had the opposite effect.

Over the coming years, the Chinese tightened their hold on Tibet, attacking sacred institutions like the monasteries, mentioned previously, as well as dismantling Tibetan infrastructure.

Resistance to the Chinese grew, with the Khampa warriors and other tribes fighting the PLA.

The Dalai Lama was cognizant of the unrest in his country but at the same time he was bound by duty and tradition to continue studying to attain the highest qualifications a Buddhist monk can achieve. It was his destiny, and he needed to earn his place as the religious leader of the Tibetan Buddhists. He needed to make the sacrifices and undertake the necessary diligence that had started when he was discovered as a child incarnate. Though he was surrounded by political strife, he also had to carve time out to follow the path chosen for him.

The Dalai Lama and his siblings had taken to their childhood training in different ways. While initially, the Dalai Lama had got bored at times and was not so committed to his studies, he later developed a fascination for academic learning.

On the other hand, the Dalai Lama's youngest brother, Tenzin Choegyal, was always full of surprises when he was young. Even now, so many decades later, he is often jokey and unpredictable.

Author Stephen Talty describes how, as a thirteen-year-old in the Drepung Monastery, Tenzin Choegyal was a monk with mischief on his mind. He is depicted carrying a needle and cotton thread. When sitting on the floor behind monks who were deep in prayer, he would sew their clothes together without their knowledge. When they tried to stand up after their contemplations, the monks were confused as they'd find that their robes had been inextricably joined together.

While Tenzin was having fun and making mischief in the monastery, he was also aware of a darkening atmosphere in Lhasa. Tenzin told Talty that he and his classmates could sense a brewing unrest among the Tibetans. The Dalai Lama's youngest brother felt that this might result in a battle between the Tibetans and the PLA.[7] Tenzin was picking up on the inevitability of armed conflict, but his patriotism convinced him that the Tibetans would win.

This observation by Tenzin ties in with what happened at one of the weekly lunches between the Dalai Lama and his mother. The young man's family would come to meet him since he was not allowed to leave Norbulingka Palace.

Around the beginning of 1959, before the Tibetan New Year in February, Diki told him that Khampa rebels were now populating Lhasa, and that there were frequent clashes between them and the PLA. The Dalai Lama was twenty-three. The PLA soldiers must have been of a similar age.

Talty writes that the young soldiers often missed their homes and felt alien in this new land. Even though their faces remained impassively neutral and they were highly disciplined, the truth was that they were unhappy because the Lhasans resented them. The PLA represented a controlling and oppressive power.

It was uncomfortable being agents of the powerful in Lhasa.

The Tibetan capital, by the Kyichu River, was not considered a popular posting by soldiers. They often got depressed because most of the surroundings was downbeat. Even the famous river on the outskirts of Lhasa was no picnic spot; in places it had a sombre and morbid atmosphere. This was because poor Tibetans, unable to afford the more expensive ritual of sky burial, consigned their dead to the Kyichu. But the PLA had to obey instructions and stay put.

Outside the city, to the south-east, on the shores of the Kyichu River, some of the Khampas pitched their tents. The warriors were plotting their next move.

For as long as anybody knew, they had always presented a striking image wearing leather belts, guns held firmly in them; high boots and hats.

Away from the river, the atmosphere in Lhasa was growing febrile. The Dalai Lama, holed up in the Norbulingka, had a glimpse of what was happening, but he was not part of it.

The Dalai Lama has a presence that fills any place he is in.

I appreciated this myself and felt a sense of peace and tranquillity when I visited Dharamsala, where he now lives. It was palpable on landing at the tiny aerodrome. There is a stillness, a calm in the air. A feeling that this is the domicile of someone special. Similarly, back in 1959, the Lhasans felt hope as long as the Dalai Lama was in his palace, even if they could not see their Precious Jewel. They derived strength and energy from the fact that he was among them.

Because of the devotion of the Tibetan people towards their ruler, the Chinese leadership had been feeling for some time that it was important to have at the very least, a sympathetic, and at best, a subservient Dalai Lama, and had issued several invitations to him to go to Peking and visit the country again. But stories abounded of senior monks accepting invitations and then disappearing.

The Chinese continued their overtures to the leader of the Tibetans, hoping to win him across to their side. For this to happen, it would be easier if he was among them. Perhaps he might become more malleable and even agree to give up his role to his second in command, the Panchen Lama.

The US expert on South Asia, Bruce Riedel has written about this period in Sino-Tibetan history. He observed, 'What the Chinese wanted was pretty clear. They wanted the Dalai Lama to be a docile, complicit collaborator, a participant who would cooperate with their takeover of Tibet. That he would bless it, both spiritually and practically, and they would therefore find their occupation of Tibet was made easier.'[8]

By February 1959, Radio Peking stated that the Dalai Lama would be going to Peking, a piece of news that was as much a shock to the young leader as it was to his terrified people. He had no intention of leaving Lhasa and was determined to sit for the exams he had been preparing for since the age of thirteen. If he passed them, he would become a Master of Metaphysics. The Dalai Lama did not go to Peking.

During this period, he received an invitation from the recently promoted PLA Commander in Chief in Lhasa, General Tan Kuansen, to attend a new dance performance at the Chinese army camp. The Dalai Lama demurred, but the General pursued him for an appearance at his headquarters at Yutok. So, a date was set—10 March 1959.

As the head of the Tibetan people, attending long, drawn-out evenings of entertainment and speeches by ambassadors and royalty from all over the world was tedious par for the course for him. He knew that avoiding the event would not be acceptable since he felt that diplomacy demanded a courteous relationship with the Chinese.

As the invitation had been extended through a direct conversation between the Chinese official and the Dalai Lama, coordination of the visit did not pass through normal protocol.

The Dalai Lama's head of security was called to Yutok on 9 March. He was forbidden from informing the people of Tibet outside the Kashag about the visit, and, more importantly, the PLA told him that none of the Dalai Lama's bodyguards would be allowed to escort their beloved leader on the occasion. So, the Dalai Lama's gatekeepers only found out about the show the night before the event. It seems that no one had told them. They became alarmed.

They feared for their leader's life because sometimes it had happened that the Chinese would extend an invitation to a senior lama, only to kidnap or kill him, or both. The Dalai Lama's courtiers were frightened that their leader too would be abducted, never to be seen again. This fear fuelled a growing paranoia and rumour mill among Lhasans, who, every day, imagined a new threat to their Precious Jewel from different Chinese agents.

On the day of the event, when the people of Lhasa learnt about the invitation, they decided that it must be a trap. They ran towards the Norbulingka.

One of the concerned Tibetan government officials was a young man called Barshi Ngawang who consulted the most important of the oracles, the Nechung. The oracle was said to house the spirit that kept guard over the Dalai Lama and his government.[9]

The Nechung Oracle, Talty says, first gave a non-committal answer as to whether or not the Dalai Lama was in danger. Barshi pushed him to be more definitive. Then the Nechung performed his rituals again, allowing the spirit to enter his body. This time he told Barshi that the 'Guru' ought not to leave his quarters. This was the signal Barshi had been waiting for. It indicated a clear threat to his leader.

This was not the only sign that scared the gatekeepers. The Dalai Lama had twenty-five Khampa warrior bodyguards, but the Chinese, for the first time, had instructed them to leave their principal two miles from the Chinese military headquarters, giving an order that the PLA would take over and handle the Tibetan leader's security themselves.

The Dalai Lama likes to keep his family close to him even today. Probably, then as now, they are among his most trusted people. At that time, his chief bodyguard was his brother-in-law. He was the one who had been given the order to leave the Dalai Lama's bodyguards behind on the day of the dance performance.

Phala, the Lord Chamberlain, and other staff, advised the young leader not to go. But the Dalai Lama was, and is still, not keen on formality and will dispense with official procedures if he feels like it. Back in March 1959, he did not see anything wrong in attending the performance in an extemporaneous fashion and insisted on going.

Barshi was desperate. He was more concerned for the Dalai Lama's safety than the Dalai Lama himself. Barshi reacted quickly. He sent an unidentifiable letter to two local monasteries, telling them that their leader was going to the Chinese military headquarters. Then, he cycled frantically to various places in Lhasa city, including Potala, telling residents to collect and encircle the Norbulingka to stop the Dalai Lama from getting out. They had to keep him safe.

Barshi was not the only devotee to take it upon himself to highlight the potential threat to their leader. Several individuals spread panic among the people that led to a call to collect, to physically prevent the Dalai Lama from leaving his home and from riding into danger.

Early the next morning, word reached the Dalai Lama's mother that her son was at risk. She was not too worried because she knew that he was well guarded with a security team and was behind ramparts. Instead, Diki immediately thought of her youngest son, Tenzin Choegyal, who had left for the Chinese military headquarters to attend the event. She was terrified for him.[10]

When the Chinese military transport arrived to take a retinue of the cabinet, religious heads and Choegyal to the Chinese headquarters, they suddenly became aware of noisy crowds streaming towards the Norbulingka. Though the elders were fretting, Choegyal found it all very exciting.

The crowd was angry and some of them were vengeful. The people did not have just one target for their wrath. They were mad at the Chinese for being in Lhasa but they were also cross with their government for standing by silently. The crowd was frustrated at corrupt officials. They knew the officers were being bribed by the Chinese into acquiescing to their mighty neighbour's whim.

At the Chinese military headquarters, the top officials were growing impatient. The noise of the Tibetans could be heard from afar, and the atmosphere at the barracks was tense. Hours passed by.[11] A short version of the entertainment was put on, and Choegyal watched with enjoyment.

While all this was happening, PLA soldiers marched into Diki Tsering's home. They were blocked by her staff from entering her inner quarters. They left in high dudgeon. Knowing that Diki may be in danger, the Dalai Lama's chief bodyguard had quickly smuggled her out and escorted her down the road to Norbulingka.

Still watching the show, Choegyal did not know that his mother was being moved to safety. Meanwhile, Diki, worried about Choegyal, sent emissaries to the PLA headquarters, but they could not find him.

After the entertainment and a very strained lunch, Choegyal was released by the PLA at 4 p.m. He was found and taken to Norbulingka, where he was reunited with his mother.

When I ask the Dalai Lama what happened that day, he starts off by describing the people who had gathered in Lhasa and the suffering that many of them had gone through. He says that because the Tibetans had found it hard to resist the Chinese, they assumed the worst of their neighbours—rightly or wrongly—and felt that if the Dalai Lama was with the Chinese unprotected, he would likely suffer in some way. Their own experience of becoming refugees—when they escaped from eastern and north-east Tibet—played into this narrative. Nonetheless, rumour, fear and ignorance spread among the crowd.

The Tibetan leader says that Lhasans were recalling how easily the regions of Amdo and Kham, in eastern Tibet, had fallen to Chinese troops.

The Dalai Lama knew that the Tibetans who were protecting him on the streets around Norbulingka had their own local leaders. He was concerned that a Tibetan attack on Chinese soldiers would trigger a retaliatory massacre. He tried to quell the passion of the leaders of the rebellion by talking to them directly. 'After a few days I called the leader of these people. They had set up some kind of committee. And I told them, "Please, don't stay here. If you remain like this, it's causing more tension, so better to return. Some of your representatives, a few of them, can remain in Norbulingka. I won't go", but they would not listen.'[12]

A Chinese eyewitness, Shan Chao, who was just outside Lhasa, described how, for the first time, he could see rifles pointing out of Potala Palace's windows. There is a mountain between the middle of Lhasa and the Norbulingka. Chao observed Tibetans staggering up the mountainside, nearly collapsing under the weight of ammunitions and the accoutrements of war. He watched other Tibetan soldiers move into place on the steep slopes, alert and ready.[13]

Meanwhile, the Dalai Lama was considering a speedy departure from Lhasa.

*

Namgyal Lhamo Taklha had settled in India by the time of the Tibetan uprising on 10 March 1959. Speaking about this story and the Dalai Lama's escape at her home in Dehradun during the inaugural Valley of Words Literature Festival,[14] she said, 'It was 10 March 1959 when the Tibetans rose against Chinese oppression and occupation of our country. I was in school in Darjeeling, it was an international school, a missionary school . . . and some friend came up to me and said, you know, in the newspaper there was a write up about Tibet, there was a revolt going on in Tibet. Many Tibetans were being killed and the Tibetans rose up against the Chinese. Also, there was bombing in the Norbulingka, which is the palace of His Holiness the Dalai Lama and it was just sort of, we were so . . . it was shocking. I had my younger sister with me there and it was very disturbing and so we were both crying. Then our teachers and school friends were really very caring and understanding and they consoled us. [The newspaper said that] many people have been killed, the Summer Palace office assumes the Dalai Lama had been bombed . . . we kept looking at the newspaper and then one day, a few days back they said that Dasang Dadul Tsarong [who had been the commander in chief of the Tibetan army] had been imprisoned and he had died. And that turned out to be my grandfather. It was really such a shock saying oh, you know at home my grandfather's gone, now what's happened to the home, what's happened to my aunt and the other relatives at home. What is going to happen to Tibet? That's when His Holiness the Dalai Lama came out. Then, what happened to His Holiness the Dalai Lama . . . and then you know it was just really traumatic for us.'[15]

7

THE ESCAPE

In March 1959, around 90,000 Tibetans visited Lhasa to celebrate Losar, the Tibetan New Year.

But the reformist work of the Chinese government, combined with the continuing presence of the PLA troops in Lhasa was causing bitter resentment, and there was tension in the city.

For a few weeks, Diki Tsering and her daughter had been discussing a means of escape[1] as they had been observing the rising temperature in Lhasa.

The Dalai Lama's brothers and US-trained Khampas were in communication with the CIA. America wanted, strategically, to have the Dalai Lama declare himself an ally. They also wanted him as a figurehead for the support it had been providing the Tibetan rebels.

In the recent years leading up to 1959, the Dalai Lama had been sending messages to Tibetan-friendly societies in India and other countries. He had sensed that his people were in desperate need of support from the international arena. But Talty says that the Chinese grip on the region was so effective that news of what was happening in Lhasa was prevented from reaching the outside world.[2]

Some news of the battles did leak out via a *Daily Telegraph* journalist, George Patterson, who was stationed in Delhi and who also had contacts in Kalimpong. Tibetan refugees had been escaping to Kalimpong for years. This town was also the place of one of Gyalo Thondup's two homes in India. (The other is in Darjeeling). It was a hotbed of information and intelligence, with a network of agents living among the newly arrived Tibetans.

Rebels had been gathering in Lhasa and picking fights with the PLA whenever they could. Outside or inside Lhasa, when they scored a rare win against the Chinese, there was always a backlash. More and more PLA troops would be mobilized as a result.

By now, there were 40,000 PLA soldiers in and around the city. The Chinese camps were fiercely defended by electric wires, artillery weapons and mounted machine guns.[3] Angry and insecure Tibetans that could lay their hands on arms lost no time in attacking and killing any Chinese that crossed their paths. It led to a febrile atmosphere in which violence could erupt at any minute.

By the morning of 10 March 1959, the mood in Lhasa had turned ugly. The Tibetan blood was up; nothing would be allowed to hurt the Dalai Lama, the Precious Jewel. The Tibetans marched to his palace with rocks in their closed fists. They would fiercely protect their leader with whatever they could muster. Molotov cocktails and ancient rifles were used.

By the time the uprising had taken hold, the Indian consulate in Lhasa was in continuous contact with Delhi. Nehru, however, wanted peaceful relations with China above all else and insisted to all who listened in India that the only issue in Tibet at the time was a clash of ideology, not of people and weapons.[4]

'I think that Nehru was always sympathetic to the . . . Tibetans, to the Dalai Lama in particular . . . He must have been torn between his responsibilities as a ruler of India, protecting its strategic interests and his sympathy for the Tibetan people who were being potentially polarised by the Chinese. It's a great irony that at a time when imperialism was in retreat around the world, Chinese imperialism took over Tibet,' Bruce Riedel commented.[5]

The outside world was hearing disturbing rumours and half truths about what was going on in Tibet. But back in Lhasa, witnessing the agitations by the Tibetans, the Dalai Lama was so worried for the safety of his people that he began to pray.

Talty posits that the Chinese probably had little intention of hurting the Dalai Lama or kidnapping him at the dance event. They actually needed him as he commanded Tibet, and in any case, the Seventeen-Point Agreement had been signed as insurance for them.[6] Since the canny young monk leader was not outwardly endorsing rebellion, and had even agreed to Peking's demand that he nullify the residency of his two brothers, Gyalo Thondup and Thubten Jigme Norbu, who had defected to India, he did not seem to pose a threat.

Perhaps, says Talty, the young leader was just playing for time.

The Dalai Lama did refuse a Chinese demand, however, which was to summon his own Tibetan soldiers to quash the rebellion.

Talty writes that about 5000 Tibetans amassed at that time to protect the Dalai Lama at Norbulingka. They had elected seventeen representatives to work with the Tibetan government.

Later, on 10 March, the Dalai Lama received a letter from the Chinese representative to Lhasa, advising him that given the situation with the 'reactionaries', it was better that he did not attend the PLA show.[7] It was an attempt by the Chinese to save face, given that they had, in effect, been snubbed.

In our interview, he explained, 'Meantime, I received one letter from Chinese military commander in Lhasa. I also wrote two or three letters. I politely mentioned I would like to take refuge, or something like refuge, to Chinese military headquarters, I wrote. That's one lie! A monk, a Buddhist monk, should not tell lies, but under difficult circumstances a little, little lie, I think, is permissible by Buddha. So then I received one letter. It mentioned Norbulingka summer palace.' According to the Dalai Lama, the letter from the PLA was asking him to identify and mark the location of his living quarters. '"Where do you live? Please mark it and then send us." They mentioned they will protect me from artillery.' He ended by saying that he wasn't sure whether the PLA wanted to protect him or make him a target. 'It's difficult to say.'[8]

By then, more crowds had gathered. Some young, trainee monks even had arms, though they had to share one ancient British rifle between two men. They allowed themselves to handle the Molotov cocktails the lay Tibetans were using. At that moment, the novices ignored the fact that Tibetan Buddhism forbids bloodshed and violence.

*

By 15 March, Phala, the Lord Chamberlain, was sure that he needed to get the Dalai Lama away for his own safety. The young leader would have none of it. He felt he could not betray his people by leaving them; it was not the brave thing to do. He wanted to stick it out and remain rooted in his beloved homeland.

Dunham says that the Lord Chamberlain faced three hurdles: the PLA, the Tibetans surrounding the palace, and his own recalcitrant young leader in training. Nonetheless, he came up with a plan, a route and the date.[9] He did this privately, without telling the Dalai Lama.

He arranged for horses to be placed at the other side of the river running close to the palace.

His scheme involved bringing Diki Tsering and Tenzin Choegyal to Norbulingka. Meanwhile, he instructed his tailor to make soldier's clothes for the Dalai Lama and other disguises for some of his family otherwise if the Tibetans saw him leave, they would have stopped their Precious Jewel and his cover would have been blown.

But for confirmation that this was the right course of action, the hallowed mystical voice of state authority, the Nechung Oracle, needed to be consulted.

When I asked the Dalai Lama about seeking the Oracle's opinion, he referred to 'others' having 'mysterious ways of investigation'.[10] He said that he always consulted the Oracle on important matters.

'Then, finally, the indication was "now better to go". Before, the Oracle had insisted I should remain in Norbulingka. Then, on 17 March, [sic] Oracle just said, "Now the time has come. Leave."'[11]

Two days before, a PLA platoon had arrived, marching close to the palace. Tenzin Choegyal remembers they patrolled so close that he was able to see the faces of the Chinese soldiers. All this he witnessed while accompanying the Tibetan defence corps, even though his mother Diki had expressly forbidden him from being with them.

On 16 March 1959, the Dalai Lama received a note warning him that the Chinese would capture him if he tried to leave the palace. He sent conciliatory messages to the Chinese, which threw his enemies off guard.

Dunham describes how at 4 p.m. on the critical day of 17 March, the Dalai Lama and the Kashag were in formal conference when they heard the sound of two mortar shells landing from different directions. One crashed into a decorative pool just outside, and another, says Dunham, just beyond a wall to the north of the palace.[12]

This unnerving and intimidating salvo was a physical and terrifying final message of intent from the PLA's General Tan to the Dalai Lama.

Phala saw these threatening signals and decided that it was important to leave then and there.

In our interview decades later, the Dalai Lama told me, 'Since 11 March, every night, there was more Chinese troop movement, because Norbulingka was quite close. There are two roads from mainland China up to Lhasa. One through Kham, one through Amdo. That road from Amdo was very close to my place. So, we could hear the sound of trucks or cars. Every night. Also, some people were just watching; a lot of Chinese military cars each night with guns, big guns.'

I asked if he could hear the trucks from his window, to which he replied, 'From my room? No, my room window faces only south, not to the north. But every day, every morning you see people saying, "Oh, now last night, a lot of trucks. A lot of troops."

'And then one serious matter, one noticeable thing is, I think around 15–16 March 1959, on the other side of Kyichu River, there was one Chinese artillery division. We could see it. For the last few years, their big artillery had been kept there, covered. On 15–16th, all the covers were removed. People from Potala noticed through binoculars that the artillery was being cleaned. On 17th morning, two mortar shells were lobbed into Norbulingka. Things were then very, very serious.'[13]

And so, considering all that was going on, 17 March was chosen as the date of the escape.

The Lord Chamberlain forbade the use of flashlights, so that no citizen might inadvertently discover that the Dalai Lama was in front of them. He also sent a summons, via a horseback message, to the south east of the country to the CIA-trained Khampas, Athar and Lhotse. It would take just under a week to get to them.

Athar was in the south mobilizing rebels and was in constant touch with the CIA, having been snubbed by the Tibetan government. Little did he know that the Chinese had been intercepting his messages and had even caught one of his CIA-trained colleagues.

*

There were many uncertainties ahead. Where would the Dalai Lama and his retinue find refuge? What would happen to the Tibetan people? But as the noise of the shelling and bombing continued, the plan for the escape was set in motion.

Phala told everyone in the room to set their watches to his. As far as was possible, he had planned everything down to the last detail. He sent the Dalai Lama's beloved cook Ponpo and his team away to a designated ferry point to await the rest of the party.

He wrote to the Indian representative in Lhasa, broaching the topic of the group coming to India as refugees. The letter never reached its destination. Then, he sent a message to the south of Tibet, where the Khampa rebels were mobilized, to say that they should expect significantly important people to be arriving soon.

Around the same time, Nehru was telling the parliament in Delhi that stories of civil conflict in Lhasa were nothing more than rumour.[14]

Three days later, on 20 March, the PLA shelled the Indian Consul's offices in Lhasa.[15]

At the decided time, everyone followed the instructions they had been given. The Dalai Lama was dressed in his soldier's attire. Diki and Tenzin Choegyal were dressed as male servants.

Tenzin recounted the incident in detail. 'All the elders were very tense. My mother and sister, they were dressed as men, you know, in men's clothes and moving about. I just found it extremely funny. Earlier on my mother had told me that we are going to a nunnery in southern Tibet, but then I knew that we are escaping, rather than just moving. Then she told me to go and put on my lay clothes, so I went.'[16]

Phala had organized for small groups to leave at different times. The first party included Diki and Tenzin Choegyal. They were to exit via the south gate. 'At about nine o'clock we left Norbulingka and started to walk. Time to go. Soldiers came, His Holiness's bodyguards came. I think there were three or four of them. I had two monks who looked after me when I was in the monastery. I said goodbye to them and both of them said, "Don't forget what you have memorized. Try to recite and don't forget", because I had done quite a lot of memorization back in the monastery. We started to walk towards the riverbank.'[17]

As Tenzin Choegyal mentioned the next part, his voice rose, 'Then we left and my mother,' he pauses, 'she walked, and then after some time she was provided with a pony. It's not completely dark. After having crossed the river, I went down the river, saw Dewan Monastery afar, then I prostrated three times. I could see the outline on the right.'[18]

Next, it was the turn of different officials, hidden under a tarpaulin cover in a truck, to leave.

Finally, it was the Dalai Lama and his immediate retinue's turn. There was Phala, the chief abbot, the commander of the Dalai Lama's personal bodyguard, Kusing Depon.

Meanwhile, lookouts returned to report that Diki and Tenzin had travelled safely to the river ferry.

Dunham says that the Dalai Lama was aware of the occasion's significance. Citing the Dalai Lama's biography, he says that the young leader, having changed into disguise, read the scriptures, acutely taking note of an extract about the need to focus on bravery and confidence.

The Dalai Lama needed to carry a limited number of his own possessions: one of these was an ancient painting, dating back to the time of the second Dalai Lama, that was rolled up in a long tube with a cloth handle.

There was a high wind; he could barely see, but he was given a rifle to carry as he approached the gate. With two soldiers to escort him, he left his compound.

A group of rebels recognized the Dalai Lama and insisted on forming a protective phalanx around him. Phala strictly forbade it, saying it would render the escapees too conspicuous. While the Lord Chamberlain and the devoted Khampas were arguing, the Dalai Lama slipped out and away.

This last party soon got to the coracles and crossed the Kyichu safely.

I asked the Dalai Lama how he was feeling the night of the escape, whether or not he was frightened to leave Lhasa and if he feared for his life.

'Oh, yes. Some fear. Of course, some fear,' he said. 'But then, before we finalized, I had some sort of hesitation. Once we finalized, then there was no hesitation.

'So, then, I think, about noon 17th [March], we decided that we had to leave. So, at exactly ten o'clock according to Lhasa time, I left from Norbulingka. On the other side, there was quite a long road beside the river. On the other side was a, Chinese military camp. We could see the Chinese guards.'[19]

With the PLA right beside them, all the escapees had to extinguish their lights and torches. 'In the dark like demons, like ghosts, we go like that. Really, really dangerous there. Danger on our lives.'[20]

The Dalai Lama then spoke of two Tibetan officials who had been going around the palace checking security the previous few nights. 'So that night also, you see, these two officials went to check. I, acting like these two officials' bodyguard, carried one gun and went like that [sic]. Followed these two officials.'[21] But the young Dalai Lama had a distinctive feature that made him stand out among people—his eyewear, 'At that time, one problem—I wore these glasses. So, if I wear the glasses, people may notice.' There was only one alternative—to remove the one item that might reveal his identity. But without them, he could hardly see. And he wasn't used to carrying a weighty weapon. 'Without glasses, really difficult. With that gun. More walks, more walks, that gun becomes heavier, heavier, heavier. Then I escaped.

'Then, these two officials, when they reached the gate, they shouted, "Oh, we are checking! Now open door." They open then salute and then go outside. And then we reached outside, the little bit of distance from gate area, then nobody now noticed.'[22]

When it was safe enough, religious hierarchy took over, and the Tibetan officials switched places with their revered leader. But the group was still in extreme danger.

'So, then I become head. These two officials then follow me. Very, very tense. Then, after, [I] reached other side of the river, even more risk. Then, few hours by a horse, but on horse there were also sound of their hoofs. We cannot prevent that. *Chok, chok, chok, chok,*' he mimed horses trotting. 'Then we saw some Chinese soldiers. They just smoked.' He mimes a Chinese soldier looking up and smoking in a nonchalant way. 'Then we feel, "Okay, now." Then, next morning we reach one pass. So then, after passing, after we cross that pass, then no danger. No immediate danger. Then, there, everybody, quite relaxed.'[23]

Within a short space of time, the Dalai Lama was able to make out in the silhouettes of his family, his tutors, his cabinet and his staff.

Thirty mounted, impressive-looking local Khampa warriors were guarding them and waiting for the Dalai Lama with arms straight out in front of them in obeisance, holding traditional white scarves of greeting.

The escape party decided to travel in three groups. Young Tenzin and his family would go ahead, next the Dalai Lama and his group would follow, and finally, a set of tutors and members of the Kashag would bring up the rear. Everyone in the party mounted their horses and rode hard through the night. They only got to their first stop as the sun was setting the next day.

They were heading for Lhoka, where the rebels, 80,000 of them, were holding strong. The fugitives had to negotiate 19,000-feet passes through the Himalayan mountains, which were still nearly impassably full of winter ice.

Though the Dalai Lama still advocated non-violence, the Tibetan rebels were armed and dangerous.

Any one of them, disgusted by the behaviour of the Chinese and frustrated with their young religious leader's exhortations of peace, could have turned traitor and informer. It would have been easy for a rebel to have handed the relatively unprotected high lama over to the PLA. But this didn't happen. Instead, villagers helped as best they could, feeding and sheltering the party in the humblest of circumstances. They would line the roads and bow. One remembered placing hay and dung across the ice to provide a safer passage to the escaping party.[24]

The Dalai Lama's mother fared terribly in the cold. Her skin peeled and she was barely able to stand. The family sheltered in a twelfth century monastery at Rame.

The horses they rode were not fit for the punishing journey as they were court animals used to being pampered. They began to collapse. As some of the steeds were dying, when the party came to a village, they asked if they could use local pack animals. But in the end, forty village men and women decided to help the escaping group by carrying the baggage across the mountains for them.

Heading south, on 20 March, the Dalai Lama and his party met some Khampa warriors who were on horseback. To their leader, Ratuk Ngawang, he offered words of encouragement, urging them not to be put off by belittling words from any authority. The Dalai Lama referred to the Khampa effort as being 'necessary' and that it would not be futile in any way.[25]

While the Dalai Lama and his party headed south, Athar and Lhotse were riding with all their might in the opposite direction towards him, having been summoned by Phala. This summons is one that did reach them.

Talty states that on 22 March 1959 they met with the Dalai Lama and gave him information about how the CIA had trained the rebels at Camp Hale, how Athar and Lhotse were in touch with Washington, and that President Eisenhower was being kept informed of events.[26]

Khampa Ratuk Ngawang made sure that the Dalai Lama and his party were escorted safely through his territory, and then turned back to fight the PLA. This was how it went. As the Dalai Lama journeyed south, Khampa rebels provided a devoted, armed escort through the areas in which they operated. But as he said farewell to each group, the Dalai Lama knew that there was only a slim chance of the rebels surviving their battles with the PLA.

*

Back in Norbulingka, the PLA's General Tan could not work out the young leader's location. And the Lhasans refused to help him. He sought permission to enter and search the Indian, Bhutanese and Nepalese consulates, but was refused each time.

Meanwhile, the Dalai Lama and his party kept up a steady pace. Even after all these years, Tenzin Choegyal remembered how he felt during those crucial days. 'Ah, the journey wasn't that hard physically, but mentally it was hell, because we never knew when the Chinese might intervene and capture us.'

Even as a child he could sense the gravity of the situation. When I asked him how he coped with that fear, he replied, 'By hoping for the best, right? When the escape took place, particularly the night we left Norbulingka, I wasn't afraid, but now if I look back I don't think I could do it again. The Chinese camps were very near, anything could have happened. It was very scary.'

The most frightening moment was when they had to cross the river. The walk from Norbulingka to the Kyichu was about forty-five minutes to one hour. In terms of distance it wasn't more than three kilometres, but they could see the lights of the Chinese camp. Tenzin says, 'I think His Holiness being able to escape was a miracle. There was a little bit of moonlight. So, we crossed the river in coracles, made out of leather.'

After Tenzin and his group had crossed the water, they waited. They had been told that horses would be brought to them. 'We were waiting, and then there's a tremendous amount of the sound of people walking, horses' hooves, and the breathing of the horses. Then someone said, "Good luck." That was the voice of His Holiness's Lord Chamberlain, who was guiding that particular party. Then I knew His Holiness has crossed, and we followed.'[27]

I asked the Dalai Lama if the Chinese soldiers he was rushing away from in Lhasa made him freeze in fear, to which he said, 'At that time it was a little bit safer. We had already crossed the river. But still, when it was dark, then there was some more fear. When I saw one Chinese soldier,' he mimicked a relaxed, smiling, smoking Chinese soldier, 'guarding their own military camp, he looked completely relaxed. So, then we felt. "Okay, they do not know now."'[28]

After he had escaped and he received news of what the Chinese were doing in Lhasa, the Dalai Lama was devastated. He said, 'I immediately reflected on all my friends, including one of my small dogs and some peacocks there. When I heard there was a lot of Chinese bombardment, I also said, "Oh, what happened to those peacocks?" They were put inside a fence. If they are free, at least they can fly to some places. And then my small dog, and then those old sweepers. Very sad.'[29]

Tragically, they also had to leave his eighty-year old grandmother behind.

8

MISSION COMMAND

The flight of His Holiness was now entering the period of its highest drama.

With the PLA in hot pursuit on land and by air, the Dalai Lama and his entourage of eight advisers, staff and family were sorely at risk. The party rode by horse and at times struggled on foot to the south of the country as fast as it could go, covering many miles in one day. The journey was exhausting and debilitating.

Meanwhile, vague instructions had reached political officer Har Mander Singh via an unreliable wireless system. The message he received said that the Dalai Lama was escaping Lhasa and was likely to enter India through the Kameng division, the area that he was responsible for. The Dalai Lama was travelling south, it seemed, so he might enter India through one of several routes. Har Mander and his staff had to work out the most likely entry point into India, using the team's network of people posted near the frontier and information that came to them from across the border. Once the Dalai Lama reached the border, he and his people would require accommodation, first aid, someone to guide them, etc. So, Har Mander and his team set about making arrangements.

'The communication channel was Delhi to Shillong, which was our headquarters. From Shillong to Bomdila was the next one step further,' Har Mander said.[1]

He remembers that passing on these messages was difficult and often done in person. A convoy of two or three people—dispatch runners from Shillong—had visited him and said that they were expecting 'the important person' at the border.

A code was worked out by Har Mander's seniors for this assignment. This code was for communication between him, the Assam Rifles and Har Mander Singh's secretariat headquarters at Shillong. This cipher would have been made by sepoys—soldiers who knew how to interpret the code—who worked in the battalions of the Assam Rifles.

Gathering intelligence was an important part of this operation, for Har Mander needed to work out what was happening at his end.

It is not overtly stated, but the whole area of NEFA/Arunachal Pradesh is of the utmost interest to intelligence personnel. China, as well as the US, keeps an eye on whatever is going on here. The region may have agents staying there due to its strategic location.

If Singh were to successfully meet the Dalai Lama and escort him back to Bomdila, from that moment on His Holiness and his party would be actively providing information of great interest to Indian intelligence.

Typically, junior intelligence personnel, like sub-inspectors, were posted in places all over NEFA. In places like the Kameng division, that were considered important. They fed information to their superiors in Shillong, where it was all collated and sent to the strategic headquarters—Delhi. But in this case, a senior additional officer was sent as escort should the Dalai Lama and his family make it successfully across the Indo-Tibetan border.

Har Mander was aware that the language barrier would need to be surmounted, and he was ready with his own interpreting team. He already knew most of the protocols that would be required, having always had Tibetan advisers in his office. In addition, he had to think of how to make the journey as comfortable as possible for the Dalai Lama and his convoy, as the route through the mountains was tough.

'The North East Frontier terrain is difficult. The roads only went so far as the lower hills. After that, we had to take the help of porters from villages for our baggage. It may have been as high as 21, 22, 23,000 feet at the border. We would cross the rivers at the lower heights, in the foothills, by riding an elephant or in a small boat. In some places, there were narrow bridges to cross. For the interiors, we would use a system of ropes and pulleys to get across streams. You would place your feet on the lower rope and take a hold of the upper rope,' Har Mander said, as he retraces the journey in his mind.[2]

Once he had a grasp of what he had to do, Har Mander and his staff activated what he calls the 'network'. This meant calling in the chief coordinators responsible for each of the inhabited areas in the Kameng Frontier Division. These coordinators would be needed all along the route he had charted for the Dalai Lama and his party. The path they would take stretched along the Indo-Tibetan border.

Har Mander was in the habit of planning ahead—a throwback to his military training—even though army men also know that the best plans often need to be changed at the last minute. As soon as he received his instructions, Har Mander Singh would have gone through the check list for his mission—planning resources, security, medical provision, and so on.

'We had some kind of setup already in the headquarters. There were heads of all these departments which we had been trying to establish so that there was a medical setup, an agriculture setup, a head of teachers and so on in the district. The first thing I did was to get the heads of each and told them what was happening. I said, "I don't have a lot of people, and what I want to do is to set up small posts ..."'[3]

If he chose to stop, these small posts were to provide what was needed along the way—succour, accommodation, food, medical attention and anything else that was vital for the visitors. At this stage, no one knew precisely what might be required, though Har Mander

Singh had calculated the need of the hour based on the intelligence he had received.

He had the cool temperament a soldier needs in battle. All he focussed on was that mission command had issued the instruction; his duty was to carry out the order.

He needed to cover a journey that would normally take seven days in less than half that time if he was to meet the Dalai Lama at a strategic point near the border. The 'dignitary' and his party could enter his territory but there was going to be a situation of jeopardy until Har Mander was sure that the area was fully sanitized. He knew there was a lot to be done till the dignitary and his retinue were in a safe place, protected by his armed guards.

The primary mission was to get the important visitor back to Singh's headquarters at Bomdila. Until then, being on the move included a degree of exposure that Singh and the Indian government were not happy with.

Har Mander calculated that the maximum distance he would be able to cover in one stretch would be limited to 10 to 15 kilometres. This was as far as a horse or pony could go in that terrain without dropping from exhaustion. The villages and settlements on the route to Bomdila were also roughly the same distance apart. So Singh would keep himself moving by using a relay of ponies. If there wasn't a village on any one stretch, Har Mander Singh set up a small group of people responsible for communications, food, shelter, medical support, administration and transport. In each of these groups, it was not laid down that the doctor or a teacher would be in charge of the whole group; they worked it out among themselves, choosing leaders according to seniority.

Next, he had ponies sent to each checkpoint, so that he could save a couple of days on the way to Tawang and beyond.

The only armed soldiers available to Singh were the Assam Rifles.

Har Mander said, 'With my army background, I know that one shouldn't interfere in the nitty-gritty of the deployment of personnel of the forces doing a particular task. They have their own commanders to assess the situation and deploy men accordingly. But here, firstly, there was no commander available senior enough to gauge the situation and secondly, there was just a handful of men. With my service background I was familiar with the distribution of manpower for various tasks. So, I made some changes in the deployment of the Assam Rifles men to ensure that the security of His Holiness was not jeopardised. Of course, I consulted the non-commissioned officer or anyone who was the leader of that group before finalising these changes.'[4]

*

Har Mander was aware that he was embarking on an important assignment, and that it should be recorded.

Har Mander opened the album with a flourish. 'I have little pictures taken with my camera . . . which are of no value.'[5] The fact that these photos now appear in any place or book relevant to the story, and that the Dalai Lama's office holds an enlarged copy of most of the images demonstrates the value of the photos.[6]

Either he or one of his staff took the photos, he explained. 'In all these pictures I must have been somewhere close at hand.' He placed the album on the round dining table. The album had many black and white photographs, one on each laminated page. His was generally the only camera present on this trip. Though he underplayed their significance, these photographs were almost the only complete pictorial record of what took place during those historic weeks on this assignment.

Har Mander is seen wearing a high-collared suit and regular town shoes at all times in the photographs; at no point is he seen in a coat, with head protection, boots or equipment usually associated with mountain travel.

'It was pretty chilly up there. How come you weren't wearing a hat?' I asked him.

'We were cold, but I suppose we were not equipped with stuff like hats and so on,' he replied.

He had owned the warm high-collared suit (*bandh gala*) that he wore for the mission for many years. On being asked if his feet were cold in regular shoes at the bitter height of 14,000 feet, he stoically replied, 'We managed.'

While the weather in March–April was not as chilly as it gets in December–January in the North-East, even so it would still be harsh. I know, as I have shivered in Arunachal in April, despite wearing at least two layers of ski clothes during the day and been grateful for warm duvets and a bhukari at night. On the other hand, the photos show Har Mander's Tibetan guests looking much more appropriately dressed for the weather. They sport fur-lined boots, jackets and hoods. Part of the reason for Har Mander's attire on this journey is simply that there were no stores or facilities to buy winter clothes—wool jumpers and coats—in the mountains. Air drops consisted of food and necessary supplies only. So, officials would usually have items of clothing they might have worn in their last posting, with no facility to add to it until they left the region.

At that time, the North-East was extremely isolated. Even now it sometimes feels that way up there, and the majority of the Indians residing in other parts of the country have never visited. Some 'mainlanders' are not even familiar with places like Tawang and Bomdila. As for communication, connecting with anyone across the region or outside the area could take days in 1959.

*

Arunachal Pradesh is still a sensitive area in today's India. Whereas previously, army presence was minimal and the limited protection resources consisted mainly of the Assam Rifles, now there are many paramilitary groups. Getting around can still be a gruelling exercise, even for those used to Indian roads. In 1960, the Border Roads Organisation (BRO) was formed to help make India's borders more secure primarily in the north and northeast of the country. The BRO also undertakes engineering work in neighbouring

countries—Afghanistan, Sri Lanka, Tajikistan, Myanmar and Bhutan—
that are 'friends' of India.

Members of the BRO do not generally engage in combat. Officers
and troops come from the Indian Army's corps of engineers, electrical
and mechanical engineers, army service corps, military police and army
personnel on extra regimental employment. These projects include the
development of roads, bridges, and airfields in hostile environments
that private companies will not work in. The BRO is called in to
troubleshoot because of security concerns related to hostilities, or
because of environmental challenges. As I have already said, landslides
occur several times a year in the mountains of Arunachal Pradesh, and
the BRO works as speedily as it can to clear the roads.

When the landslides cause floods, it becomes a major catastrophe.
All defence services combine to provide disaster relief. Though these
natural calamities are regular, ongoing and impossible to avoid, they
are accepted as part of everyday life. Local journalists are often the only
media who cover the phenomena.

As an illustration of the treacherous nature of the weather, in June
2017, flash floods and landslides hit many parts of Arunachal Pradesh,
resulting in deaths and casualties. For a week, rainfall flooded much
of Itanagar and Bhalukpong near Bomdila. For days the four national
highways—the biggest roads through the mountains[7]—became
impassable due to roadblocks. As the rivers rose and climbed valley
walls, ravines filled with water and low-lying dwellings were swept
away. Families had to leave their homes and possessions, while others
tried to stop the river flood in their own way by creating makeshift
barriers with bamboo and empty cement bags filled with sand. These
days, there is a fledgling District Disaster Management Authority that
can place an Emergency Operation Centre[8] on high alert. But even a
crisis response unit is powerless in the face of the angry force of nature.
An Indian Air Force helicopter on a flood rescue mission crashed into
a gorge killing three crew members and an Indian Reserve Battalion
soldier.[9] It had already saved around 170 civilians. It would have taken
five hours or so to get to the crash site on foot from the nearest village,

but the recovery team was hampered by bad weather, so it could not arrive at the mangled chopper remains for a couple of days.

This is how it is, trying to live and work in the Land of the Dawn-Lit Mountains. Nature always shows you it is master and that it must be respected. Even royalty and top brass public servants are powerless before its whims.

In 1959, there was no disaster management system in place, so it was left to political officers to manage events like this. It was one of the hazards facing Har Mander and his team on his journey with the Dalai Lama. The consequences of such a disaster happening during April that year did not bear thinking about.

9

THE EXECUTION PHASE

It was the end of March 1959. Har Mander and his team had put together a plan of action while trying to decipher occasional half-heard, half-understood instructions from Shillong and Delhi.

Singh keeps a meticulous record of his daily activities, writing a few lines in pencil in an exercise book. For the assignment with the Dalai Lama, however, he decided to keep a more detailed diary to record events as they were happening. He knew that the mission was momentous, important and historic, which is why he started his private chronicle. Sixty years later, in his dining room in Delhi, he takes out a plain cardboard file from among his papers. It is that very chronicle. On the light brown cover, in capitals, there is just one word written. 'SECRET.'

In 1959, the diary contents were kept between Singh and his confidential assistant, a man he took along with him to assist him on the journey. This man typed or hand-wrote events as they happened during brief pauses in the action as Singh was travelling at breakneck speed and had a lot to organize. Creating a written record was no easy task given the pace of events on the ground and how regional power structures were constantly in flux. Singh knew that he was, for a limited period, close to the epicentre of a gale force wind blowing across South and South East Asia. He describes it as a moment in time when he was called to action.

Har Mander's diary is the main day-by-day, detailed account of what happened during those weeks from the end of March through April 1959.

The contents of the diary, by permission of Har Mander Singh, can be read for the first time in this book. The original is in a vault and is not destined to see the light of day. I reproduce the diary along with all its abbreviations, and methods of spelling particular to the time and the writer. Here is the first entry from the document.

26 March 1959

ASI [an official from the Architectural Survey of India] *arrived in the morning. He informed me that [a Tibetan speaking official] Sandup has been held up in Rupa due to an attack of lumbago and was unable to move unless some transport was arranged for him.*

We made some arrangements for his travel in a jeep which was going down with the executive engineer. In the meantime, [As opposed to the diary versions, Samdup is normally spelt this way, with an 'm'] *Sandup started from Rupa on pony and arrived here at about 2.30 pm.* [For speed, Samdup had to start his journey on the mountain steed and the jeep would likely have met him en route.] *He told me that the dignitary was expected to seek asylum in our territory possibly today.*

We are not sure if he will be coming to Bumla or Chuthangmu. He said that a code name had been devised for him and signalled to us to maintain secrecy but we have not received it so far. We have also not received any instructions about the likelihood of the dignitary seeking asylum with us. Made arrangements for the ASI's journey up to Tawang.[1]

This diary extract is significant because it outlines the challenge that lay before Har Mander Singh. It also shows how Singh's team members were hurriedly deployed from one place to another, like chess pieces being moved around a board all at the same time.

*

The Chinese had already intercepted some of the messages between the CIA and the Khampa rebels, but across the border, all precautions were being taken to ensure secrecy. Not only were messages encoded, but the Assam Rifles also used code names for the Dalai Lama.

'From my diary it appears that at the local level, they thought of giving him the code name "Saigol". Saigol is one of the earliest late musicians and singers of India. I don't know how this name could have occurred to the authorities, but to my knowledge we probably never used this code name. We called him "Dignitary", etc., but those working on codes may have used the word "Saigol",' Har Mander Singh recalls.[2]

If the Dalai Lama were to be granted refuge in India, there were two possible final entry points, both were in the Kameng Division under Singh and his team.

Tawang Monastery in Kameng with its historic Tibetan Buddhist ties would be an ideal halting place for the religion's titular head.

The Dalai Lama could reach the monastery in two ways. He could ride through Tibet to Tsona, the country's southernmost monastic centre. From there he could cross the border. If he could get to the nearest Indian settlement, Lumla, he could travel on to Tawang. Or he could head for a Buddhist monastery in Bumthang, Bhutan, west of Tawang, and enter India.

On 26 March, the Dalai Lama arrived at Lhuntse Dzong, just a few days from the border. Singh therefore calculated that the Dalai Lama must be headed towards Tsona, on the Tibetan side of the Indo-Sino border. Har Mander's counterpart in Tsona was most likely in contact with Tawang already.

'My district adjoined Bhutan, situated to the west of the district. There was a possibility he might enter Bhutan. The situation was vague. Rumours were flying around. If the Dalai Lama came to my Division there were only two possible routes.

The situation was known to the higher authorities. I decided to move forward and handle the situation at the Frontier. My headquarters at Shillong was in touch with me but communication was through unreliable wireless sets and the instructions were unclear. Messages were sent through emissaries. While I had some instructions, I had to act at my own. There was some likelihood of his seeking asylum and therefore I would need to offer courtesies to him. I planned as I went along.'[3]

Singh and his men considered deployments and logistics. As ever, there was no time or room for emotion. He describes the start of the expedition matter of factly.

'It was routine for me; I needed a couple of men, and to deploy the Assam Rifles. I also needed to plan for the return journey. I had to think it out in detail and leave instructions as to where the Dalai Lama would be staying.'[4]

But deployment would be difficult due to the short supply of manpower.

It is lonely up in the mountains of the Kameng Division. In 2017, I felt daunted travelling around on dirt tracks or on the single road, especially around dusk. The green slopes in front of me were steep, impenetrable walls and I felt caught in a mountain universe. There was an eerie silence because there were no streetlights or people on the route.

Kameng is characterized by high mountain ridges along which the paths run. But Har Mander and his people were used to this terrain. They rode and trod surely, focussed and driven by their mission.

Along the routes, there were staging huts and guest houses where visitors could sleep and wash with icy stream water, using bonfires to keep warm and heat water.

Har Mander needed to plan how all of the Dalai Lama's entourage would be accommodated. Where there were village halls and guest houses, these could be made available, as well as the homes of villagers where necessary. The simple staging huts consisted of two or three rooms with the bare minimum furniture—a bed, a table and a chair.

By contrast, in more remote areas (fortunately not on the route that Har Mander was planning for the escaping party) the accommodation would often be even more rustic and rudimentary. Below the main rooms would sometimes be a space reserved for pigs. Above the pig area would be the convenience: a hole in the wooden floor, with a bucket of water.

Though the settlements on Singh's route were developed and organized, he still needed to ensure that officials would be appropriately housed according to their rank. The highest protocol would need to be observed, even in the most basic of conditions.

En route to Lumla was the dreaded Se La Pass—the highest part of the journey. Covered with snow most of the year, the pass sits at just under 14,000 feet. It can take half a day to get to the top, so it is important to descend the other side before nightfall. The cold only adds to the treacherous nature of the passage, for the average temperature through the colder months is minus 10 degrees Centigrade.

Travel at that time was on ponies or horses, with the former proving more popular as they are smaller and more suited to mountains.

*

In Buddhist areas today, the maroon robes of monks and nuns are a familiar sight. In colder climes, holy men and women may don hats and jumpers or even a hooded sweatshirt if they are younger. Many of them, however, wear sandals and are trained to withstand freezing temperatures through their practise of meditation.

While bald-headed monks and nuns are common in Kameng, it is harder to find their lapsed counterparts—monks and nuns who opted out of the rigorous system, though they retain an umbilical affection for their monastic training. One such lapsed monk is Jampa Phende, a Monpa resident of Tawang who comes from a modest background. He was a monk until the age of twenty-three.

He dresses in the latest trends but retains a devout affection for his rigorous Buddhist education. When he first met me, his hair had an orange streak in it. Jampa has always loved movies and sport, two interests that were forbidden in his monastery when he was training.

He had been put into a monastery not because of a free education, shelter and the prospect of a respected life—often the most common reason poor families choose this life for their sons or daughters—but because Jampa developed a terrible swelling in his leg at the age of three or four. It got heavy and he had to drag it behind him instead of walking normally. He was taken to many hospitals, but the situation remained the same for years. In the end, his parents consulted some lamas who advised that perhaps some bad karma in Jampa's past had resulted in the condition. Aged nine, he was put into a small monastery, Seling Gonpa, in east Tawang, and spent a year there before moving to a larger one in south India. After six or seven years, his leg got better. This seemed to confirm to Jampa's family that becoming a monk had been good for him.

'I'm a happy person, I'm a cool guy,' he says when I meet him in Tawang. He's dressed in a fashionable khaki hooded parka, jeans, loose top, belt and boots. He wears a string of prayer beads around his left wrist.

'It was a very good life, a very good education there,' he remembers. But he did not stick to the strict rules of the establishment. 'I was a very naughty monk. Not in the sense that I hurt people; I didn't, I didn't do bad things. But I broke rules for my enjoyment.'

Jampa now teaches English at a monastery in Tawang. He lives in the staff quarters onsite and is content with his life. He is still in a monastic environment but liberated from its constraints. With free food and accommodation, he is paid a modest salary that is enough for him to run a car, buy the clothes he wants from second-hand charity shops, and visit his family when he can.

Echoing the description that Har Mander Singh gives of basic facilities in far flung parts of Kameng back in 1959, Jampa talks about how one of his aunts still has a primitive convenience in her remote village home.

'In this modern world, we have funny toilets in old places. We are used to them. Our toilets have no door to close. A curtain is put at a door where we enter so that people can't see you. Among the planks of wood, there are two or three big holes for several people to use together. Below are the pigs. It's the way of the old Monpa community. They used leaves as toilet paper. Sometimes there were thorns. When there is a big family, say about ten people, then the pig will be very fat. Where there are only two or three people, then the pig is thin. The pigs look up expectantly when someone goes in. Still, these toilets are there in many of the distant villages here. Not in the towns though.'[5]

There are some basic aspects of life in rural Kameng that have not changed for decades. They add to the feeling that in some remote and precious corners of the eastern Himalayas, time has stood still.

10

THE SET UP

Har Mander Singh had a plan. He was not anxious or stressed. And even if he was, he didn't show it. For Singh, under his military code, sentiment was irrelevant to the task at hand. As I'd mentioned earlier, he'd learnt to control his feelings since he was a child. The call to action meant that he knew exactly what he had to do. Har Mander had done his best to prepare the villages along the way to be pit stops where he and his Tibetan guests would be able to change ponies as swiftly as possible, to find food and to rest.

Har Mander remembered, 'I forwarded a message, so the village had notice. In each village they would forward a message to be sent over. For example, if I were at Place A they could ask the village head to inform the village at Place B ahead before I reached.'[1]

I asked him what he said in these messages. He said that he mentioned the date and time he was expected to be at that village. He also informed the local organizer that he too, on his way up to the border, would need to change ponies so that he could continue his journey without having to take a break.[2]

The messages from Shillong continued to arrive at Bomdila, Singh's division headquarters, but they were either incomplete or hard to decipher. Since Singh's diary was never designed to be made public, it is written in the kind of language that officials used with each other. The text has many abbreviations and acronyms.

Har Mander Singh helped unravel these for me over a couple of mornings in his home. The messages give detailed insights into the structure of local governance—with general instructions emanating from Shillong—and the support team Singh used. I asked Singh to expand on his diary notes for me wherever he could. All his relevant additional notes are included in my narrative.

Diary Extract, 26 March 1959 (continuation):

Late in the evening, received a message dated the 23rd from the Administration which contained directions about receiving the dignitary if he seeks asylum with us. This was received corrupt and was, therefore, not fully understood.

Here's how Har Mander Singh explained the above entry. 'Corrupt meant that half of some words were missing, and others were distorted. Somebody in Intelligence must have told me orally that somebody was coming with more information. The information was to come to me, but because it was sensitive, the intention was that it should be shared with the smallest number of people.'[3]

Singh did not stand on ceremony with his own men. That same evening, on 26 March, he walked over to Khurana's, a staff member's, house.

Diary Extract, 26 March 1959 (continuation):

Went to see Sandup at Khurana's place in the evening.

Samdup was the Tibetan-speaking official of the Indian Intelligence Bureau who had come from Rupa. He was fairly senior. His job was to convey information back and forth, since the area is—and was— acutely sensitive.

Khurana was also one of Singh's officials, the same rank as Samdup. His official title was Base Superintendent. He was part of the chain of command that started with Singh and his Assistant Political Officer. He ran errands and took messages to villages and staff, and also passed on messages to Singh from others.[4] Khurana would create written reports for senior bureaucrats.

The message referred to in the diary had come from the Adviser to the Governor of Assam, known as the ADGA.

The ADGA at the time was K.L. Mehta, responsible for the entire NEFA. Even though the director and legal authority for administering the NEFA was the Governor of Assam, much of the administration, however, was delegated to the Adviser.

Diary Extract, 26 March 1959 (continuation):

He [Sandup] *suggested that as ADGA's message had been received in corrupt form, we should repeat the gist to APO Tawang in a coded message.*

The APO, T.S. Murthy, was a Chinese-speaking Assistant Political Officer, sent ahead by Har Mander Singh to the border towns.

Diary Extract, 26 March 1959 (continuation):

This was done. The message was cleared at 1am. Also requested OC Wing [the company of the Officer Commanding the Assam Rifles located in Bomdila][5] to get the message repeated for us.

There was another message from the Administration about C.T. La's posting on special duty to Tawang because of his knowledge of the Chinese language.

C.T. La was an administrative official of 'a not particularly high rank'.[6]

Diary Extract, 26 March, 1959 (continuation):

There were also two coded messages from CO Lokra, in one of which he had asked to be kept informed of the developments and in the other had said that if there is need to strengthen any post by going short elsewhere, he should be informed. I replied that although OC Wing was not here, I personally felt that some additional reserves should be created in Bomdi La and Tawang.

CO Lokra was the Commanding Officer at headquarters of the Assam Rifles. There was a company or wing of the Assam Rifles in Kameng, deployed to secure the route into Kameng from Tibet/China (from the border to Bomdila), under a Major stationed in Singh's HQ. There were twenty to twenty-five men in reserve in Bomdila, and at this time, soon after Har Mander's rapid march to the border, this reserve was activated so that men could be positioned along the route the Dalai Lama would be taking.

Diary Extract, 27 March 1959:

Wangdi left for Tawang.

Tibetan sub-inspector Wangdi was a functionary from the Intelligence Bureau posted to the Frontier Area. 'We had intelligence people mixed up with the security people, so he was one of the intelligence men.'[7]

Diary Extract, 27 March 1959 (continuation):

Informed CT La about his posting and instructed him to move immediately. Khurana is making special arrangements for porters for him and he will be leaving tomorrow.

One of Khurana's jobs was to arrange transport. He was responsible for the ponies and porters needed for Har Mander's journey.

Diary Extract, 27 March 1959 (continuation):

Sandup suggested that I should see the three Tibetans who had been permitted by the Government of India to proceed to Tsona. They are carrying a radio set, a cyclostyling machine and some other articles.

These men had links with the local Indian intelligence setup, Har Mander remembered.

Tsona was the last Buddhist centre in southern Tibet, just north of the Indian border. It was the place that the Dalai Lama and his entourage now appeared to be heading to. It was likely to be their destination because all other routes had been cut off. There was no way back. Thousands of Chinese troops had fanned out across the south of the country on land and in the air. Thus, they would easily spot the refugees. In escaping, the party had a few precious days to get ahead, but the PLA were now lying in wait behind them.

The Dalai Lama and his entourage had been heading for Tsona to hide out because they knew that they had friends there.

Historically, Tsona and Tawang in India were linked, being major Buddhist monasteries not far apart. Tawang answered to Tsona, which was seen as the mother monastery. Lapsed monk Jampa Phende's grandfather recalls paying taxes to Tsona monastery in Tibet. Jampa himself said, 'They used to take planks of wood, grains. One had to walk all the way from Tawang to Tsona in the forties and fifties. There were no roads. My grandfather couldn't afford horses.'[8]

There was communication between the two monasteries.

Before the Simla Convention, Tsona and Tawang worked together in the ancient kingdom of Monyal. Law and order, as well as taxation, was controlled by Tibet, and Tawang was in charge of the administration. Taxes, a summer and a winter one, were collected twice a year. The taxes were collected not in money but in kind; for instance, in food grains, as Jampa Phende remembered in his testimony. Cowrie shells and coins made of iron were the currency used for business and trade. This was before Tibetan currency was introduced by the Thirteenth Dalai Lama in the twentieth century.

The Tsona Dzong and Tawang monasteries together sent letters to the village heads in advance of the tax collections. These letters were draped around arrows, and a feather was included. They were called 'arrow letters'. The arrow, straight and perpendicular, was the symbolic ideals of dedication and honesty. The feather demonstrated the speed of a bird.

Right up until 1951, the Government of Tibet managed Tawang. It was the winter base of Tsona's district chief or king. There was a trans-Himalayan form of communication. People travelled from Tibet, through Bhutan to Tawang, and in the opposite direction. This provided a constant flow of trade and business. After 1951, India's Major Kathing took control of the town. The first Indian political post was established there and then India placed it under the aegis of NEFA.[9]

Gradually, Tsona became absorbed into the Chinese sphere and Tawang into India. But these were important stopping posts on the Dalai Lama's journey.

Diary Extract, 27 March 1959 (continuation):

Sandup suggested that as they had already been checked once by the customs authorities at the Tista Bridge, we should not search their baggage again. The impression which Sandup gave me was that they were perhaps on a special mission and the search might compromise their mission. I agreed and instructed Khurana to record their statements, which he did.

Samdup, the Tibetan official, was taking precautions here, since the Tibetans might have been carrying equipment of a sensitive nature.

Diary Extract, 27 March 1959 (continuation):

There is no further news from Shillong or Tawang. I have issued instructions that wireless network should be kept as clear as is possible so that important law and order messages may not get delayed in transmission.

Have issued warning instruction to K Lama[10] that we may need him here on special duty.

Diary Extract, 27 March 1959 (continuation):

We have no APO 1 or APO II at the Headquarters and his presence may be useful here not only to assist me but also to deal with the dignitary. K Lama knows Tibetan protocol fully.

APO 1 and APO 11 refer to Assistant Political Officers working with Har Mander Singh in his office.

Har Mander Singh's personal assistants, one of whom wrote confidential documents for him such as his diary, were known as confidential assistants. That was because much of what they were handling was sensitive due to the location. All communication was either by letter, which took days, or by wireless telegraph (abbreviated in the diary to WT).

Diary Extract, 27 March 1959 (continuation):

The Confidential Assistants kept in touch with the W T Room and I was also up until 2.30am but there was no news from outside except a message from CO LOKRA asking us to provide transport for move of one JCO and some OR proceeding to the forward checkposts.

A JCO was an Assam Rifles junior commissioned officer, a sergeant major. ORs referred to 'other ranks'.

Tibetologist Claude Arpi obtained a relevant report written by Har Mander Singh and published it on his site. It reads: 'According to the report of the Political Officer in Bomdila: On the 27th March, 1959, Shri T.S. Murthy, Assistant Political Officer, Tawang, received instructions about the possibility of the Dalai Lama seeking entry into India. He reached Chuthangmu to receive the party at 0900 hours on the 31st March 1959.

The advance party of the Dalai Lama under a comparatively junior officer had already reached Chuthangmu on the 29th March. They stated that the main party consisting of the Dalai Lama, his family, ministers and tutors were expected to enter our territory at 1400 hours on the 31st March, that there was no sign of the Chinese pursuit and that the party was bringing a small number of porters and would be needing many more from our area.

At 1400 hours on the 31st March, the Dalai Lama and his party reached Kenze Mane [Khenzimane] which demarcates the frontier in Chuthangmu area. His Holiness was riding a yak and was received by the Assistant Political Officer, Tawang. They proceeded to the checkpost without halting at the frontier.

Dronyer Chhempu [Chenpo], Personal Assistant to the Dalai Lama met the Assistant Political Officer in the evening and it was agreed that all porters brought by the party from Tibet would be sent back and that porterage arrangements thereafter would be made by us. It was also agreed that all pistols and revolvers, except those in possession of the Dalai Lama, his family and ministers (excluding their servants), and all rifles would be handed over to us for safe custody and that these could be collected at the frontier by those members of the body guard who were to return to Tibet after escorting the Dalai Lama to the plains or that alternatively, we would keep that in our custody and obtain disposal orders from the Government. It was further decided that a list of all Tibetan officers and of entering our territory would be prepared and handed over to the Assistant Political Officer.'[11]

It's clear from this extract that there was a sanitation process going on, and Har Mander Singh and his team were being as cautious as possible.

Systematic, speedy preparations for the arrival of the important spiritual fugitive and his party were under way.

11

GETTING CLOSER

Bomdila, headquarters of the Kameng Division, the area identified as the most likely entry point for the Dalai Lama, was a hive of activity. Electricity crackled through the air in the wireless room. The tension was manifest as much in the anxiety of the team members as it did in the physical power supply. The messages that were being received were the only hint Singh ever got of what might be happening and the instructions from Delhi.

Diary Extract, 28 March 1959:

There was a message from APO, Tawang,[1] informing us that the dignitary was likely to enter via Chutangmu[2] and that preparations to receive them were afoot on Tsona.

Diary Extract, 28 March 1959 (continuation):

Before we could get the last part of this message, the set went off air again. I decided that the best method to remedy this state of affairs would be to send Khurana with instructions to reach Lokra[3]

Diary Extract, 28 March, 1959 (continuation):

by tonight and explain the situation to the Commandant and impress upon him the vital need of keeping the communications open and expediting transmission of messages from Tawang and Shillong. He left accordingly at 10am.[4]

CT LA left for Tawang.

I have asked Katuk Lama to come to Bomdi La to assist me during the Dignitary's visit.

I have written again to the OC Wing impressing upon him the need for getting ADGA's message dated the 23rd March, re-transmitted.

Sandup[5] *has written to the DD SIB* [Deputy Director of the Subsidiary Intelligence Bureau] *asking for the assistance of two more SIB men in Bomdi La.*

The communications were through again in the afternoon and we got the last part of APO, Tawang's message according to which 16 men are leaving Tsona for Chongey, four stages north of Tsona to receive the dignitary.

Three more messages arrived in the afternoon from Tawang. One dated the 23rd March mentioned that the two Khampa officers who came to Chutangmu on that date with intention to visit Tawang to recruit Monpas and Tibetans for Rebel Army, had been turned back after confiscation of their papers.

The Khampa officers thought that they could find fertile recruiting ground south of the Indian border, since many Tibetans lived here. Naturally, the Tibetans, as well as the local Monpa tribes, were fiercely loyal to the Dalai Lama. But Har Mander Singh and his men could not afford for those under his jurisdiction to get involved in agitating the Chinese. As part of India's representative team on the spot, he needed to prevent any sort of conflict with Chinese troops. While he had to refer to senior colleagues on policy, being on the ground, he and his men decided who might pose a risk to stability.

They sent anyone they were unsure of back across the Indo-Chinese border.

I asked Har Mander Singh about the Khampa rebels several times during my interviews with him. I asked him directly about how many came across into India, and if there was tacit support for them. I pushed him persistently. He knew I wasn't going to give up and towards the end of my first session with him he decided that giving me an answer was the only way to stop me questioning him along this line.

'You have . . . You tried to lead me towards the Khampa question. The point is that there are two different matters: one matter is that the Dalai Lama, who was the head of government in Tibet, had sought refuge from us, and our government, in its wisdom, had decided that it would give refuge—that is one matter. The other matter is to get involved in the internal affairs of Tibet and China. Khampas were waging a war against China. They were the warriors from Tibet, and we were not concerned, nor did we want to involve ourselves to fight in the internal matters of China,' Har Mander Singh said.[6]

It was as direct an answer he could give me. Har Mander's precise and measured manner of speaking hasn't changed much in all these years, as is apparent from the rest of these diary entries.

Diary Extract, 28 March 1959 (continuation):

Another message said that two letters brought by two Tibetans via Chutangmu for Gompatse Rimpoche had been intercepted. The third message requested that henceforth Dalai Lama should be referred to as Saigal for local security.[7]

Here's the Saigal code name in this diary entry, the code name that Har Mander mentioned earlier.

Singh clarified that while the letters referred to in this entry were intercepted, they were not confiscated.

Singh's assistant decided to write the following diary entry by hand instead of typing it out perhaps because it was written in a hurry at the end of the day. Singh introduced the extract to me by saying that there were firm indications that there was the possibility of the Dalai Lama getting to Tsona. So, early next morning, he called a meeting and gave instructions to his staff about taking care of affairs at headquarters. He made arrangements to leave at 10 a.m. with a relay of ponies every 10 to 15 kilometres.[8]

Diary Extract, 28 March 1959 (continuation, handwritten):

At 1 am a message from the Admin was delivered to me. It said that the DL was expected to be in Tsona at any moment and that . . . . shd move out and receive him simultaneously I shd move forward. It also said that the wing comdr was expected to move forward with me to . . . (he is not in station at the moment) and that CO Lokra –CS0,[9] HQ IGAR[10] will move forward to Bdr.[11] I decided to move early next morning.

Given the urgency of the mission and the need to reach the border, the Indian team needed to find a way to get there much quicker than was possible. The journey would usually take seven to eight days. But on the strength of the information Har Mander Singh and his staff were receiving, they needed to get to a meeting point in three days.

Yet in Kameng Division, however quickly you tried to move, the topography slowed you down. You could not possibly canter along on the dirt tracks skirting the mountains without endangering yourself and your steeds. There was only one way to get to the border quickly and that was by keeping their rest periods to a minimum.

Har Mander Singh and his men decided that over 29 and 30 March they would ride hard and fast. They would make up time by creating longer legs of the trek than anyone else normally would.

Before they left Bomdila, Singh briefed his staff.

Diary Extract, 29 March 1959 (handwritten):

Called a meeting of . . . STO [station transport officer] *and BS* [base superintendent] *. . . and gave them instructions to look after the affairs in the Divisional HQ during my absence. Also met DIS* [district industries officer], *DMO* [district medical officer] *and DAO* [district agricultural officer] *individually.*

Har Mander Singh needed to involve these men in this operation because he had set up base camps with his staff for the fleeing Tibetans.[12]

Diary Extract, 29 March 1959 (continuation, handwritten):

Met Sandup and informed him about the latest instructions from the Admin.

After this came the most intense part of Har Mander's journey. On foot or on pony it is impossible to go over mountain peaks directly in this part of the Kameng Division. The dirt tracks follow the steep mountains and are little more than animal paths that have appeared over time rather than being man-made pathways. Looking across from one side of a mountain to another, you can't even see them.

The journey from Bomdila to Tawang is a steep ascent, climbing higher and higher, deep into the Himalayas. Here, the danger to travellers from snow blocks and landslides is perhaps at its highest. At night it is pitch black, with the threat of a sheer drop only an arm's distance away. The rigour of the terrain necessitates two-night halts along this route so that one can rest before continuing the journey. Har Mander Singh decided to save time by tarrying as little as possible at these two stopping points.

He and his men thus crossed two major stages of the route to Tawang. It's only briefly described in the diary, but he dealt with it more fully in his interviews. It was one of the critical strategies deployed to accomplish the mission.

He and his men had over 180 kilometres to cover to get to Tawang.

Diary Extract, 29 March 1959, (continuation):

Left BDL [Bomdi La] *at 10 am and reached Drg* [Dirang Dzong]
at 7pm. *I rested for the night and left early)*[13]

On the way, Har Mander passed through a village called Rahung,
which is on the path to Dirang Dzong, a fort that is over 150 years old.
In Rahung, he spoke to the village head to ensure that arrangements
had been made for hosting the Dalai Lama's retinue appropriately for
the return leg. The conditions were primitive. The village consisted
of ancient stone houses, some of them 500 years old. To enter one,
Singh would have had to take care ascending an uneven, cobbled stone
staircase.

Travelling onwards, Har Mander must have navigated sheer drops,
as the narrow ridge gave way to the tips of deep, dark forests. To any
city dweller, the view is breathtaking and frightening at the same time.
However, this was Har Mander Singh's patch; he would walk these
ledges as routinely as others might go to the market.

Diary Extract, 30 March 1959

Left Drg at 7am and reached Sangedzong at 3pm.

To cover this leg, he skipped a village called Nyukmadong before
getting to Sangedzong.

The route to Sangedzong is treacherous and the utmost patience
is required to keep on track. Like a mind-bending maze, it crosses back
and forth, back and forth, seeming never to make any real progress.
The track seemed to have appeared along the ridges of the Himalayan
mountains as if by magic. Singh asked the pony man escorting him to
take care that he did not fall off his mount. When he was tired, he
dozed or rested on the obedient animal, keeping his feet in the stirrups

for safety. He may even have dropped off to sleep for a few minutes, but otherwise he was alert.

Diary Extract, 31 March 1959 (handwritten):

Left Sangedzong at 5am and Tawang at 8.30pm.

'I moved on my own; I may have had one or two people with me, but I expected to get porters and Assam Rifles at the other end if and when we had to care for His Holiness,' he recounts.

Diary Extract, 31 March 1959 (continuation):

Murthy has moved forward and is expected to be in CTM today.[14]

Singh and his team were desperately seeking confirmation that the Dalai Lama had crossed the border. In readiness and anticipation, they had prepared a wireless message saying that this had already happened.

Diary Extract, 31 March 1959 (Continuation):
We got information through operators that the dignitary had arrived in CTM. Sen was in the W.T. room till late at night but we could not get this [news] *confirmed.*

Ever since we became convinced about the dignitary's entry inside India, we prepared a message for transmission to the Administration on the following day.[15]

When I heard about the journey and read the diary entries, I wondered how Har Mander made the trip, considering he didn't have the convenient travelling tools—equipment such as appropriate headgear, handy torches and trekking apparel—we have at our disposal today. In fact, the pictures show that even his clothes were not really suited to the journey.

Singh is a man who has always taken care of his appearance. He is known for his slim-cut, matching jackets and trousers. Though he needed to be prepared for any eventuality, he did not consider it important to dress in a particular manner for the terrain he was about to enter, as it involved expending unnecessary time and energy. He and his men would be riding into alpine forest, travelling through the night, experiencing dicey narrow paths and ridges with steep drops. Even so, Singh kept to his uniform of a sharp, high, round-collar jacket and matching trousers that would be fit for any formal function. He looked smart, but at the same time his clothes were those of a relatively senior Indian official. In the photographs, one can see that Singh even wore dark city brogues for this assignment. He would have stood out in clear contrast to the tribals but he was maintaining, by means of his meticulous attire, what he perceived to be his dutiful official persona.

12

TAWANG TO LUMLA

Har Mander Singh barely slept on the journey from Bomdila to Tawang. He was focused on gleaning any information that could help him in his mission to get to the Dalai Lama.

He needed indisputable confirmation from headquarters that the dignitary had crossed into India. Singh checked with his wireless team at every opportunity, hoping for news via the Assam Rifles from Shillong. But as communications were down, all that came through was a deafening silence from the other end. In 1959, the terrain was too high and the conditions too poor for full and coherent wireless messages to get through.

Even today the residents of the area face communications problems. They often complain that their telephone connectivity and internet access are too sporadic. I found the same problem when I was there in 2017.

Going back to the journey of 1959, some 78 kilometres from Tawang, Har Mander Singh crossed the Se La (La means pass) that is sometimes blocked. At just under 14,000 feet, it is nearly always under snow, and witnesses sudden changes in weather. Subject to landslides and other hazards, the Se La takes a day to traverse.

The Se La may be dangerous, but it is still special to Tibetan Buddhists. For them, the spectacular lake there has significant properties.

Diary Extract, 1 April 1959 (handwritten):

Sen and I were in the WT room[1] since early morning. Sen tried to send a log message[2] to APO Tawang[3] to get information but we could not find out very much except that the dignitary had reached CTM the previous afternoon at about 3.30pm and that he was accompanied by about 20 soldiers who had been disarmed. This information coincided with the message to the Admin which we had prepared last evening [the one saying that the Dalai Lama had arrived in India] *but the operators could not transmit the message to Shillong until the 1st evening. Later we got a message from Murthy dated the 31st from CTM en claire* [in diplomatic speak, en clair is an uncoded or unciphered message] *telling us that the dignitary had entered Indian territory at about 3pm, and he was accompanied by about 80 men.*

Murthy was a critical player in Har Mander's intelligence gathering team as he was collecting information for his boss on the Dalai Lama's movements. It was now apparent to Har Mander that the Dalai Lama had entered India. This meant that there was no longer a critical need for secrecy in communications, though caution was still necessary.[4]

As advised by the Political Officer, Murthy and his team had the twenty soldiers disarmed. While this was being done, India's Fifth Assam Rifles took over so that the Dalai Lama's protection was not compromised.[5]

In Arunachal Pradesh, the Losel Nyinje Charitable Society based in Tawang has studied the early days that the Dalai Lama spent in the Kameng Division. The group shared its findings with me in a book, *The Crossing of the Frontiers*, it recently published. It also shared memories orally.[6] In their narrative, they describe how a small, welcoming formation of locals and officials stood in line with scarves in their hands, their heads bent with respect. Even today, wherever the Dalai Lama goes, people, dressed in their finest traditional clothes, stand with their heads bowed, holding scarves in their hands in supplication, with their elbows bent.

After the Dalai Lama entered India at Khinzemane, he walked one and a half kilometres to Grong-Kukpa. Here, according to local historians, the Dalai Lama planted his walking stick firmly into the ground. In its place now a large tree has grown, the base of which has a protective casing. Next to the tree, a *stupa*—a commemorative monument associated with saintly individuals like the Buddha and the Dalai Lama—has been built.

One grainy photo shows the Dalai Lama walking along a line of happy locals.

After Khinzemane and Grong-Kukpa, the Dalai Lama's party moved through Ngang-Chung-Kang to get to Chutangmu. It was here that the twenty or so Tibetan guerrillas were disarmed and asked to hand their weapons over to the Assam Rifles. The way ahead was wild and forested just as the path behind them had been. The guerrillas had been faithful soldiers and would even have given their lives for their leader.

The Dalai Lama also blessed his new protectors, the Assam Rifles, with these words: 'May your luck increase to the size of a mountain. May your name and fame be such as to cover the whole universe. May your knowledge be as deep as the sea. May your life be long and healthy.'[7]

*

The Tibetan visitors spent their first night in tents erected for them by Indian officials.

Namgyal Lhamo Taklha remembers hearing the news in her school in Darjeeling. She told me:

'We had news that His Holiness the Dalai Lama had crossed over to the border. So we felt, "How good that he has been able to come across to India, and was saved" and otherwise he would have been captured, taken to Peking or maybe even killed, so he was safe.'[8]

Diary Extract, 1 April 1959 (continuation, handwritten):

From another message we learnt that the dignitary was moving in slow stages and will be halting at Gorsham, Shakti[9] and Lumla[10] before moving forward. We passed this information also to the Admin, and the message was cleared in the evening.

Despite the best efforts of Singh and his team, the protracted nature and lack of communications was frustrating. He was able to contact Shillong, the next link in the chain of command to Delhi, but not his own office at Bomdila.

Diary Extract, 1 April 1959 (continuation, handwritten):

Sen and I paid several visits to the WT room but contact with CTM could not be established till evening. Messages from CTM dated the 31st from Murthy were received on 1st evening and our messages to the Admin were transmitted late in the night. There was hardly any contact with Bomdi La.

We got instructions from the Admin that the strength of the escort for the dignitary should be increased to two sections [24 men] and that it would be preferable to accommodate him in Pungteng. I had already decided that he will stay in Pungteng.

By the end of 1 April, Har Mander Singh had reached Tawang.

Diary Extract, 2 April 1959 (handwritten):

There was a message from the Admin in the morning telling us that the dignitary should stay in Tawang only for two or three days and should then move to Bomdi La.

Har Mander Singh's colleagues were equally anxious about the Dalai Lama being placed in a safe environment as soon as possible.

The closer the Dalai Lama stayed to the Indian border the longer there were chances of him being reclaimed by the Chinese in one form or another. Being in proximity to Tawang, a huge Buddhist centre and the most populated settlement along the route back to Bomdila, also put the Dalai Lama in peril. Singh knew that apart from the many monks in the monastery, hundreds and thousands of devotees would throng to receive their leader.

Diary Extract, 2 April 1959 (continuation, handwritten):

DST[11] had sent a message asking to let him know what relief commodities should be dropped in Tawang.

Gave directions to Sen about accommodating the dignitary and his party.

Since Murthy was Singh's team member closest to the border, Singh had sent him there to report on the Dalai Lama's movements. Time was of the essence. Singh needed urgent confirmation of the identity of the charges who were now on Indian soil. This was for diligence as well as security—theirs as well as India's.

While Murthy was at the border, Singh followed closely.

Around 20 kilometres away was a place called Lumla. It was the nearest inhabited settlement to the Tibetan border.

Singh described what happened. 'Now beyond Lumla there were a couple of places that had names: Gorsham, Shakti, but no population. They were recognized places because of the pasture. Local farmers and agricultural workers would bring their animals to these places for grazing.'

On 1 April, the second day of his exile in India, the Dalai Lama moved from Chuthangmu in the direction of Zimethong. At Gorsham, the Dalai Lama and entourage stopped for a night.

Diary Extract, 2 April 1959 (continuation, handwritten):

Left Tawang at 10.30am and reached Lumla at 6.30pm.

Singh was now on the verge of events that would change his life.

While Har Mander had been riding hard towards the border, the Dalai Lama and his party had been roughing it out, travelling south across Tibet, hoping to find shelter along the way and praying that India would grant them refuge.

The Chinese were already laying the foundations for a substitute Tibetan leadership to fill, they hoped, the vacuum and the vacancy left by the Dalai Lama. On 28 March 1959, the Chinese leadership installed the previous second to the Tibetan religious throne, the Panchen Lama, as a figurehead for Buddhists to turn to. Whether this strategy would work or not, indeed whether the Panchen Lama himself would cooperate, remained to be seen.

In 2019, at thirty, the current Panchen Lama, Gedhun Choekyi Nyima, who was recognized by the Dalai Lama when he was six, remains captive in China and prevented from interaction with the outside world.

13

MEETING TENZIN CHOEGYAL, AND THE CHASE

On 20 May 2015, the day after I had my second interview with His Holiness the Dalai Lama, I went to a well-known residence that is also an accommodation for paying guests called Kashmir Cottage. It sits on one side of McLeod Ganj, on a long hill road that leads away from the Dalai Lama's residential buildings.

This small, historic compound is where I spent my first few nights in Dharamsala. It is a place I have fondly returned to since. Here, I saw no security guards, cameras, metal detectors and lines of waiting devotees. The Dalai Lama's youngest brother, Tenzin Choegyal, lives here with his wife and staff. Some of the rooms are rented out to visitors. This is also the same house where the Dalai Lama's mother, Diki Tsering, lived with her youngest son when she first settled down in India. Today, it is an attractive complex in peaceful surroundings. A raised building to the right contains Tenzin's private quarters, and across it, a building houses the office, with a dining area beyond some spacious suites. The dining area sits in a manicured garden, and on its right, there are more bedrooms for hire on two levels.

Though only a few miles separate Kashmir Cottage from the hub of McLeod Ganj, the two locations feel very different. The narrow roads of the small town are sometimes so congested that waiting for the traffic to clear can feel like an eternity. Even the minutes seem to slow down as vehicles inch past each other, sometimes perched precariously on sharp hairpin bends. When the road is blocked, horns blow. At those moments the fresh air of the hills of Himachal Pradesh can feel polluted.

By contrast, Kashmir Cottage felt like an oasis. The only noise in this tranquil place with its tidy garden and quiet, devoted staff was the sound of the birds. Here, all seemed right and peaceful with the world. Looking out over the Dharamsala valley the sun shone on small dwellings dotted here and there. A silent sense of history was palpable. I thought of the danger and the adventure that the Dalai Lama's mother Diki and the rest of the family went through to get here, and the stories they would tell if they were present.

It was a surprising, and slightly surreal, gift that Tenzin and his family live here and that I was in the dwelling of these figures who carry so many memories.

On my first night in the house, I was invited to meet Tenzin in his private drawing room. I was struck by his languorous air and intelligence. He is a serious and thoughtful man, but jovial and humorous too.

To my surprise, I found that Tenzin Choegyal would enjoy ribbing me.

Later, when I went to his place days for an interview, Tenzin was waiting for me outside a room at the front elevation of the ground floor.

It was a large space with its own special, calm atmosphere. There were Tibetan pictures and a striking Tibetan tapestry on the walls, a calendar in one corner, a mirror, and a picture of a tree. Low lamps were placed on wooden tables by the arms of the sofas and a corner fireplace that could warm the whole room with a comforting flame made of freshly cut logs.

Tenzin was neatly dressed in trousers and a shirt, looking tall and youthful for his sixty-nine years.[1] At all our meetings, I'd noticed that he gestured frequently, and had the same tendency like the Dalai Lama to raise his voice at certain points in sentences.

When he talked, he made eye contact often and held the other person's gaze for much of the sentence, frequently adding a 'right', or a 'yes'. But he has a special way of communicating with his eyes, his body still, his back straight.

That day, he made sure he had my full attention.

Tenzin's charisma is different from his elder brother's, who is magnetic in his own way.

In a friendly exchange before the interview, I asked questions about his mother's quarters and the suite we were in. Tenzin Choegyal mischievously called me a 'nosy parker', to which I replied that it was part of my job. I then asked about his name and title. He told me that in Sanskrit, his name means 'protector of the faith, religious king'.

'So, what shall I call you?' I asked.

'Multi-purpose rascal,' he replied, making both of us laugh, and putting me completely at ease. He continued, 'Rinpoche is a reincarnation title. It means "precious" and is given to teachers. I'm supposed to be one of the thousand reincarnates in Tibetan tradition. There are so many who are reborn to do service for people. I don't believe I'm doing anything much, anyway.'

We talked a little more, and finally arrived at the topic of what it was like to flee Lhasa, the Tibetan capital, as a thirteen-year-old with the Dalai Lama and the rest of his family.

At that stage in the story, his elder brother had been travelling towards a place called Lhoka.

I will return to Tenzin Choegyal's interview in the next chapter.

Now let's move to when the Dalai Lama reached the Indian border.

The Dalai Lama and his party had arrived at the Gorsham grazing ground on the Indian side of the border and were installed in basic accommodation for the night. Villagers from two or three neighbouring hamlets rushed across for a glimpse of their revered leader and to seek blessings.

There was a thirteenth-century stupa at Gorsham that had never been consecrated by any senior lamas or Tibetan priests. Now it could be. It was as though the stupa itself had been waiting for the right moment.[2]

While Har Mander was setting off from Bomdila, the Dalai Lama and his entourage left early the next morning for Shakti, another grazing ground with little to recommend it. At this point, the Dalai Lama's party was accompanied by Murthy and the Assam Riflemen. The climb was steep and hard. The *Crossing of the Frontiers* research team, led by the Losel Nyinje Charitable Society, Tawang, has studied the Dalai Lama's route through their district. The team's research describes the route as so gruelling that the party's steeds could not complete the journey.

Villagers from nearby Zimethang formed an outer ring escort as the group passed through another village, Kobleteng. Those who could not get to the Dalai Lama's party due to distance or illness burnt incense in honour of the auspiciousness of the occasion.[3]

Residents of the Shakti settlement went out to welcome the Dalai Lama at Manegom. As mentioned earlier, it is a Tibetan tradition to welcome and bid farewell to guests with a whole group of people. (I first experienced this myself when I was welcomed by a group while visiting the Tibetan village of Bridim on the Tibet–Nepal border).

At Shakti, a doctor from Lumla attended to the Dalai Lama and gave him some medicines.

Har Mander and his staff had arranged for someone from his team to maintain a presence ahead of the holy group by twenty-four hours. This was to ensure that all logistical arrangements were in place. Singh had organized for the Tibetan leader to stay at an Inspection Bungalow in Shakti. Even now, the place is primitive and mainly green shrubland.

Lumla sits on the same National Highway that links Tawang and other townships along the route. There's no other way to get from

Tawang to Lumla or from Lumla to the border by car. The road itself snakes and winds around the mountains like a string of white liquorice.

*

In April 2017, the Dalai Lama and his entourage returned to Tawang District in Arunachal Pradesh. A set of teaching engagements there had been announced in the Indian press a few months earlier.

The international media ignored the event until it happened. The Chinese, however, immediately protested what they saw as a provocative act by India. The reason for their objection, they said, was that Arunachal Pradesh (according to them) was disputed territory. By sending the Dalai Lama there, India was creating mischief, adding that there would be repercussions.[4]

I had always wanted to follow in the footsteps of Har Mander Singh at this location; to tread the path that he took. The Dalai Lama's visit gave me the perfect opportunity to do so. But finding out the exact dates of his visit was a tall order due to the secrecy surrounding his event. Being so close to the Chinese border meant that he was in just as much danger in 2017 as he had been in 1959. The dates and locations were known only to a handful of Indian government officials. And those dates changed, again and again. Arranging international and domestic flight dates and accommodation was a logistical challenge.

I was to travel by a civilian helicopter service from Guwahati in Assam to Tawang, where I would wait for the Dalai Lama, who was due to fly in in a few days. From there, I would then follow him to Bomdila.

There were twelve passengers, including me, in the helicopter. They included Lama Lobsang Topgyal who was known to a couple of people close to the Dalai Lama. There was also a senior Indian state official and his wife. The official sat at the chopper's rear, giving up his front seat for me so that I could take in the stunning views as this was my first visit to Arunachal Pradesh.

When we were airborne, we crossed the Brahmaputra river and saw many settlements below. The sun reflected on the white body of our aircraft, bathing everything in a magical glow. Twenty-five minutes into the flight, we were level with dark green mountain peaks. Roofs glistened and a yellow-orange road contrasted starkly with the green track on the ridges. It felt as though that track was a protest against nature itself. Half an hour into the flight the peaks were steep, though some of their sides flattened out. Where there were no trees, the earth was aged, sandy-red rock.

The Himalayas were constant companions, inspiring feelings of awe and reverence. Some peaks were barren with no roads or paths, and others had sparsely scattered villages. It seemed like a little miracle that any roads had been carved out at all.

After fifty minutes, I landed on the Tawang helipad.

Waiting for us was lapsed monk, forty-year-old Jampa Phende, who is a friend of Lama Lobsang Topgyal. I talked about Jampa in an earlier chapter. Jampa wore a fitted blue jumper, faded jeans and boots, and a mala round his wrist.

Jampa first took us to a Buddhist shrine located close to the helicopter landing pad. It was the last place the Sixth Dalai Lama visited before he left for Tibet, saying that he would return. He did return, Buddhist believe, in the form of the Fourteenth.[5]

Inside, there were portraits of all the previous Dalai Lamas. Jampa showed us a tiny, decorated water well protected by a yellow canopy. There, he ladled out some sacred water for us. He told us that the goddess Tara Devi had come to this place, put her finger in a stone and caused water to immediately gush out from it. Tara Devi is considered by Mahayana Buddhists[6] to be a female Buddha, known as the 'Mother of Liberation', representing success and achievement.

Jampa drove Lama Lopsang and I into the main thoroughfare of Tawang that is known as Nehru Market, where he treated us both to a tasty lunch of typical Kameng food—soup, rice and noodles, before dropping us both off to our next stops.

I settled into the Forest Service Guest House, arranged for me by the Tawang Division Forest Officer, Abdul Quayum. The room had spectacular views across the town to the Tawang Monastery. Directly behind my quarters was a symbolic and famous landmark, a giant golden Buddha, which overlooked Tawang District.

In the meeting room of the guest house, there were many photographs on the wall, mostly of senior officials and ministers, but in the centre I was surprised to find a black and white image from 1959 from Har Mander Singh's own photo collection. It was taken with his camera, and showed a young Dalai Lama, his two tutors—Ling Rinpoche and Trijang Rinpoche—and an interpreter sitting on the ground in Tawang. Har Mander is also in the photograph, attentively listening to what the Dalai Lama is saying to him. The Tawang District local administration had been given the image and there it was on the wall, for all to see. My story was right in front of me. This photograph became the first tangible piece of evidence I would find in Tawang of the sacred journey that was undertaken through this district in 1959.

When night fell, the place became a bit eerie. There were no streetlights; only flickering house lamps could be seen here and there. The electricity flow in residential areas is regularly suspended to save power. On Saturdays, electricity is always off from morning until 5 p.m. for the same reason. I was freezing and dizzy on my first night due to the sudden adjustment in altitude. I could not rest or sleep. My phone had suddenly stopped working too.

But I got through the night.

I began the process of requesting security access to the place where the Dalai Lama would be teaching in the coming days. The process involved visiting the Superintendent of Police (SP). The SP mentioned in passing that the area around Tawang was being sealed off till the Dalai Lama left, indicating the sensitivity of the visit and the hidden dangers implicit.

While I was waiting for my pass, my helpers found out that our whole schedule had been turned back to front. The Dalai Lama had been due to fly to Tawang by helicopter the next day, but the weather had suddenly turned inclement. So, he and his entourage were going to travel by car via Bomdila to Lumla and were going to start their tour from there rather than from Tawang.

This meant that we needed to get to Lumla as soon as possible. We were short of time. We needed to get passes made and secure accommodation. So, we raced in our jeep along the perilous mountain highway up to Lumla, assured that passes would be made on arrival.

The Dalai Lama's event at Lumla was to be the consecration of a new statue and temple to Tara Devi. Arranging for the press passes for Lumla and Tawang was our biggest headache, for without them we could neither access the temple area in Lumla nor the grounds in Tawang where the Dalai Lama would be giving his three-day teachings.

We arrived at the Tara Devi temple to find officials discussing security procedures. It took all afternoon, running back and forth, to get the formalities done. We waited for hours, exasperated. It started to get cold with heavy downpours. There was nowhere to eat or find respite. The rain soon turned into a hailstorm. Finally, by mid-evening, we were given the requisite permissions.

We raced back to Lumla. The jeep took a forty-five-minute drive into a forest to drop me off to the BRO at Lumla. It was a compound with welcoming bright painted letters on a stone wall in front of green roofed rooms. I was greeted by the commanding officer of the 117 Wing of the Road Construction Company of BRO, Lieutenant Colonel Prerit Rawat. I began to relax. An orderly served me dinner, complete with a banana as dessert.

Lieutenant Colonel Rawat briefed me about the dangers of the local terrain and the BRO's work. It made me realize how much the lack of a BRO team must have hampered Har Mander Singh and failed to prevent hazards from occurring.

Even now, the BRO has its work cut out for it. It cannot prevent the frequent landslides and earthquakes, but it can get to the scene of a hazard and clear it quickly.

During our recce trip of the Tara Devi statue and temple, it seemed as though there was going to be little media present besides us. That was great news because it meant that we might get a good position right at the front to the side and not be penned off, as it happens in larger events.

Lumla is a bit of an outpost compared to Tawang, with fewer accommodation and facilities available. It explained the absence of outsiders there.

The next day, we arrived at the Tara Devi temple to find a host of devotees all seated on the ground in front of the temple, patiently waiting for the Dalai Lama. We grabbed a prize spot right next to the building at the front. It was likely that the Dalai Lama's party would have to pass by us to enter the temple complex. That would be my chance to ask questions.

The atmosphere brimmed with excitement. We saw the SP from Tawang discussing security with officials and other uniformed personnel.

Suddenly, we got word that the plan had once again been changed. The Dalai Lama was postponing his Lumla visit and would be heading straight for Tawang.

The devotees, dressed in their best clothes, looked nonplussed but did not protest. They remained seated, waiting, and when instructed, stood up and filed out quietly from the ground. It felt as though a bubble had burst.

We had to switch to plan B for the day.

14

DREAM WARRIORS
AND THE OLD TOWN

It was almost fifty-eight years to the same day, 4 April 1959. I was mirroring events in Har Mander Singh's diary, walking in the same places as he had once done.

Since the Dalai Lama would be travelling straight to Tawang instead, I did not want a wasted trip. I decided to explore Lumla and see if there might be any relevant buildings dating back to 1959 still in existence. I had heard that the original rooms where the Dalai Lama had first met Har Mander Singh were still standing. After asking around, I was told that the first encounter occurred in a place that later became the old State Bank of India building in Old Lumla (Lumla, though small, still has an old and a new part).

Old Lumla feels like a set from an American Wild West movie, with its quiet and near-deserted streets.

We found the old State Bank of India building located beside a car park. But there were no markings or any sign of it having been a significant historic structure. While we were looking around, a man came running up to me and said, 'I heard that you are searching for the original building that the Dalai Lama came to in 1959. I can introduce you to someone who knows.'

We were surprised by this because we thought that we had found the right building. The Lumla resident then introduced us to a young man, who took us to a row of small houses up a steep hillside. From here, we could look down on all of Old Lumla. He led us to a disused, decrepit one-storey unmarked building surrounded by a fence. It had a small porch above five stone steps, leading to a green door with a sloping V roof. The windows were dusty and some were broken, while there was debris scattered on the wooden floors inside.

The young man told me that he had heard from neighbours that this was the Inspection Bungalow where the Dalai Lama and Har Mander Singh first met in April 1959. He had been informed that since it is an historic building, a temple was going to be built at this location, which is why it had been requisitioned.

I asked him for evidence, but he told me that that's what he'd heard. He spoke earnestly, and since he lived in the area, he did not seem to be lying. With a largely oral culture in these parts, it is difficult to believe that a mistake could have been made over a building of such significance in the history of the one revered as a god-king in this region. The story must have been passed down through two or three generations, carefully preserved in the annals of human memory.

This decaying construction had been identified as the one to be turned into a shrine, not the former State Bank of India that we had first been sent to. This demonstrated the likelihood of the claim, since local devotees are meticulous in noting and recording every place a Dalai Lama visits. The respect that the local population have for the Dalai Lama pervades every aspect of their day-to-day existence, including their lifestyle, food and drink.

Monpas organize their lives around their faith; observing not only holy days and festivals but even structuring their weeks around their Precious Jewel—the Dalai Lama. This quiet reverence extends to the Buddhist Monpa diet.

Initially, I could not understand why there was no meat available in the restaurants of Tawang on a Wednesday. Then ex-monk Jampa Phende told me that a no-meat rule is observed on that day in schools and government offices out of respect for the Dalai Lama. Children, staff and officials also wear traditional Monpa dress on Wednesdays. Further, Buddhists across this region recite a special prayer for the long life of the Dalai Lama on Wednesdays.

We went back to the 117 BRO mess. Captain Jaffri, then number two to the commanding officer, Lt Col Rawat, organized a BRO jeep to take us to a nearby bridge where a landslide had recently devastated the landscape. It was a dramatic vista, for just behind the wide road and the strong bridge were boulders. In the environs of the BRO, I was reminded of the inescapable presence of the forces of nature. The silent landslide was a stark reminder of what can happen at any time due to the rains and the wind. We stood on a new road built by the BRO division, but next to me were big rocks the same pale colour as the road. They could easily have killed us if they'd come loose and rolled down. At that moment, I felt that however much modern India tries to reinforce and protect its north-eastern flank, nature will always win.

Not long after, we drove back to Tawang in a hurry because we were told that the roads to the monastery town would be sealed off to create a sterile bubble for the Dalai Lama to drive into.

In Tawang, I moved to the BRO accommodation. My bedroom had a bhukari. I was in good hands for the next three days and could refocus on discovery, learning and the main reason for my visit—to interview the Dalai Lama.

Horticultural Development Officer, Koncho Gyatso, managed to get a dignitary pass made for me so that I could be within talking distance of the Dalai Lama during his teaching and prayer sessions in Tawang.

I had also asked Lama Lobsang Topgyal to introduce me to someone in the Dalai Lama's inner circle.

That night Lama Lobsang took me to Tawang Monastery. There are no path or streetlights around the monastery, but at a couple of strategic points in the monastic complex, bright lamps lit up walkways and entrances.

In 1959, the Dalai Lama chose to seek comfort here. These cobbled stones and the ancient temple area both are familiar to him. Most of it is still intact.

While we waited for our meeting, we were invited to eat with the senior monks—an honourable and rare occurrence. The copper dishes were placed buffet-style on a central table, full of nutritious, delicious food. After we were done, I finally received a message that the New Delhi Representative of the Dalai Lama, Tempa Tsering, would see me.

Lama Lobsang introduced us. I talked about the project I was working on, and the fact that I was Har Mander Singh's niece.

A thin man, Tempa Tsering has a soft, kind face and white hair. 'Of course, I know Har Mander Singh,' he said, smiling. 'I know his son too: Harsh Mander.'

I showed him Har Mander Singh's diary that I had brought with me. 'I would be very interested to read that diary,' he said excitedly.

That night, I went to bed happy that things had fallen into place, even though our plan had been turned upside down.

*

I am now going to rewind the story back to the American sphere of operations.

During the eventful period when the Dalai Lama left Lhasa in the last week of March 1959, the US moved Tibet to the top of the White House agenda. Matters in Tibet were considered so critical by the US that President Eisenhower's daily Current Intelligence Bulletins featured Athar's reports.[1]

The CIA didn't want to complicate matters by making direct contact with the Dalai Lama. In any case, their trainees, Athar and Lhotse, were still accompanying the ruler south and were in constant contact with Washington.

Athar and Lhotse informed Washington that a critical mass of PLA troops was coalescing in north Bhutan. From there, the army would fan out to block all escape routes to the border.

The only place left to run to was south Tibet. At this point, there was no permission for any kind of asylum from India. The last time the Dalai Lama had asked, he had been refused by Nehru and received a verbal metaphorical slap on the wrist for his seeming impudence.

Once he had headed south, the Dalai Lama had set up a temporary Tibetan headquarters at Lhuntse Dzong, a large fort built of stone. The Indian border was to the south, sixty miles away. There was an old business route to India from Tsona in Tibet to Khinzemane–Jimethang in India, which might be needed for an escape route for the Tibetan aristocrats.

Here, the Dalai Lama had been receiving news of the tense situation he had left behind.

'After March 20th, the bombardment started at Lhasa. That news reached me, 21st or 23rd,' he told me. He also said that his Private Secretary had fled the Tibetan capital. 'He wrote a letter to me about the situation, what had happened.'

The Dalai Lama said that on reading the letter, he and those with him, felt sad for the individuals left behind.

At that time, said the Dalai Lama, he and his advisers were contemplating about staying back in southern Tibet. They thought they could still negotiate with the Chinese military authorities in Lhasa.[2]

On 25 March, the Dalai Lama and his party made it to Chongye Riwo Dechen. While there, the lead Tibetan Khampas trained by the CIA, Athar and Lotse, arrived. They were met by the Dalai Lama's Lord Chamberlain, Phala, who asked if they could provide any security or cover to their leader. The pair reassured Phala that the rebels commanded the whole area. Furthermore, the place was without roads. This meant that it was near impossible for the PLA, accustomed to moving in large convoys, to transport its troops and tanks down there.

The CIA agents also informed Phala that weapons were being provided to the rebels by the Americans and that the plan was to train more insurgents, away from Tibet. They also told the Dalai Lama's gatekeeper, chief liaison and chief minder that the Americans wanted to establish direct contact with his charge. If that could happen, it would encourage the US to become more active in the field. Endorsement from the Dalai Lama would be an advantage for the CIA.

The next day, the two guerrillas were granted an audience with their ruler. As instructed by Washington, they asked the Dalai Lama about his plan. He replied that he intended to set up a preliminary government based in Tibet at Lhuntse fort.[3]

Athar told the author Mikel Dunham that he and Lhotse then described their CIA training to the Dalai Lama.[4] They talked about the weaponry, air drops, and the plan for further training with the CIA. They even informed him about their most precious and vital weapon—the RS-1 radio. Athar told Dunham that the Dalai Lama became 'excited' by this news. The young god-king expressed his gratitude and presented beads to the pair.

After the audience was over, dutiful to his training and his new masters, Athar followed instructions and radioed the US to inform the CIA that in Lhoka, the person of special value that they sought to reach was safe and sound.[5]

When I first interviewed the Dalai Lama in McLeod Ganj in 2015, I questioned him about the extent of his knowledge of the Tibetans being supported by the CIA.

'You found out that the CIA was supporting the rebels. How did that make you feel?' I asked.

The Dalai Lama responded, '1956, when I was in India, my two elder brothers casually mentioned that they tried to have contact with the CIA. I didn't pay much attention and after I reached Lhasa, some of my officials said, 'Oh, now some Tibetans have already gone to the United States for training.'' The Tibetan leader was further informed that these CIA-inoculated rebels were dropped inside Tibet.[6]

The Khampa rebels were, to some, dashing figures, inspiring courage through their daredevil reputation. They pushed themselves and were motivated and disciplined. They were attractive and appealing to the young Tenzin Choegyal.

In my interview with Tenzin, he described the geopolitics around the Khampa rebels and their important backer. He also commented on the then increasing international involvement in the Tibet issue.

'Then at that time there were many countries involved. The Americans were helping the Tibetans, and making it look as though the Government of India didn't know,' he looked at me deliberately as he spoke.

'But people who really should know, they knew.'

'So who were the people who knew?' I asked him.

'I think the Cabinet Secretary. IB people, Intelligence Bureau,' he replied. 'Eisenhower was there at that time, and, I believe, reading books written by Americans who were involved in the Tibetan operation. Every day Eisenhower was briefed. Then Americans also had big things happening during that time in Cuba. Of course, it was during Kennedy's time the great disaster took place, but the Cuban operation was there during Eisenhower's time,' he added.[7]

Bruce Riedel confirmed that at some point the Dalai Lama was informed about the CIA's support. He told me, 'The Dalai Lama knew he was being assisted out . . . by people trained by the CIA. He knew through his connections that the CIA was training people over operations in Tibet. I think it'd be a safe assumption that the Indians, who had even better access, must have had a fair understanding. They may not have known all the details, they may not have known how many people, they probably didn't know the tactics; when people were flown in and out, but I think they had some idea of what the Americans were up to. They, as far as I can tell, never confronted the Americans with this but I think they had a broad understanding that the Americans were engaged in supporting the Tibetan underground . . . certainly by 1962.'[8]

While tumultuous events had an impact at a macro level, on a micro level, Tenzin was fascinated with the Khampa rebels, mostly because they had guns, weaponry and were heroic fighters. I asked him how he would describe them, and he laughingly replied, 'They're dream warriors.'

He explained that during the escape, he always hung out with them. He said that he wanted to be like them. Tenzin would ask the Khampas about their equipment; what they used compasses, handguns, grenades and books for. They would show him their penknives and also how they were taught to communicate in Morse code. He would ask them about the purpose of Morse code. Tenzin even remembered seeing the radio, though he did not see any messages being sent. He recalled, 'During the day they used to separate themselves from the pack and go into some gully, and then join us later after about one hour. Then they used to go inside because they had fixed timings. The machine, the transmitter was not big.'

While Tenzin was enjoying the company of the Khampas, the Dalai Lama was preoccupied with more serious matters. They were getting close to south Tibet. They had left behind carnage, while the road ahead was unknown.

The Dalai Lama recalled, 'When I reached south Tibet, it was difficult days.' One of his high officials then revealed that he had known about the CIA's work with the Khampas for some time but had kept the information from his leader. 'Then, one of my high officials told me; he seems to have had some contact since '56 but he never told me these things. When I reached southern Tibet, now there was no longer any danger; so then he told me. He said, "They are some of the so-called Khampa guerrillas." He says he saw some of them trained and also some weapons dropped, including some [he mimes holding a walkie-talkie] communication instruments. Then, only after that, did I get the full knowledge and picture.'[9]

During the late 1950s, the Tibetans who fled Tibet as a result of the PLA advance took different routes across the Himalayas. Many travelled to India by an eastern route that took the refugees perilously near Mount Everest, bringing them to Nepal. There were many Khampas among this group.

Some of them settled south of the Tibetan border in Mustang, Nepal.[10]

Back then, a king ruled Mustang and he gave permission for the Khampas to stay. They continued their Tibetan warrior way of life in their new home. The CIA continued to help them from Mustang too.

But the Chinese, whose influence in Nepal had steadily been growing over decades, objected.[11] They pressurized the Nepalese government into sending soldiers to Mustang in 1974 to force the Khampas to give up their arms and surrender to the government.

The Khampas were unwilling to give in and wished to create an armed rebellion. The Dalai Lama was against further violence and told me that he had sent a letter to the Khampas saying, 'Don't do that! If the Nepalese government comes, give it your weapons.'[12]

There was likely also a taped message sent.[13]

Most of the Khampas acquiesced. Some, however, committed suicide to avoid disobeying their spiritual head or risk dishonour by surrendering to the Nepalese army.

In his first interview with me, the Dalai Lama said that after the failed Tibetan uprising in 1959, many Khampas moved to mountainous countries bordering Tibet, such as Nepal and Sikkim.[14]

But no matter where they lived, the Khampas still had a desire for battle. The Dalai Lama told me that he and his close advisers felt that the Khampas fighting on their behalf in neighbouring nations could be detrimental to the Tibetan cause.

One such country that the Khampas chose as a possible venue for fighting was the neighbouring kingdom of Sikkim.[15] The Khampas travelled there, along with former members of the Tibetan army and even some monks. The Dalai Lama referred to them as 'sometimes short-sighted'. He and some of his close officials successfully deterred them.

The Dalai Lama also remembered the Khampas and their motley crew of supporters making for the Bhutan border. He told me that the

Khampas and their helpers considered that, as they were armed and ready for battle, they might as well try to conquer Bhutan.[16]

The Dalai Lama remembered that a Tibetan leader had managed to extinguish the Khampas' enthusiasm for conflict, describing the rebels as having 'too much emotion, too much anger'.[17] He said that it was 'senseless' to consider such violence. He quoted the Tibetan official as saying, 'We have one enemy already, and the Khampas want to create another enemy!'[18]

While the Dalai Lama appreciated the loyalty of the Khampas, he knew that they also needed to be reined in.

But in south Tibet, the Khampas would not be much use as a defence against the advancing PLA. The Chinese felt they needed to control and rein in the runaway Tibetan leader. Whatever it took, they decided, he needed to be stopped.

The Chinese were determined to make the Dalai Lama account for his behaviour.

'I think they would have probably pressured him to collaborate and probably threatened that if he didn't there would be a price paid by his family or by the innocent Tibetans,' said Bruce Riedel. According to Riedel, the Chinese would have used extortion against the Dalai Lama and that he would have been jailed had he been caught. 'The only question would be the manner of the jail. I mean you can go from a pretty horrific circumstance to being jailed in a palace with all the amenities of home. But still a jail. I think all depended on the level of his collaboration.'[19]

The PLA deployed as many assets as they could to search for the Dalai Lama by air and on land.

It was difficult to see how this deadly manhunt could not fail to catch its vulnerable, weakened, slow-moving target.

It wasn't even that the prey was camouflaged; at times, walking across ice-white, glistening snow, they were easy marks for the Chinese. Looking down from the skies or across mountain slopes, they could easily be spotted in gun sightlines.

15

THE MIRACLES

The Dalai Lama had suddenly vacated his throne in Lhasa. The entire Tibetan leadership was on the run, nowhere to be found. This left a vacuum.

So, the Chinese laid the foundations for a substitute Tibetan leader that they hoped would fill the vacancy. Around 27–28 March 1959, the Chinese administration installed the previous second to the Tibetan religious throne, the Panchen Lama, as a figurehead for Tibetan Buddhists to turn to. It remained to be seen if this strategy would work, or indeed whether the Panchen Lama himself would cooperate with the Chinese plan.[1]

Meanwhile, the Dalai Lama had arrived at Lhuntse Dzong. There, he heard on his own radio a report from Peking saying that the Tibetan cabinet was no longer legitimate, and that the Chinese had placed the Panchen Lama in charge of Tibet.

The Dalai Lama issued an official public statement repudiating the Seventeen-Point Agreement. He proclaimed that the dismissal of the old and the creation of a new Tibetan government by the Chinese was invalid. A document stating these points was signed by the Dalai Lama and messengers rode to every major Tibetan town, distributing copies.[2]

The Dalai Lama's rejection of the Seventeen-Point Agreement pleased his supporters and the Americans, but it did not solve the problem because the sanctuary he needed in India had not yet been granted.

In fact, Nehru had been playing down the Tibetan woes. Not long before, he had told his parliament that all was reasonably well across the border in Lhasa. Talty quotes him at first refusing to admit to the country's lawmakers the existence of any 'large scale violence' in Tibet till the battles in Lhasa were out in the open and became common knowledge.[3]

*

In Washington, the CIA's John Greaney asked Athar if he had obtained indication from India that the Dalai Lama would be granted official permission to cross the border into India.

Athar found out from Phala that no such permission had yet been granted. On receiving this information, the CIA went into overdrive.

Former CIA Operations Officer, Roger McCarthy, told author Mikel Dunham that when the CIA realized that the Dalai Lama might be stopped at the Indian border, it decided to act swiftly and proactively. Under normal protocol, the American ambassador to Delhi would have been consulted and would likely have acted as liaison. But there was no time for that.

'Top priority for the handling of this piece of correspondence was given. Specifically, it went quickly from the Agency, to the State Department, to the White House, and finally to Prime Minister Nehru.'[4]

Eventually, the Dalai Lama was granted refuge. As Athar and Lhotse watched the Dalai Lama with his eighty-people entourage head south, they radioed Washington that the Dalai Lama was near the border, and safe.

In fact, that was far from the truth. The Khampas, strong, proud, devoted, committed and highly prepared, had been a buffer between him and the outside world till now. Moreover, the biggest superpower of the time (the US) was watching and working to support the Tibetans, albeit for its own interests.

But bereft of his circle of security, the Dalai Lama was left more vulnerable than he had ever been. In his retinue were his family, aged tutors, old ministers, and a handful of bodyguards.

The toughest part of the journey down to the Indian border was still to come. What he would experience would test his physical stamina to the limit. Ahead of them were two of the highest mountain passes by the border. There were icy winds, and cruel, biting snow blizzards. And the Dalai Lama was already exhausted and cold.

*

In the Dalai Lama's first interview with me, he told me about the difficulty he faced near the Indian border. In his words, it was 'a very high pass. And snowing. Quite tiresome. And also, the horse really found difficulty'.[5] He remembered a clear day when all he could see was snow around him. The party was travelling quickly through the white fields, fleeing as fast as possible.

'Then, one aeroplane comes. So everybody is frightened.' It was a Chinese aeroplane. The Dalai Lama and his men were all easy targets for the plane's guns if it chose to shoot. He recounted, 'We were in the white snow. Horse is black and dress is also black. So we were very clear targets. Everybody was really frightened. But then that aeroplane, it comes and then goes away. That's one occasion that was quite frightening. That very night we slept, all ready to run.'

There were many occasions, he said, when the group was scared out of its wits. 'Right from the beginning, we believed in truth. So, no matter how difficult it was, we carried on, as we believed in Buddha.'[6]

The sighting of the aeroplane affected both the Dalai Lama and Tenzin Choegyal who cited the same episode when I spoke to him about his journey through the mountain pass in our interview at his home.

Initially, he had found the escape, the disguises, the hiding and hanging out with the Khampas exciting rather than daunting. But the group's naked exposure and the threat from the skies on those Himalayan mountain peaks left even the adventurous, wide-eyed Tenzin gripped by a sense of fear. He recalled, 'Yes, there were a number of passes. I think one of them is over 21,000 feet. You know, on the highest pass a plane flew over and the plane had no marking. Now, looking back, I think it was a Skymaster. You know, the same frame, same style as a Dakota, but bigger, with two more engines. It had no marking and it flew right on top of the pass. I don't think it was higher than 1,000 feet, and it had no marking and it flew towards India.'[7]

As the plane veered off, the group breathed a sigh of relief that its crew had not chosen to shoot them dead.

From the snowscapes, the party descended into steaming tropical forests. The Dalai Lama and his group began to think they were safe and made the near fatal mistake of starting to relax. The Dalai Lama explained how his party felt. 'We crossed that pass, then no danger—no immediate danger. Then everybody was quite relaxed. When I reached southern Tibet, at that time there were no Chinese soldiers, because obviously Tibetan guerrillas had already carried out some activities.' He said that the Chinese avoided placing even small groups there as this was guerrilla territory. 'Only in one place they concentrated their army—in Lhasa. So we felt quite safe. But when we received the information that now the bombardment [in Lhasa] has already started. Then, we had no hope. We escaped towards the southern border.'[8]

At the southern border, there was warm rain and it brought colds and illness. On 30 March, the bedraggled group reached Mangmang, the last village before the Indian frontier.

There were a few houses around, each had a stable covered by wooden planks, on top of which people slept. The stench from the stables and unhygienic conditions was terrible.

The Dalai Lama slept in a tent that night. But the combination of foul, contaminated water and decomposing food was a cesspool of germs. Aided by the warm winds and the already weakened immune systems of the Tibetans, the germs found new homes. Already fatigued and weak, the Dalai Lama was soon wracked with chronic dysentery. Back then in Tibet, the disease was usually terminal. And here, among the poorest, sparsest population, attempting to host a group that had fled with only the bare necessities, there was no medicine to treat the Tibetan ruler.

The Dalai Lama told Choegyal that his stomach hurt badly and that he could not travel. So, his retinue transported him to a more solid structure nearby, but there was no time for him to rest and recuperate because word soon arrived that the Chinese were hot on their tail and had reached the big monastery town of Tsona, which was not far away.

There was no option but to flee. The Dalai Lama, unable to walk or support himself, was taken in a makeshift stretcher. He slumped, trying to stay on the dzo,[9] the animal that would take him to the border. He had never felt more dazed, sick, weary and unhappy in his entire life.

Throughout the Dalai Lama's journey, he received continual reports of the atrocities towards his people. There are differing reports of his reaction to news of the various episodes. Author Stephen Talty suggests that the Dalai Lama's first reaction approached anger on at least one occasion.[10] But the religious leader calmed himself by remembering the Buddha's teachings—that an enemy can also be a teacher.[11] I asked the Dalai Lama how his belief helped him deal with news of the massacres of his people. Surely, I asked, he got a bit angry with the Chinese at that time?

His emphatic response to my question was: 'No. No. Not angry. There's no use. Yes, when we were together: my mother, my eldest sister, my youngest brother, we said a lot of criticism or negative things.'[12]

I then asked him about his spiritual challenge. 'What tested you? For instance, you said that you heard about the Chinese bombardment on Lhasa and that your grandmother died there. Didn't that test you?'

The Dalai Lama said, 'No, no, no. You see, we believe that everything, all our experiences, are due to our own karma. So, for

Tibetans, there is a common karma and individual karma. So now, for example, when they're under the same sort of bombardment, it's the same situation. Some people, even with some injuries, they're alive, they escaped. Particularly some Tibetan soldiers. Later, they escaped to India. And I listened to their individual stories. A lot of Chinese bombardment. A lot of bullets. Artillery shell exploding. But nothing happened. Because, you see, we have a special experience. Some didn't get hurt. They were protected.'[13]

The Dalai Lama spoke of a monk who had swept his room every day while he had been in Tibet. The man had had a lucky escape to a safe place. Later, when the monk was changing his clothes, he found a Chinese bullet lodged in a pocket, which had thus been stopped from entering his body. The pocket and the jacket must have been padded well. The Dalai Lama told me about another security guard who had experienced the same kind of miraculous escape thanks to the extra padding on his clothes. In his own words, 'It actually happened. A bodyguard was in the same group. When they escaped, some bullets touched his body. There was some bleeding. But something happened. His main body was protected. He's still alive. Now he's eighty.'[14]

The Dalai Lama explained that such escapes from serious injury were not just by chance. 'They were due to individual karma. Tibetans, as a whole, have common karma. So, we believe that we need immense help to reduce anger towards those people who created the problem.'[15]

I wasn't convinced because I was sure that some among them, perhaps even their leader, must have felt angry at some point. I asked him, 'But it wasn't easy for you. Tell me how hard it was.'

The Dalai Lama then told me a story about another top monk. As he was describing the feelings of this priest, it felt to me that the message of compassion was and is important to him. 'There was one Tibetan monk. Now his age is ninety-six or ninety-seven, he's still here. After '59, he was he was in Norbulingka. And then he became a prisoner. Seventeen to eighteen years he remained in a Chinese prison, a Chinese gulag. In the early eighties, like some other Tibetans, he had the opportunity to come to India with Chinese permission. On one occasion, we had a casual talk. He mentioned that during eighteen years in the Chinese prison, he faced danger. I thought he meant danger to his life, and I asked, "What kind of danger?" His answer was: "Danger of losing compassion towards the Chinese." He's a practitioner. Practitioners need to stay very seriously concerned about keeping compassion and forgiveness. It's so important. So, when the situation is that difficult, then there is the danger of losing that practice. They consider it a dangerous situation. Wonderful. As a result, that old person is mentally very happy.'[16]

But the Tibetan monk had clearly been punished physically and his quality of life was severely affected as a result. The Dalai Lama said that he could not lead a normal life.

'Physically, he cannot live like that because of Chinese torture. Otherwise, he's mentally very happy.

Hearing this tragic story, my next questions seemed obvious, 'Did you manage to keep your sense of compassion for the Chinese all the time?'

'Of course,' he answered. 'It's really for my own selfish reasons. If I keep that sense, I get the maximum benefit. If I let anger in, then I suffer more. That's not only a religious practice. It's common sense. If you ask some medical scientist when you face a problem, "Is it better to keep anger or better to keep a calm mind?" The medical scientist will certainly say, "Better to keep a calm mind,"'[17] he replied, with all the poise and wisdom he is known for. It seemed that he genuinely believed he felt that way.

When I asked him what the most difficult thing was throughout the whole journey, he said, 'I heard of this bombardment and a lot of killing. It made me really, really, very, very sad. One of the Chinese scholars carried out some research on how many Tibetans were killed since '59. That person, that scholar checked against Chinese military documents. That person found out that more than 300,000 Tibetan people were killed. From March 1959 until September 1960, around 87,000 people were killed in the Lhasa area through military action. That's really terrible. In the early eighties, according to the information, we guess over 1.2 million people were killed since the 1950s, including starvation, suicide and jumping into the river.'[18]

In the following exchange, the Dalai Lama revealed how he feels that many Tibetans perceive him.

'You are the Precious Protector of these people.'

'Yes. Precious . . . Tibetan people, I think more than 99 per cent trust me.'[19]

The Dalai Lama had been discussing the physical and spiritual challenges he encountered journeying through southern Tibet. The spiritual leader also gave me his impressions of travelling through the poverty-stricken hamlets he came across. 'Local people. All Tibetan. Each place, whenever we're passing through their village. They're full of spirit. They're faithful.'[20]

I witnessed this during the Dalai Lama visit to Kameng in 2017. The ethnic Buddhists of the region are completely devoted to him.

In 1959, by the time the party was nearing the Indo-Tibetan border, the Dalai Lama had been exposed to poor conditions and food that had most probably not been cooked in a hygienic environment. He had stayed in rough accommodation where water was in short supply. The constant travel and stress had weakened him and his physical condition had deteriorated dangerously. He needed rest and medical attention, but neither was at hand.

The group had still not heard if refuge had been granted to them.

'Mao Zedong did not handle this as anything other than treason,' Bruce Riedel explained to me.[21]

With no word from India, it looked as though the border would form a natural cul de sac, ending their journey. Having sent a formal request to India for help, the travelling party decided that they would proceed towards India. Finally, Nehru sent them a formal message of welcome. 'When we received that, then, very happy, very safe,' the Dalai Lama said.[22]

Tenzin Choegyal remembered that the next day, he heard the All India Radio announce that the Dalai Lama was heading towards India.[23]

16

ACROSS THE BORDER

Having been granted permission to cross the Indian border, the Dalai Lama and his party staggered across the India-Tibet boundary. On 31 March 1959, they made their way to a clearing where a small group of Indian Gurkha guards[1] was waiting for them. As dawn arrived, so did the religious leader of Tibet.

Tenzin Choegyal has vivid memories of that day. One of his immediate recollections is the uniform of the Indian guards. At the time, it seemed to him heavy and inappropriate for the weather and the terrain. 'We were provided with two Assam Rifle soldiers. They were carrying their caps as they were feeling hot, and their leggings looked very warm,' he said, shaking his head.[2]

Tenzin Choegyal and his family members were on four horses. He recalled, 'Now, when we crossed the border I wasn't with His Holiness's group, I was with my mum. Just moments after he [the Dalai Lama] crossed over and shook hands with the Indian official and all the welcome party who are welcoming His Holiness into India, including soldiers from Assam Rifles. There was a tremendous sense of relief on His Holiness's face.' He continued, 'There is a particular photograph—he has taken his cap off and is holding it. There's tremendous relief, joy, happiness and forward-looking; satisfaction. I could sense how happy he was. As for my mother, my sister and me, it was just tremendous. You know, taking a tremendous heavy load off my shoulders because then there was no danger on our life.'[3]

The constant threat of capture had made everyone permanently stressed. The group finally felt safe and relieved. With the relative calm, said Tenzin, came a sense of relaxation combined with exhaustion. This caused people to fall asleep and slowly slip off their horses. He remembered one man in particular who had felt so relaxed that he swung both his feet to one side of the saddle and dozed off, swaying wildly. When he finally slipped off his horse (to no harm) the Tibetans, including Diki, found themselves laughing for the first time in days.[4]

When they stopped for the night, there was a lot of animated talk, a lot of laughter. Tenzin remembered that the fear in people's voices had now gone. 'For many, I think, they were looking forward to starting a new life as a refugee,' he said.[5]

Choegyal also recalled why it was a significant moment for the Dalai Lama. 'I think it's very important because when he first crossed into India and subsequently in towns and larger towns, His Holiness was still recovering from his bout of dysentery and also had fever.'[6]

The bedraggled group was escorted to Lumla, the first properly populated settlement on the Indian side of the border. Tenzin Choegyal, his mother and his sister were part of an advance party, and thus they reached Lumla first. Har Mander Singh had reached the outpost with the help of his team.

The revered leader had reached sanctuary not a moment too late. His health and his body were failing. Singh recorded every historic moment in his dry, matter of fact way.

Diary Extract, 2 April 1959 (continuation, handwritten):

The mother, sister and brother aged about 12 years, of the dignitary accompanied by 12 servants had arrived a couple of hours ahead of us. They had 35 mules with them.

I confirmed with Tenzin if the first place he remembered meeting Har Mander Singh was Lumla.

'Lumla, yes,' he said. 'Thereafter he came with us and His Holiness was escorted by Indian soldiers.'

'Tell me about your first impression of meeting Har Mander. Can you remember? It was at the camp?' I asked.

'I thought for a young person he was rather bald.' Tenzin's face creased with laughter. 'I'm sorry. Because among Tibetans who are not that old it's quite rare that you find bald people.' He broke into chortles.

This was such an unexpected answer that I too burst out laughing.

Seeing my reaction, he said, 'Now stop. Just looking at you I feel like laughing. I hope I didn't say something bad.' We both composed ourselves.

I urged Tenzin to tell me if he recalled anything about Har Mander's personality.

'I thought he was very gentle, and his steps were very deliberate. The way he walked, you know, you can almost say he walked like a cat. He also always had a smiley face, very warm. It was good to see somebody smiling like that and we felt very reassured. He was really dressed very cleanly. We were in rags. Not rags, but dirty. But his trousers were always pressed, and his shoes were always shiny.'[7]

I asked Tenzin if he remembered asking Har Mander anything, but he said that he was just thirteen at the time and faced a language barrier.

Through my interviews with the Dalai Lama and his brother, it struck me that they could not have conversed easily with the Indians without interpreters. Even today, the Dalai Lama always has one with him in public and in interviews. He relies on these trusted aides, most of whom he has known for a long time, and he often looks at them while he's talking. They listen carefully and offer the occasional word to him when he suddenly stops mid-way through a sentence. They sit close to him on stage or on platforms where he can see them. They study every movement of his face and are so closely focussed on what he wants to say that it looks as though they are trying to read his mind.

So, interpreters played a vital part in this story in April 1959. It was because of this that the royal Tibetan brothers told me about their memories of activities or actions rather than long discussions between them and Har Mander Singh. For the actual, possibly unique recordings of those talks, we have the diary as evidence of the exchanges between the Indian representative and his guests.

Har Mander had duties to perform, and the first task was to effect protocols while being mindful of the need for protection. He wrote in his diary:

Diary Extract, 2 April 1959, (continuation):

I called on the mother and assured them of Government's protection. Checked up security arrangements for her.

In other words, Singh was making sure that there were enough people to guard the Dalai Lama's mother. The Tibetan leader's family, particularly his mother, ranked second in importance only to him. They too could be high-value targets for assassination or kidnap, so it was vital that India keep them safe. From here on, Har Mander Singh and his colleagues were on the alert for anyone or anything that could harm their charges.

Diary Extract, 2 April 1959, (continuation):

Sent five Assam Rifles men who could be spared from Lumla, forward to reinforce the dignitary's escort. The four men whom I have brought from Tawang will reinforce Lumla.

Sleepy Lumla never had so much attention focused upon it. It suddenly became a bustling hive of activity.

Har Mander Singh explained, 'Lumla was the first place where we had accommodation because there was always an official there, and there were offices and structures where people could stay. So maybe some [Tibetan guests] stayed in the dispensary and some in the agriculture office. There was also accommodation for officials. It was marked out according to the warrant of precedence as to who would stay where.'[8]

Singh later told me that although he was working as a Political Officer then, he drew on his army background when considering the deployment of manpower, such as the small number of soldiers available to him on guard duty at Lumla.

Diary Extract, 2 April 1959 (continuation):

There are about six men left here who will do guard duty at night and two of them who have been accompanying this advance party will move forward with them. Instructed Sub Inspector Wangdi to go with them as they have no official accompanying them to look after their comforts.[9]

At this point, Singh was anxiously waiting for news. Although he had found the Dalai Lama's family and the rest of the advance party, the revered leader was yet to arrive. He reckoned that the Dalai Lama and his group would be at or near Shakti, the grazing place nearest to the Indian side of the border. It was an identifiable stretch of ground, even though it had no human settlers.

The next diary entry illustrates how hard it must have been to figure out what was going on. It was tough then, as it is now, to get messages across the mountains unless it was by foot.

Diary Extract, 2 April 1959, (continuation):

There was no confirmation from Shakti about the arrival of the dignitary there.

Har Mander Singh was not receiving the information he needed to track the Dalai Lama's location.

From the time the young Tibetan ruler crossed into India, he needed to be kept safe until he was delivered to the representative of the Indian Ministry of External Affairs (MEA). But back then the Indian Kameng officials did not even know where he was.

No journalist or members of the public could access the NEFA; to get this far into sensitive territory, one needed special permits that were usually never granted. Even today, permits are required, and permission is only given to certain persons.

Journalists could only get as far as the distant foothills, from where they conjectured hard about what was going on. Rumours abounded but with little substance. Newspapers and magazines printed anything on the subject that they received. Virtually none of the stories reflected what was actually happening in Kameng, but the outlets did not seem to care. Tibet was novelty news, and the West could not get enough of it.

One correspondent, Noel Barber, travelled to Tezpur, Assam, far to the south east in the lowlands. He hoped to hire a plane and fly over Kameng to circumvent the problem of permits. He had figured out that he was unlikely to be granted permission to venture up to the border by land. However, he thought that no one could stop him flying over the area where he could figure out the on-ground situation for himself through binoculars. He did not succeed in his quest.

Singh had stopped everyone from getting into Kameng, whatever the mode of transport. A few journalists who filed made-up stories later got into trouble and suffered tarnished reputations as a result.

Diary Extract, 3 April 1959 (continuation, handwritten):

Pakistan Radio quoted Peking Radio to have broadcast that the dignitary had entered Indian territory on Tuesday in the Assam area.

Depon Rahakhar, Shri Sanam Topgey [a top ranking official in the Tibetan hierarchy] *accompanied by two office servants arrived at 11 am. He said that he was a Garrison Commander from Lhasa and has been travelling one day ahead of the dignitary. His family is in Gangtok and he is anxious to join them early. He has got a permit issued by PCP* [police check post]*, Chuthangmu allowing him to stay in Tawang area for a month. After a brief halt he proceeded to Thuonglang. I made arrangements to watch his movements. I was suspicious as he did not seem to know about the dignitary's party.*

Har Mander Singh told me that this garrison commander knew nothing about the Dalai Lama's escape and that the commander had independently fled Lhasa. He had organized his own, small-scale escape. Though the Tibetan was watched, intelligence personnel at the police check post allowed him to stay a month in Chuthangmu. Singh said that somebody with authority had given him permission to move ahead, which indicated that there must have been an understanding he had formed with the Indian intelligence services.

Diary Extract, 3 April 1959 (continuation, handwritten):

Got a message from CSO [chief signal officer] *informing me that he had been able to establish direct W.T. communication from Bomdi la with HQ IGAR.*

Got a letter from Sen. He has received a number of messages from Chuthangmu. One message said that a wounded Khampa soldier had arrived Chuthangmu and was given first aid and pushed back.

Being 'pushed back' meant being sent back across the Indo-Chinese border. Har Mander followed a clear policy about the Khampas as he was in a delicate situation. He said that he would not deal with the Khampas at the time in order not to exacerbate a tense situation. Instructions from Delhi indicated that relations between China and India should not be harmed or there could be a backlash from the east.

'At this point, we didn't want to complicate matters by letting the whole world in,' he said.[10]

*

On 3 April 1959, the Dalai Lama was heading for Lumla. On the way was a village called Sharbang. Though there was little advance news of the Dalai Lama's arrival at villages along the way, whenever word got around, people ran to find the party and seek its leader's blessings.

Devotees expressed themselves in different ways. One old man at Sharbang took off his traditional Tibetan *chuba* (jacket) wrap. He placed it carefully underneath a piece of flat stone that he expected the Dalai Lama to walk over. After the Dalai Lama did so, the old man kept the chuba as a treasured holy memento. Other villagers asked him for pieces of the cloth so that they could keep them in their homes to ward off evil.[11]

At this point, Nehru also sent a telegram to the Dalai Lama via Shillong, which was then sent to Har Mander Singh, who read it to his distinguished visitor. It said:

To the Dalai Lama: Welcome

I received Your Holiness' message dated the 26th March only yesterday on my return to Delhi. My colleagues and I welcome you and send you greetings on your safe arrival in India. We shall be happy to afford the necessary facilities for you, your family and entourage to reside in India. The people of India who hold you in great veneration will no doubt accord their traditional respect to your person.

Kind regards.
Jawaharlal Nehru[12]

The following orders for the adviser to the Governor of Assam K.L. Mehta, were included after the communication to the Dalai Lama. They were:

A village settlement, Kameng, 1959.

A settlement that is probably Dirang Dzong, halfway between Bomdila and Tawang, 1959.

Forest landscape, Kameng, 1959.

Vicinity of Tawang, 1959.

A settlement in
Kameng, 1959.

The landscape and
roads in Kameng in
1959.

Inside Tawang Monastery. To the left is the Abbot of Tawang Monastery, 1959.

The twenty-three-year-old Dalai Lama resting in his tent during the journey to Bomdila, 1959.

Dirang Dzong monastery, 1959.

In front of the Political Officer's house, Bomdila, 1959. Har Mander Singh (centre left), standing, and T.S. Murthy (centre right), standing in hat and dark glasses, with local officers.

The Dalai Lama (riding a horse towards the front) and his party travelling from the border along a mountain trail with the Assam Rifles escort, April 1959.

The Dalai Lama on his horse with important Tibetan ministers and the Assam Rifles escort in Kameng, on their way to Bomdila, April 1959.

Locals witnessing the Dalai Lama (centre, on his horse), and party on the journey to Bomdila, April 1959.

The Dalai Lama (centre, on his horse) during the journey to Bomdila, April 1959.

The Dalai Lama (centre, on his horse) and Har Mander Singh (left, on his horse) during their journey to Bomdila, April 1959.

The Dalai Lama approaching the Political Officer's house in Bomdila, April 1959.

On the lawns of the Political Officer's house, the Dalai Lama is greeted by a guard of honour of the Assam Rifles. From left to right: Guard Commander, Mr Menon, the Dalai Lama and Har Mander Singh, April 1959.

The Dalai Lama sitting on a wooden throne especially designed and constructed for him in the Political Officer's house in Bomdila, April 1959.

The Dalai Lama (centre) and his interpreter in conversation with local guests in Bomdila, April 1959.

From left to right: Probably one of the Dalai Lama's tutors (standing), probably three Tibetan ministers (sitting) and the Political Officer's Tibetan interpreter in the Political Officer's drawing room, Bomdila, April 1959.

Important members of the Dalai Lama's retinue in the Political Officer's residence. The figure in the bottom left corner is probably Diki Tsering, the Dalai Lama's mother. Wearing glasses to the right is an Indian Intelligence official from Delhi, Bomdila, April 1959.

The Dalai Lama (sitting) in the Political Officer's residence in Bomdila, April 1959.

From left to right: Mr Menon, the Dalai Lama's interpreter, probably a Tibetan cabinet minister, and probably a significant Tibetan monk in the Political Officer's drawing room. Narinder Kaur, Har Mander Singh's wife, is serving tea, Bomdila, April 1959.

From left to right: Narinder Kaur wearing a traditional local outfit, the Indian Political Officer's Tibetan interpreter and the Dalai Lama in the Political Officer's residence in Bomdila, April 1959.

Local officials, heads of departments in the Kameng Division. In the centre, wearing glasses, is the Anthropological Officer, Bomdila, April 1959.

The Dalai Lama and the Anthropological Officer in the Cottage Industries Emporium in Bomdila, April 1959.

The Dalai Lama and Mr Menon (right, holding a bowl) in the Political Officer's house in Bomdila, April 1959.

From left to right: Mr Menon, members of the Dalai Lama's retinue, the Dalai Lama's interpreter (with his back to the camera) in the Political Officer's residence in Bomdila, April 1959.

'2. In transmitting the message, the officer concerned should also inform the Dalai Lama and his principal advisers that the Government of India are making the necessary arrangements for the Party's travel in India.

3. If the Dalai Lama wishes to halt at Bomdila or Tezpur for rest you should fall in with his wishes. We are sending P.N. Menon, formerly our Consul-General in Lhasa up to Bomdila within the next day or two. He will be in charge of the party during their travel to destination in India. We have not yet decided where the Dalai Lama should reside but obviously Shillong, Kalimpong or Darjeeling is out of the question. We shall send you a further message about this at the earliest possible.

4. We hope you have made the necessary security arrangements. We propose sending a senior IB Officer from here. We shall also send one or two interpreters. Please let us know if you want any other staff, which should be kept to the minimum.

5. No person, whether Indian or foreigner, should be given Inner Line permit to meet the Dalai Lama and his party. When the Dalai Lama reaches Assam, we cannot altogether prevent press correspondents from approaching him. P.N. Menon will be instructed how best to deal with them.

6. We are instructing P.N. Menon to inform the Dalai Lama orally that it would be best for him not to issue any long statements to the press here at this stage. The Dalai Lama will undoubtedly appreciate the inadvisability of saying anything which would cause embarrassment to him and to us. Similar advice will also be given to members of his party. Since no press correspondent can meet the Dalai Lama until he comes out of the NEFA area, it is not necessary to convey this advice immediately, even if it were possible to do so. We should like all our officers who will be with the Dalai Lama and his party to observe the utmost discretion in what they do or say to others.

7. [T.S.] Murti who is now in the Party should be with them until they reach their final destination in India. Instruct him accordingly.'[13]

From the letter, it is apparent that Nehru's public comments and instructions to Har Mander Singh were designed to circumnavigate India's precarious relationship with China. It seemed that the prime minister was nervous, so he was being cautious.

'I think that Nehru was always sympathetic to the . . . Tibetans, to the Dalai Lama in particular . . . He must have been torn between his responsibilities as a ruler of India, protecting its strategic interests and his sympathy for the Tibetan people who were being potentially polarised by the Chinese. It's a great irony that at a time when imperialism was in retreat around the world, Chinese imperialism took over Tibet,' said Bruce Riedel.[14]

The situation at the border was balanced on a knife-edge. There was an overwhelming force of Chinese troops, far outnumbering their Indian counterparts, a stone's throw away. In any case, China would be displeased with India for granting refuge to the Dalai Lama. Singh, therefore, needed to ensure that nothing provocative happened because it might encourage the Chinese to declare all-out war.

17

THE ENCOUNTER

It was 3 April 1959. The track to and from Lumla was mostly barren.

There was still no sign of the Dalai Lama.

Events had started to accelerate, and this is reflected in Singh's diary. Instead of entries about the difficulty of communicating with his bosses, now the content is about who arrives when, and how Har Mander Singh and his team dealt with arrangements for their well-being.

Diary extract, 3 April 1959 (continuation, handwritten):

Another message said that Lobsang Thagey, cousin of Dalai Lama had been permitted entry at his request. Another message said that Tsona Dzongpen[1] [a fort commander] *had arrived at Chuthangmu and had requested permission to accompany the party but was turned back.*

The last message was that the Dalai Lama had requested permission for his brother Gyalot [sic] *Dhandup*[2] *to come to Tawang from Darjeeling earliest.*

For interpreting conversations and receiving messages from the Dalai Lama, Singh relied on one of his junior officials, Lhendup, who spoke fluent Tibetan.

Diary extract, 3 April 1959 (continuation, handwritten):

Sen[3] informed me that the gist of these messages has been repeated to Admin and Bomdi La.

Holser Palden, an officer of the third rank with 12 servants also arrived ahead of the Dalai Lama. I tried to persuade him to stay for the night in Lumla but he said that he had instructions to move ahead. We came to know later after the main party arrived that his instructions were to move one stage behind but that he was too panicky to do so. The Dalai Lama arrived at about 12.30pm. I received him and took him to his home.

The place where Singh received the Dalai Lama was the small building I had discovered in Lumla. Singh told me that the Tibetan leader was housed in whatever building was deemed the best place at the time. Since Lumla was a staging place, the Dalai Lama's room there was fairly spartan. It was sparsely furnished, with just a bed, table and chair.

At Lumla, in 1959, crowds came from near and far, just as they did in 2017. Here, the Dalai Lama invoked the Mani Lung blessing[4]— an explanation and a mantra requesting a long life for the person or people for whom it is said—for the people of Lumla. It was the first time that the Dalai Lama invoked this blessing since leaving Tibet and since being granted refuge in India. It was a watershed moment; the Tibetan spiritual lantern physically crossing the border and now shining in India. Continuing the theme, the Tibetan guru asked those in his audience to feel compassion and warmth for one another.[5]

Kameng, then and now, is poor and relatively underdeveloped compared to mainland India. Despite this, at that time, the villagers offered up their most precious items to their spiritual leader. These were religious beads, holy textbooks, flour and rice. The Dalai Lama would accept none of it.

Those who could not receive the Dalai Lama's blessings physically, sent special scarves tied on sticks through acquaintances and relatives who could travel to him. As before, the elderly and the infirm burnt incense in their homes, lit lamps and prayed.

What was Har Mander Singh's impression of the Dalai Lama then? Was his spirit moved like the people of Kameng?

He described his observations pragmatically. 'Actually, he was an extraordinary person, because he had faced huge personal danger; his life was in danger, and he had undertaken several days' journey through mountains and forests, and yet I can testify that he was as fresh as ever. I think, quite frankly, it was not a spiritual moment for me. It was more a relief moment because the Dalai Lama had safely reached me, and now it was up to me to take him safely to the plains and see to it that he's okay.'[6]

Diary extract, 3 April 1959 (continuation, handwritten):

We carried out formal [the word 'discussions' is crossed out] *conversation for about an hour with Khandup interpreting, during which we discussed mainly about his journey beyond Lumla.*

Also met Chickyap Khempu and other officers on the personal staff of the Dalai Lama.

Here the handwritten text finishes and the next part is typed. Perhaps the diary was handwritten when there was less time to record what was going on.

Diary extract, 3 April 1959 (continuation):

Chkyap Khempu has cabinet rank.

Two of the three Shapes[7] who are accompanying the Dalai Lama arrived in the afternoon.

Shapes were members, or ministers, of the Kashag (which means 'lotus foot'), the highest political authority in Tibet after the sovereign, that is the Dalai Lama or his regent. The Kashag comprised only five members. These people were among the most politically powerful men in Tibet.

Protocols were still important between leaders and representatives of governments, even in this rough, alpine terrain. Singh, his team and the Tibetans maintained decorum. The Tibetan cabinet members were of such a rank that, if protocol were to be strictly observed, the Indians present at that time would need to show them respect appropriate to the rank. This respect would be shown by the Indians going over to see them, rather than have them walk to where they were. But the Tibetans themselves dispensed with these formalities and before Singh could step out, they were already at his door.

Diary extract, 3 April 1959 (continuation):

The third Shape who is accompanied by his family and the two tutors of the Dalai Lama who rank next in precedence, are travelling a stage behind. A couple of hours after their arrival the two Shapes sent word to me that they were coming over to see me. I got ready to go over and see myself but in the meantime they arrived accompanied by the Chickyap Khempu.

These two Shapes are known as Lingsha Shape who deals with foreign affairs and Sawang Shape who is nearly 64 years old. I thought that the meeting was of a social nature but it turned out to be a formal one. I have recorded a separate note on my discussion with the Shapes.

The 'separate note' mentioned here is no longer available. Singh recalled that the tutors, Ling Rinpoche and Trijang Rinpoche (who were referred to as 'Their Excellencies'), confirmed to him that things had been getting very difficult in Lhasa, to the extent that they feared for the life of His Holiness. It was for the sake of his safety that they decided to escape and seek refuge in India, they explained.

Diary Extract, 3 April 1959 (continuation):

In the afternoon a messenger brought a letter for Yonzone[8] from Dr Kharchung, Lekhung of Tashigong in Bhutan.

Dr Kharchung was Har Mander Singh's counterpart, a district officer of Bhutan.

The Bhutanese messenger may have been an official called Sri Legthong, arriving to pay his respect as well as deliver the note to the party.[9]

Diary Extract, 3 April 1959 (continuation):

It acknowledged receipt of letter from OC PCP[10] Pungteng (Chuthangmu) and stated that he was prepared to render all help to the Dalai Lama to pass through Tashigong District on his way to Delhi.

It also stated that he had received instructions to permit fifty persons of the Dalai Lama's entourage to pass through Bhutan and as there may be more than fifty persons in the party, he had referred the matter to his Government for instructions. I was surprised to find that OCPCP has apparently been in touch with the Bhutan authorities to obtain passage for the Dalai Lama to pass through Tashigong when there has been no talk whatsoever of his going through that country. I shall be asking his superior in Tawang to look into this matter.[11]

It was clear that although the Bhutanese were willing to help in every way, they were being careful with their response because they were wary and respectful for their powerful neighbour, China.

The Bhutanese are mainly of the same faith as the Dalai Lama. Thus, the Tibetan leader held—and still does—a very high rank in their ecclesiastical order. They wanted to support the Dalai Lama's passage in every way possible. But because they were a small nation, the Bhutanese would have wanted to safeguard their own interests against the susceptibilities of the powerful Chinese.

The tiny nation's devotion towards the Dalai Lama continues. Even today, as I witnessed in Tawang in 2017, thousands of Bhutanese patiently travel across the border into India just to catch a glimpse of their guru.

*

In 1959, while decisions about destinations and diplomacy were taken by governments at a high level, on the ground, appropriate transport was being organized.

Up in the mountains these days, jeeps are a necessity for navigating the rough terrain, mud and floods, but back then such vehicles were a rare sight.

Anywhere else in the country a jeep was an unremarkable vehicle, an army staple and a normal carriage in the mountains. But Kameng was far from an average mountain settlement; there were few roads and certainly no access to the border for a four-wheel drive. So Har Mander Singh had imported a jeep from the plains to the foothills, had it dismantled, and brought up to Tawang.

Across the border, the Chinese had constructed many wide roads. 'At least we could make a show of one tiny jeep,' said the Political Officer. It would come in handy now that he had a VIP to look after.

He described the conveyance as something to impress local people, to boost morale. He wanted to show them that the Indian government could produce transport despite the challenging terrain. The bulk of a jeep's components constituted one human load or one pony load. 'I wanted the people to know that we could dismantle the larger parts of a jeep, take it across the mountains, and reassemble it.'[12]

Meanwhile in New Delhi, a debate about the Dalai Lama's arrival in India was raging in Parliament.

Prime Minister Nehru was telling MPs in the Lok Sabha that the previous day, 2 April, he had received some unconfirmed reports. He had wanted to wait until they were confirmed, he said, before bringing them to the House. He also felt that Parliament should know about it before the media got wind of the information.

'The facts are that on the 1 April 1959, i.e, day before yesterday morning, we received a message via Shillong dated 31 March 1959 evening that an emissary with a message from the Dalai Lama requested us for political asylum and that he expected to reach the border on the 30 March 1959, The same evening, i.e., 1 April 1959 evening, a message was received by us again via Shillong dated 1 April 1959 that the Dalai Lama with his small party of 8 had crossed into our territory on the evening of the 31 March 1959. Expecting that some such development might occur, we had instructed the various checkposts round about there what to do in case such a development takes place. So, when he crossed over into our territory, he was received by . . . Tawang sub-division, which is a part of the Kameng Frontier Division of the North East Frontier Agency, he said.'[13]

Nehru's speech explained that a party of eight had 'come with or after' the Dalai Lama, and that on 2 April, Nehru had been informed that the group was moving in sections towards Tawang, the sub-division's headquarters. He said that they were expected there in two days' time—Sunday, 5 April 1959.

One MP asked if granting the Dalai Lama asylum meant that he would still function as the spiritual and temporal head of Tibet. Nehru demurred from answering directly, saying that '[. . .] it was a complicated matter which will have to be considered. But there is no doubt that he will receive respectful treatment.'[14]

After the debate was over, India's foreign secretary gave China's ambassador in Delhi a copy of Nehru's speech in Parliament. He also let the ambassador know that the Dalai Lama had entered India.

Har Mander Singh heard about the prime minister's speech on All India Radio.

Diary Extract, 3 April 1959 (continuation):

The 9 O'Clock AIR News was that the Prime Minister had given a statement about the entry of the Dalai Lama via Chuthangmu. He had said that he could not announce this earlier as the information had reached him late. He said that the VIP was receive by APO, Tawang and was expected in Tawang on Sunday.

There it was. The Indian prime minister had announced that his country was providing shelter to the Dalai Lama. Now that the rumours were confirmed, the attention and danger to the Dalai Lama had just increased a thousand-fold.

But all Har Mander Singh focussed on was to keep the party on the move, away from the danger zone, as quickly as possible.

18

LUMLA TO TAWANG

Diary Extract, 4 April 1959

A ceremony was organised in the morning where the Dalai Lama gave blessings to the people of the Lumla area. After the ceremony he took me to his room. While I was present there, the second Lekhung of Tashigong by the name of [an underline was left and his name clearly added later by hand in the diary] *Kocka*[1] *and two of his subordinates obtained permission to have audience with the Dalai Lama. They said that they had come as Maharaja's messengers who had sent word that as the route through Bhutan was very difficult, it would be preferable if His Holiness goes through the Indian territory during his entire journey. The Dalai Lama replied that his thanks should be conveyed to the Maharajah and he should be told that he had already obtained Government of India's permission to pass through their territory and that he was having a comfortable journey.*[2]

I also met the Lekhung separately. He expressed his thanks for the help which we had given in supplying vaccine when there was a small pox epidemic in Bhutan. He said that another epidemic of smallpox had broken out in his area and that he may be needing

159

further help. I told him he should let me know his requirements and
we shall be very happy to do whatever we can.[3]

This letter is an update on the one that arrived the previous day, 3 April
1959. It subtly highlights that a smallpox epidemic had broken out in
Bhutan. The outbreak of such a disease might have acted as a deterrent
to a group of travellers, already exhausted from a long journey.

*

The party set off from Lumla on a small track. The Dalai Lama rode,
and Har Mander Singh walked beside him, leading his steed. The
Dalai Lama had many questions for Singh, who did his best to give
appropriate answers. Lhendup, the portly local Indian intelligence
officer attached to Singh's office, acted as interpreter for the Tibetan.

Singh's 4 April diary entry covers the best part of two pages. He
knew that the first conversations between the Dalai Lama and himself
were critical. On a dirt track, in primitive conditions, surrounded by
tribespeople, a handful of officials and soldiers, two individuals were
meeting. It was a time of familiarization, of habilitation and of two
young men getting to know each other. A little bit of a dance was
also involved, for each man had to make his point while maintaining
equilibrium, taking care not to offend the other.

Diary Extract, 4 April 1959 (continuation):

*We left Lumla at about 8am and reached Thongleng at about
11am. During the journey the Dalai Lama asked questions about
the tribes in the Division, the school and system of education,
agriculture and self-sufficiency and script for the medium of
instruction which I replied suitably.*

At Thongleng, the overnight accommodation was a thatched-roof,
government Inspection Bungalow made of bamboo. The Tibetan

leader was a little too weary that day to meet many locals. Despite this, a Mani Lung blessing was granted to the village.[4]

Singh told the Dalai Lama about the main local agriculture crop—grain—and described the various Monpa language scripts that were used in the area. The Dalai Lama remembered being curious about education in the area and talking a lot to Har Mander Singh about it through the interpreters. Seeing children and schools along the way triggered conversations about the subject.[5] It's a theme that he has taken up with his government—both previously in Tibet and now in exile in India as well.

In the Dalai Lama's own words, 'Education, it's right from the beginning. I have a keen interest in education and I think around the early 1950s I had some serious discussions with concerned Tibetan government officials about education. So, naturally, when I saw some children, some schools, naturally I expressed some concern on these things, yes.'[6]

The Dalai Lama's concern about education has translated itself into many meaningful projects over the years. When I was in Tawang District in 2017, I saw how the Dalai Lama's enthusiasm for the education of local children had found expression in remote settlements.

In April 2017, ex-monk Jampa Phende drove Lama Lopsang and me from Tawang to a school for girls in the remote mountainside. It took over an hour to get there. On the way, we passed a famous nunnery that Jampa had told me about in Tawang.

It was late afternoon when we'd arrived. We were welcomed onto the premises set in wide, open grounds. With dusk falling and a chill in the air, it was a bit eerie. The buildings were scattered over a vast area, and there was hardly anyone around. The one thing that Tawang and greater Kameng do not lack is space. Nearby, there was a reassuring, throbbing, well-lit BRO hub. Their engineers were building a proper road to this remote place in a bid to improve the local infrastructure.

The school we had come to was run by the Abbot of Bomdila. He was personally asked by the Dalai Lama to come here and run the institution, primarily set up for poor rural girls who would otherwise never have had a chance to receive an education. The Dalai Lama had had this school built among the farming community because its people could not get to towns to attend educational institutions. Here, survival and the preservation of tradition are the watchwords for simple local families. Before this institution was established, the few families located here might not have been inclined to get their girls educated.

The Abbott greeted us in his maroon robes and a maroon woollen beanie hat. He showed us around. We drank tea in the Abbott's office, with boxes of sweets and sugary treats sitting on the table in front of us. We bought them on the way as Jampa and Lama Lobsang told us that they would always carry nice things for the girls to eat whenever they visited. The Dalai Lama, the Abbott told me, always felt happy coming to the Tawang region because of the special connection with the Great Sixth.

'We had a very good relationship with the Fifth Dalai Lama. Because of his blessings and his prayers, the Sixth Dalai Lama was born in this region. So apart from the lineage there's also a connection between the Dalai Lamas and the people of Arunachal Pradesh,' he said in Tibetan, with Jampa translating for me. 'The Fourteenth, the first time he set foot outside his own country, he came here. If he was still in Tibet, we would not be able to get advice and blessings from him.'[7]

Apart from the Abbott, there were no male staff members, due to the need to protect vulnerable young schoolgirls. Since I had visited during the vacations, I had been welcomed by empty dorms. I saw little lunchboxes, little shoes, little school uniforms and books in the classrooms, which gave me a sense of the place during term. Some of the staff members walked about in casual pyjamas and track suits, seeming to be completely at home in the cold.

The Abbott told me that the girls who attended this school were all Monpas, except for a small quota of 'non-believers'. 'Nomadic parents don't think to educate girls,' he explained, 'they just do their work. Monpa children here are financially backward. Parents cannot send them for better education in better schools.'

I asked him at what age the girls start attending the school and he replied, 'Currently, the school is for children above the age of six. Some parents of four-year olds fake birth certificates to have their girls enter the school before they are supposed to, as they may not be able to care for them at home.'[8]

Education here, endorsed by the Dalai Lama, followed a modern curriculum as well as 'ancient' methods too. 'If he or she is a Buddhist there are some prayers we have to do when we get up about respecting elders, humanity; the main thing is taking care of other people. Only modern-educated children don't grow up respecting their parents, they don't respect their own region, they don't respect their own caste and creed,' the Abbott said with conviction.

The school encourages traditional arts and crafts with purpose. 'When they grow up, they learn to knit things like clothes. The ancients—our forefathers and foremothers—made clothes themselves by knitting. We teach this way of knitting to the girls. Monpas knit with thread made from wool, mostly sheep and yak's wool. If we continue to do these things, there will be the preservation of sheep and yaks, leading to more work for everyone and more caring for the animals,' the Abbott added.

Apart from creating more work locally, giving the girls a means of livelihood and teaching respect for livestock, the school's main aim is to bring up good, kind, right-thinking people. The school also gives them basic education and inspires them to become doctors, teachers or businesspeople if they wish. The school plans to teach to as high an age group as it can. Over a hundred girls study here currently.

'This is all because His Holiness came here,' explained the Abbott.

The Dalai Lama was taught by the best when he was young. When he entered India, he once again had to learn many things. That may be one of the reasons why he encourages a modern Buddhist/Tibetan education wherever it is relevant. He is anxious that Tibetan culture is preserved and brought into the twenty-first century.

He adores being with children all over the world and sits in rapt attention when they perform for him. I witnessed this during a private visit the Dalai Lama made to Newton Preparatory School in London. I sat next to Tenzin Choegyal, watching the Dalai Lama on stage, captivated by a child performing a shadow dance for him. She beautifully mimed holding a dove, signifying peace.

The Tibetan leader was moved to tears by the performance.[9]

*

Har Mander Singh remembered the Dalai Lama's keen interest in education and teaching. In his private photo collection from 1959, there is an image of Singh, the same picture I saw in the Tawang Circuit House. From Har Mander Singh's distant memory and description of the event in this photo and its location, the place might have been Thongleng, but there is no certainty. Har Mander told me that the Dalai Lama usually sat alongside his tutors.

'It's the tutors who make him the Dalai Lama. Actually, once the Dalai Lama is discovered as a young boy, he has to be tutored on everything; philosophy, religion and languages, everything. So he has two tutors who rank above the cabinet ministers,' he remarked.[10]

*

Diary Extract, 4 April 1959 (continuation):

After arrival in Thongleng when I was alone with the Dalai Lama in his room (except Lhendup who was interpretting) [sic] he asked me as to what was the average number of Tibetans crossing over on either side in any one month. I gave the figure and explained very briefly the relevant provision of the Sino- Indian agreement on Tibet.'

Before the Dalai Lama crossed the border, only a trickle of Tibetan refugees had managed to reach India. But afterwards, the number of Tibetans crossing into India swelled to about 100 every month. Singh and his team had the task of processing these refugees. They had to determine who was genuine and who was not. Medical, health, food and in some instances temporary accommodation needs had to be considered.[11] But the Dalai Lama also seemed to be concerned about another set of people, as is apparent from the extract below.

Diary Extract, 4 April 1959 (continuation):

His Holiness said that although it was rather delicate for India to give assistance to the Khampas and others fighting for the Tibetan cause, he would like us to consider whether it was at all possible to give any kind of help to the Khampas. I said that any Khampas who were close to our Border and needed medical aid were welcome to come to our checkposts for this purpose. Similarly we were always prepared to consider cases of genuine refugees particularly women and children seeking asylum in India. In regard to the armed rebels it was rather difficult for us to allow entry to them for if armed rebels in any number entered our territory and/or use it as a base for operations, it may easily provide a legitimate excuse to the Chinese to violate our Frontier to deal with them which would make things very awkward for us.

It seemed that this topic was on the Dalai Lama's mind, despite the personal difficulties he had faced.

Singh remembered that the Dalai Lama did not talk much about the difficulties of his journey. The Tibetan leader was relieved that the ordeal was over. 'Almost all the time he was optimistic about his future while feeling concerned about his people left behind. He was concerned about the Khampas being defeated or destroyed. But apart from that I don't think he mentioned very much.'[12]

Har Mander told me that the Dalai Lama probably understood that his Indian host was not senior enough to make a strategic decision about whether Khampas should be allowed to enter India or not. Singh knew that officials that were senior to him would be making those kinds of decisions and that too, behind closed doors. 'And in any case, the rebels don't seek permission to fight their war. They do what their philosophy is,' he said.[13]

I asked if he found any Khampa rebels crossing the border, to which he said that the few who had made it to the border were sent back.[14]

Diary Extract, 4 April 1959 (continuation):

The Dalai Lama asked if we had passed a message to the Government that he would like his brother Gyalo Thendup to come down from Kalimpong and meet me in Tawang. I said that we had sent instructions to that effect from Chuthangmu and that I shall check up whether this has been done on my arrival in Tawang. I said that it may not be possible for his brother to reach Tawang in time but that he may be able to come as far as Bomdi La.

Har Mander explained why the Tibetan leader had constantly asked for his brother, 'Dalai Lama's brother Gyalo Thondup was a senior person and was in India. He was senior enough in age and relationship to provide advice to His Holiness, who had taken a huge decision to escape from Tibet and take refuge in India. How has this worked for him? He probably wanted to consult and take advice from somebody who was totally independent on the next course of action. So, it was only right that he wanted Gyalo Thondup to be in touch with him as soon as possible. He was absolutely the right choice to advise His Holiness on a further course of action. The Dalai Lama had a lot of faith in his brother to handle political matters.'[15]

Diary Extract, 4 April 1959 (continuation):

The Dalai Lama said that he had decided to spend a couple of days in Tawang and that he would like to halt for a much longer period in Bomdi La ro [sic, to] recoupurate [sic] from the strain of his journey before going down to the plains. I told him that I shall convey his wishes to the Government.

The Dalai Lama said that he wanted to have a longer discussion with me about the circumstances under which he escaped from Lhasa.

I went over individually to the various houses where the senior officers were accommodated to see if they were comfortable.

Kusung Depon, commandant of the Dalai Lama's bodyguard mentioned that he was in charge of a thousand men in Lhasa. He had brought thirty of them to guard the Dalai Lama. Twenty of them had been sent back from the Frontier and three more would be sent back later leaving seven men to xxxxx guard the Dalai Lama. He spoke about his friendship with [Indian] Counsul General, Lhasa, and said that he was a very reliably [sic] person. He said that two Shapes, including the Shape Incharge of the armed forces of Tibet have been left behind in Lhasa and have been captured by the Chinese.[16]

When I went to call on the two Shapes travelling with us, they reiterated that their escape was intended to save the person of the Dalai Lama and was in the nature of a religious crousate [sic] They had nothing to gain personally from the escape. The Chinese were treating them and the Dalai Lama very courtesy [sic] and were paying them handsomely but they could nto [sic] tolerate their interference in the religious affairs of Tibet. If they had allowed the state of affairs to drift, religion would have been got uprooted from Tibet and the future generations would have held the people at the helm of affairs responsible for it. They said that they expected not only sympathy but active help from the Government of India in their cause.

I also called on the Chickyap Khempu.

Two messages have come from the Administration. One asking me to persuade the Dalai Lama to stay in Tawang for minimum possible time in the interest of his safety and the other permitting me to decide where he should be accommodated in Tawang.

The Dalai Lama asked to stay in Tawang because there were many followers living there, and it was a famous monastery. The Tawang Monastery is important for several reasons. It's one of the biggest in Asia and was founded at the behest of the Fifth Dalai Lama.

As mentioned earlier, the Sixth Dalai Lama was born in Urguelling Monastery, not far from the Tawang Monastery. Har Mander believes that the Dalai Lama must also have thought of the need for recuperation with the Tibetan party, having had such a gruelling journey and thus asked to stay on. However, he was also aware that he needed to reach the plains as soon as possible and must have weighed the two.

I asked Har Mander to tell me what kind of danger the Indian officials thought the Dalai Lama might have been in.

'The Dalai Lama had escaped from Lhasa, and we didn't know what the Chinese were going to do about it, so our task was to get him away from the border as soon as possible so that [the likelihood of] anyone doing any harm to him was reduced. So, to the extent that we could, we took precautions,' he said.[17]

He showed me a photograph of the Dalai Lama surrounded by soldiers—tall, swarthy, serious-looking men in suits who could only be security personnel. The world over, these unsmiling men form an invisible ring of steel around the Dalai Lama, the prominent person whom they are protecting, in the same way as other principals are protected. They are always scanning the surroundings for potential threats. They tend to be slightly turned away from the principal they are close to. These marked characteristics are clear in one of Har Mander's many photographs. The Dalai Lama is looking out at his people, while devotees or the members of the audience gaze at him in adoration.

Har Mander added, 'For example, from these pictures you will notice that a circle of four or five people always surrounded him. But if there was a fifth column [people working for or sympathetic to India's enemy], I felt that that was a remote possibility, because he had come far away from the Chinese presence without their getting knowledge of it.'[18] However, there were some who were disarmed at the border by Singh's men and sent back across 'as a precautionary measure'.[19]

But the security personnel were not the only ones on a lookout. Though Har Mander said he rested, he was on watch almost twenty-four hours. As I mentioned in my preamble, my late mother Parsan, his younger sister, had told me it appeared that he hadn't slept at all. She also told me that he would taste the Dalai Lama's food to check for poisoning. Raj Mander considered it highly possible that this occurred. Singh himself would not admit to this.

Singh and his team also needed to have a 360-degree awareness of what was going on at the border so that anyone who could threaten the security either of India or the Dalai Lama could be repelled.

They needed to be alert every moment that they were with the dignitary. And they needed to be aware of what might happen in future.

19

TAWANG IMPRESSIONS

Given the high-risk scenario, the Dalai Lama, his entourage and Har Mander Singh needed to cross Tawang as soon as possible and proceed on their perilous journey.

It was important to sterilize the environment around the Dalai Lama, but the world's news reporters were beating a path to NEFA's borders. There was little by way of hard fact in international newspapers about this story, but there was a general perception that the Dalai Lama, from the faraway, mystical land of Tibet, had made a dramatic getaway from the Chinese.

Over in NEFA, Har Mander Singh needed to clamp down on access routes to stop prying journalists unnecessarily interfering in what was going on in Kameng division. They could wait in the foothills until he and his colleagues had made sure that the Dalai Lama was fully debriefed. The Inner Line, the demarcation that closed off a sensitive area a certain distance from the Indo-Tibetan border, became off limits to news hounds. This is reflected here in Singh's diary.

Diary Extract, 4 April 1959, (continuation):

The Administration have directed that issue of Inner Line passes should be stopped. No newspaper correspondents should be permitted to come till the VIP leaves NEFA, that the Border should be completely sealed.

Har Mander Singh explained to me how he and his team kept the press out. Only the local population was allowed within the Inner Line. Certain Indian officials were also allowed, but the Indian public, and foreigners certainly, were forbidden without full scrutiny and background checks.

Today, Arunachal is sometimes difficult to access. In my case, permissions and assistance were only granted after issuing authorities had thoroughly vetted me and secured personal references from those they trusted. I took nothing for granted until I had the various permits in my hand. My authorisations were also checked once I was in Arunachal; at checkpoints and in offices. The closer I got to the Dalai Lama, the more scrutiny tightened.

Back in 1959, Singh had swiftly pulled the drawbridge up on his patch, and he indicated where this was with a pencil on a sketch he drew of how the north-eastern zone was divided.

'These were all hills and there was the North East Frontier Agency divided into six divisions,' he drew a rounded rectangle with three vertical divisions, at the bottom of which was the Inner Line, painstakingly marking out where he was stationed, Lumla, Bomdila, his headquarters, the border, the line and the place that the Dalai Lama crossed into India. 'Now, an Inner Line was drawn, beyond which anybody who was not resident of these areas couldn't come in. The officials who were working there were given an Inner Line permit. So, there was no possibility of anyone, very little possibility in fact, of anybody infiltrating these areas. Kameng Frontier Division was the westernmost division of the north-eastern divisions. There was the Inner Line, and then there was Assam. Anybody could come up there. All the press came to Assam. But on this line and beyond, nobody could come,' he said.

'How did you deal with the press at this time? What did you do about news?' I asked him.

'The world's press was agitating with all their paraphernalia to speak to the Dalai Lama, to take his picture and so on. But all of them were held back beyond the Inner Line. That meant, this area where he was moving, was closed,' he replied, pushing both his hands beyond the Inner Line that he had drawn for me.[1]

This was why much of the detail of this story has remained private until now.

Diary Extract, 5 April 1959:

I called on the Dalai Lama in the morning. He asked me if I had listened in to the news. I said that I had.

He said that he had learnt from the radio that fighting had broken out between the Chinese and the Khampas some 60 miles South of Lhasa. He said that this area was inaccessible to the mechanised transport and was ideal for gurella [sic] type of warfare. He was, therefore, confident that the Chinese would not be able to over-power the Khampas in this area.

The Khampas, Singh told me, had lured the Chinese to the area 60 miles south of Lhasa so that guerrilla fighting could take place there.

Diary Extract, 5 April 1959 (continuation):

I mentioned to the Dalai Lama that the Tawang Monastery would be arranging a reception for him enroute between Thongleng and

Tawang and since Tawang was one of the largest monasteries in India, I shall be grateful if he would stop for a few minutes to attend the reception and also show special consideration to the Khenpu.[2] He agreed to do so.

Diary Extract, 5 April 1959 (continuation):

Before leaving, the Dalai Lama gave blessings to the villagers of Thongleng.

After leaving Thongleng early in the morning, the abbot of Tawang Monastery, Katu Lama, met the Dalai Lama and his entourage at Kidung Tse. The Losel Nyinje Charitable Society recorded that the Dalai Lama was welcomed inside a tent with tea and snacks. The leader and his abbot discussed the religious workings of Tawang Monastery. Local villagers, then and now, bowed and sought blessings from their guru. Historians[3] recorded that the Dalai Lama proceeded to leave Thongleng with his entourage and climbed a hill to get to Tawang.

On the way to Lama Tsii-Kang, they stopped to meet other Indian government officials. A famous Rinpoche was specially invited and arrived on horseback. When the Dalai Lama saw him, the Tibetan ruler alighted, and they exchanged words.

Diary Extract, 5 April 1959 (continuation):

The party left at 7am, attended reception by Tawang Monastery enroute and arrived in Tawang at 12 noon.

I had already noticed that the Monpas who have been lining the road side in thousands to see the Dalai Lama, are going through a . . . of spiritual experience. One can see quite clearly that with this spiritual experience, the faces of people have brightened up and they are feeling greatly elated having been in the presence of the Dalai Lama.

While Singh was observing how local tribespeople rejoiced at their guru being among them, he and his team were on alert for any signs of danger and never allowed themselves to relax.

'What kind of fear were you dealing with? That somebody would assassinate him?' I asked Har Mander.

'That somebody would harm him,' he replied. 'But the loyalty of people in those areas; they are of the same stock as Tibetans. The Monpas. It was a very far-fetched fear, yet we had to take precautions.'

On Friday, 7 April 2017, the Dalai Lama arrived in Tawang. Devotees from all over the area, stood patiently behind a rope barrier that extended on both sides of the road all the way along, through Nehru Market and right up to Tawang Monastery. Everyone was wearing their best clothes, and many pilgrims had trekked all the way from Bhutan. The Bhutanese could be easily identified by their red clothes and Monpas by their red or black chubas. The arduous journey takes two days just to drive through the mountains, so on foot it takes twice that long. But the devotees filing into Tawang would do anything to catch a glimpse of the spiritual leader of the Buddhist Himalayan belt. For some of them, especially the elderly who most probably fled Tibet in the late 1950s like him, it could be their last chance to do so.

Police and paramilitaries strode up and down the roads, asking stray observers to move behind the cordon. Media teams found vantage positions on steps. We chose a strategic corner just by the information point in central Tawang. We waited for ages.

Suddenly, a flurry of security and police personnel came running in. When the official cars carrying the Dalai Lama and his entourage arrived, he could be seen smiling and waving to his followers along the route. His devotees bowed in respect. Immediately, the atmosphere in Tawang was transformed.

It was the same feeling I had experienced in Dharamsala when I had landed there in 2015. It seems as though the Dalai Lama's presence spreads an aura of calm and warmth to his environs.

The next day, Saturday 8 April, was the first of the three teaching days in Tawang. The large Yiga Choezin grounds were expected to hold up to

40,000 people and there was an excited, picnic-like atmosphere among those in the devotee area. Families sat on large plastic mats. Up a steep bank were steps on which camera crews could stand facing the front stage with a red carpet where the Dalai Lama would enter with his entourage.

Behind that platform was an area, mainly enclosed in glass, leading to a building. Open to the public and not enclosed in glass was a throne, with cushions placed alongside it. To the throne's right were cushions for all the senior monks and to the throne's left were cushions reserved for officials. To the left of the throne and a little behind it was one for the chief minister, who had a prominent role during these three days. When Tempa Tsering, the Dalai Lama's representative in Delhi, saw me, he ushered me into the VIP area, and I quickly placed myself behind the chief minister.

The Dalai Lama entered from the front, walking up a gently sloping stage so that the public could see him. He entered the room, meeting as many as he wished to, and then he walked towards the heads of departments who were sitting just behind the glass enclosure on a glass-walled slope.

As he came back to his throne, I stood up and reminded him of my name and my reason for being there. As though he had all the time in the world and the masses waiting for him to ascend his throne did not exist, he spoke to me of staying with Har Mander Singh and his family in Bomdila. He told me about his memory of Singh and his wife Neena, and of a four-year-old Harsh Mander, their younger son, running around in Monpa dress.

'Now older,' said the Dalai Lama, touching his head, referring to my cousin, 'bald, like Har Mander and me,' and, chuckling loudly to himself, he smiled at me and went and sat on his throne. I felt as though time had stood still when his attention was on me. I was a bit emotional. Security officials, the chief ministers and 40,000 visitors had been waiting patiently.

The teaching began, and the Dalai Lama spoke in Tibetan to the assembled multitude. Some of the prayers he recited were familiar to the crowd.

I observed the Dalai Lama's two personal security guards that were with him all the time. They tended to place themselves in a way that they formed a triangle, with the Dalai Lama at the apex. Photographs taken of him over the years will sometimes feature both these smart-jacketed Tibetans who usually look serious and innocuous. As the prayers started, the bodyguards too, moved their lips, quietly saying the prayers.

These feared security men, trained to the highest level, able to neutralize most threats to His Holiness, were in communion with him—the one to the left of the triangle even closed his eyes for a few seconds at a time. Though seated, they remained alert and poised, ready to spring into action should the need arise. Observing their devotion shifted me away from journalist mode towards more of a place of feeling.

During the teachings, sweets, religious threads and other items were handed out each day by monks to the multitudes in the grounds. Figures or pictures of goddesses and gods were brought round to bless each one of us and held to our heads. In between, we were kept supplied with sweet tea in paper cups and *prasad* (religious offering).

*

On another day, I was curious to visit the Deputy Commissioner's residence that the Dalai Lama had visited in 1959. I asked for directions and was guided to a complex just above the Superintendent of Police's compound.

The place was just a left turn uphill from Nehru Market. Now, both buildings were patrolled with armed security. It still had a rustic feel. On entering the driveway of the Deputy Commissioner's residence, on the left, I found a tree with a plaque on it. It read: 'Planted by H.H. the 14th Dalai Lama on March 1959.'

The Dalai Lama has made several visits here over the years, and tends to plant trees on these excursions. Around the corner from the 1959 tree and the accompanying plaque, inside the Deputy

Commissioner's garden itself, there are other plaques from his tree plantings in 1997, 2003 and 2009—his last visit to this region.

The Deputy Commissioner's residence stood grandly atop a hill looking out onto the Himalayas and the rest of Tawang. In the sunshine, Tawang looked bright but the benign view could not be allowed to beguile—the closeness to the border here bred an air of electricity and watchfulness that was palpable.

On Sunday, 9 April 2017, the Dalai Lama conducted the second day of teachings at the Yiga Choezin grounds. This time, as he stopped to hear my question about being in Tawang again, he said, 'I like to help people', as one of his reasons for visiting. Separately, he spoke to me of having an emotional attachment to Tawang. Not only because Arunachal Pradesh Buddhists follow the same sort of tradition as exists in Tibet, dating from the eighth century, but also, as detailed in this book, because Arunachal Pradesh was his first major destination when he crossed into India.

*

Diary Extract, 5 April 1959 (continuation):

After xxxxxxx arrival, the Dalai reminded me again to find out xxxxxxxxxxxxx if any reply had been received about his request to permit his brother Gyalo Thondup, to come up to Tawang.

Lt Col Dorabji has reached Tawang and was introduced to the Dalai Lama along with the other senior officials.

Singh remembered that the twenty-three-year-old Dalai Lama seemed to keenly miss his brother's presence. He told me, 'He would ask me, when he met me, for his brother to join him. He wanted his political advice. He would ask insistently, all the time, "Have you conveyed my request to the higher authorities about Gyalo Thondup?" To this I would patiently reply, "Your Holiness, I have already conveyed your request to the higher authorities."'[4]

At Tawang, the Dalai Lama chose to stay at the monastery too. Singh remembered that the monks gave him the best rooms. Though the plethora of monks milling around provided some level of protection, Singh was never fully relaxed and made sure that security was always provided. He stayed close by and remained watchful.

At Tawang, the jeep that had been carefully imported from the plains was deployed for the dignitary. If the Dalai Lama needed to be taken somewhere, for instance between the official premises at Tawang and the monastery, the jeep was used.

In this small town, the Dalai Lama's family started to relax, unwind, and integrate into society. They were able to shop and look around the area of their new home.

Though language was a superficial barrier between Singh, the Dalai Lama and his youngest brother Tenzin Choegyal, strong bonds were still formed. All three have vivid memories of the impact each had on the other.

Tenzin felt that Singh reminded him of a certain kind of man that he was familiar with: one with old fashioned manners.

Tenzin Choegyal recalled, 'I think everything looked very orderly, and I think officials functioned in a different way in those days.'

'In what way?' I asked.

'Just orderly; everything was done properly. They didn't have a "why do I care?" attitude,' he said with a laugh. 'During that time, men like your uncle, they behaved like Englishmen.'

I asked him what he meant by that.

'In the way they talked and their mannerisms; everything. As I said, you know, people of that generation who worked in government services, particularly the Ministry of External Affairs, they behaved like Brits. Yes, they were gentlemen, definitely. They knew how to bite the bullet. They had a stiff upper lip. You look at this picture, you don't get people like that today. Even among Tibetans it's worse. See, I'm at an age, when I left Tibet I was thirteen, now I'm sixty-nine, I have seen a certain generation go and new ones come and take root. There's so much more difference. It's all over the world. I think it's like that now. Even in English society,' he said.[5]

While Tenzin Choegyal was respectful of his Indian government rescuer, it didn't stop him from being mischievous.

Tenzin remembered that he had a bit of fun at Tawang. He didn't need his fur-lined *chuba* or dress anymore because he was no longer completely exposed to the elements or on icy slopes. So he sold it. 'Fifteen silver dollars,' he said. 'Now with that I went to buy Amul butter, crackers and jam. I mean with part of the money.'[6]

*

Though Tawang was the biggest stopover en route to Bomdila, the need to get to base was paramount. The tension was high for the local Indian administrators.

'How anxious were you about that stopover? Didn't you want to keep him moving?' I asked Har Mander Singh.

'Actually, mutually, a decision was made that he will stay there for that long. I think it was three days. And to have taken him from Tawang, where hundreds of Lamas of all ranks say their prayers, would have been unfortunate,' he replied.

He stayed for the shortest possible time, Singh continued, and people from the surrounding villages came to see the Dalai Lama. 'I think God is great and this period passed off exceedingly well, and the Dalai Lama was able to make his journey as he wanted it.'[7]

The Tawang stop seemed to do the Dalai Lama some good. Up until then, he had been feeling pretty weak. He told me, 'Then, when I reached Tawang, day by day my physical condition improved.'[8]

Har Mander Singh did not reveal the tension that was palpable in the air as he watched over the Dalai Lama in this highly exposed monastery town. There, the young, vulnerable leader, under Singh's protection, felt as though he was among his own people.

But Singh had a problem–the Tibetan ruler was too much in public view. The highest Lama of Tibet was a sitting target.

20

THE ORCHID

Local historians tell how two days before the Dalai Lama's arrival, part of Tawang Monastery collapsed due to high winds.[1] This was interpreted as presaging an important event.

And so it came to pass, they say, with the visit of the Dalai Lama. Another omen occurred when a hurricane smashed three branches of a tree to the ground. Locals linked this event with the prediction that the sixth Dalai Lama made when he went to Tsona in Tibet from India wherein he said that he would return to India as a reincarnation.[2]

In 1959, just as I saw in 2017, everywhere the Dalai Lama went, his followers crowded around him, overjoyed to see the holy leader.

Har Mander Singh did not permit himself to show impatience at the discussions and religious formalities. He allowed the process, also because Tawang was the most developed and populated resting place for the escapees since they had reached the Indo-Tibetan border. The Tibetan visitors needed the space to feel secure and comfortable, even if it was only for a brief while.

Significant messages were flying back and forth between Singh and the chain of command, as shown in Singh's private diary where events were noted as soon as they happened.

Singh felt that the Great Fourteenth appeared rejuvenated on entering Tawang.

Har Mander Singh told me, 'His spirits were high and all along the route people lined up because these were the most important spiritual moments in their lives. People had come along with a village band and carried incense sticks. l can only imagine what those people must have felt while the Dalai Lama was crossing their path. I think they must have felt very blessed that this kind of moment came into their lives.'[3]

To the Losel Nyinje Charitable Society interviewer, Rinchin Norbu, Har Mander Singh said that it felt as though the experience of the people of Tawang could only be compared to a situation in which his own god were to come before him and say 'I am here'.

So, it was with the Monpa people, he felt. They were amazed and would keep that moment as a sacred memory for the rest of their lives. He saw them bent over, their eyes closed, murmuring Tibetan prayers. They would not allow themselves to raise their eyes and look at their guru since that might be considered disrespectful.[4]

*

In 1959, the Dalai Lama exerted complete spiritual and temporal leadership over his people. Though he has now given up temporal power and handed it over to the head of the Tibetan government-in-exile, President Dr Lobsang Sangay, his spiritual influence still reigns supreme.

In my interactions with followers such as former monk Jampa Phende, I found that their devotion to the Dalai Lama was non-negotiable and apparent. Apart from the *mala* the ex-novice wears on his wrist, he told me how his relationship with the Dalai Lama was helping him become a better person.

'The important thing in this world as a human being is to be happy,' said Jampa.

So, he bettered his behaviour in steps, improving himself stage by stage each time he was in the presence of His Holiness. 'I am grateful to be a Monpa,' he said. 'We are great followers of His Holiness; he's a great guru and spiritual leader.'[5]

Jampa's behaviour echoes that of his predecessors who have watched the Dalai Lama over the sixty years that the Tibetan leader has been coming to the Kameng region. They all express unfettered, complete devotion. Such scenarios provide an insight into the relationship the spiritual leader of the Buddhist Himalayan belt has with his followers.

To be a better person, Jampa liked to give things up that he described as being 'not good for me and not good for society'. The Dalai Lama is the motivator. 'I used to smoke—I was not addicted—a little bit.'

Jampa explained that when he attended a teaching session at Bodh Gaya in Bihar conducted by the Dalai Lama, he was inspired to give up smoking.

Similarly, he once loved non-vegetarian food. 'But being a lover of animals, respecting others' souls, you cannot take their meat to fill your stomach,' he commented. Jampa stopped eating meat for seven years but suffered from a lack of protein so he resumed. 'Still I was not happy. Somewhere in my mind or my heart I felt guilt for those who give life for our sakes,' he said.

After the Dalai Lama's visit to Tawang in 2009, Jampa renounced alcohol. 'If we promise in front of His Holiness then we can keep the promise much longer than if we promise in front of our friends or anyone else,' he said.[6]

Equally striking is Koncho Gyatso, a Horticulture Development Officer in Arunachal Pradesh.

He ensured that the farmers' land is productive and sustainable. This Monpa sophisticate has a passion for the promotion and development of plant management here among the stern, unfriendly Himalayan peaks. With the rough terrain, all-mountain topography and low numbers of individual landholdings, his outreach work with farmers is critical. But he faces hurdles. With a desire to earn money quickly, farmers like to lease or sell their land for road construction and development purposes. Koncho persuades farmers to plant fruit orchards so that, as the Dalai Lama desires, the land is cultivated with produce and the Himalayas remain cared for.

Koncho told me that his grandfather remembered that in 1959, the main crops were millet, wheat, rice and at certain places, potatoes. The bulk of the necessary rations, meat, and household needs had to be air dropped.

Now, Koncho encourages the growth of kiwi, apples, oranges and guavas. Rice, though, is still brought in. Koncho said, 'We buy rice from fair price shops outside the district. Rice is sold at a reduced rate by the government. It is the one item we mainly do not grow ourselves still. All individuals are issued with ration cards. Every month, some rice per head is provided to a family.'[7]

Persuading the farmers to have an awareness of their horticultural potential is an uphill struggle for Koncho's team, but the officials have made progress. Koncho's family is from a village near Lumla. His grandfather was a religious teacher-monk, and his father was in the SSB armed forces.[8] I asked him what the the Dalai Lama meant to him.

'Buddhists all over the world consider him as a living God, a living Buddha. He's our spiritual leader. We worship him. If you visit our houses in the Monpa community, you will see a separate puja room in every home. There we put his portrait, we worship him, the same as we worship God,' Koncho said.[9]

*

Back in April 1959, Har Mander Singh was accompanying the Dalai Lama to the Deputy Commissioner's compound. It was the most comfortable building they had been in for many weeks. The Dalai Lama's body was still weakened from the dysentery he had contracted in Tibet, so to be able to stretch out on a comfortable bed in a solid building with many rooms, well-guarded, away from the town but with a clear sight-line to the historic Tawang Monastery, allowed him some space for the first time.

Wherever the Dalai Lama travels along roads in Buddhist areas, at key junctions, decorated archways of cloth are constructed to welcome him. At the top of the archways, over the arch itself, portions of sacred Tibetan texts are usually inscribed. They were put up in 1959, and modern versions were in place when I saw them in 2017. In the main Tawang market, I noticed that prayer flags were hung from house windows across the streets, and a Tara Devi statue by the Information Centre was decorated in Tibetan colours too.

*

Diary Extract, 5 April 1959 (continuation):

Several code messages have arrived from Shillong. The most important contains the Prime Minister's reply to the Dalai Lama's request for asylum.

Prime Minister Nehru had granted sanctuary to the Dalai Lama due to the weight of various factors. From a trenchant position of non-cooperation over providing refuge to the spiritual leader, he had taken a 180-degree turn. India now changed its official position, mainly because of tensions emerging from the shifting Asian political scene and American concerns over the rise of the Communist dragon.

Diary Extract, 5 April 1959 (continuation):

P N Menon, formerly Counsel General Lhasa will be meeting the Dalai Lama at Bomdi La and will be ascorting [sic] him from there to his final destination in India.

In the evening I went over to see the Shapes and check up arrangements for their accommodation and security.

Murty has been promoted as Additional Political Secretary, Tawang.

Diary Extract, 6 April 1959

Obtained audience with the Dalai Lama at 9 a.m.

In this audience, Har Mander Singh believed he may have explained about the Government of India's hospitality arrangements for the next stage of the journey.

Diary Extract, 6 April 1959 (continuation):

The Shapes were waiting in the adjoining room. He explained to me the circumstances leading to his escape. from [sic] *Tibet and his future intentions.*

I was curious to know how much the Indian Division Political Officer and the Tibetan ruler had communicated with each other on the journey. When I asked Har Mander, he tried to underplay it. He was Nehru's representative, the Government of India's senior-most official in the division, but this was what he said: 'I think there was small talk all the time. There was also serious talk, in the sense that I was the only senior Indian representative there and he thought that he was talking to some very high up Indian with all the formality and protocol. I was the only one he could talk to.

'The Dalai Lama had just started learning English, and during the journey he would identify something with the English word. For example, if there is a flower he would say, "Flower", and then say, "Ha, ha, ha, ha", as if he'd conquered something.'[10] As Har Mander spoke, his soft skin crinkled, and his skin, fold by fold, and allowed a smile to gradually form.

Har Mander Singh also mentioned that the Dalai Lama talked about a particular flower. Kameng is famous for its orchids, and it was most probably this flower that the Dalai Lama had noticed.

I asked if that was why the Dalai Lama associated Har Mander with an orchid. Har Mander replied, saying that it was possible, and told me that the entire area around Bomdila was rich with different varieties of orchids.

I asked Har Mander if he thought the Dalai Lama appeared nervous at arriving in his new home, to which he replied, 'No, he wasn't, it's surprising but now that you ask me this question you make me think about it. He was completely at ease right from the beginning. He did go through the protocol for the first few days until we became, until we started knowing each other better. But apart from that he was alright.'[11]

In other words, Har Mander soon discovered the natural, playful side of the Dalai Lama that caused the young leader to break with formality whenever possible.

When I interviewed the Dalai Lama, I wanted to go to places other writers had not reached. I knew that the precise weeks of the story I was covering had not been written of in much detail. I also wanted to interview the Dalai Lama in a location rarely visited by other writers. One of the members of my assisting team tipped me off about the Dalai Lama's garden, through which a path runs uphill from his sleeping quarters to his official offices and meeting rooms where interviews often take place. I knew that he loves flowers and that he was fond of his garden. I was told that reporters and correspondents were not usually granted interviews in this private, peaceful space.

At the end of the first part of my interview, the Dalai Lama rose from his chair. As he took a tissue from inside his maroon robe and wiped his head with it, I started my pitch.

'Holiness, thank you very much for talking to us today. I know that you have a great love of flowers and of your garden, so I wanted to ask if I could spend some time with you later in the day? We're just here for a couple of days to talk.'

He responded, 'Over the coming three days, every morning, I'm going to come here and do some sort of work. So each morning or after that, when you have passed through the gates you can take some pictures of my flowers and my greenhouse.'

'Can we join you?' I asked.

'Okay, that's okay,' he acquiesced.

A few hours later, an email arrived from Tenzin Taklha, nephew of and personal secretary to the Dalai Lama. He managed the Tibetan leader's diary.

I had been granted my garden interview.

The next morning, I passed through security and was asked to wait in a small, elegant wooden room halfway up the steep winding driveway to the Dalai Lama's official quarters. Finally, we were ushered through to the garden area. Down the path, I could see a low-rise white and glass building with two storeys and a white roof with curves. Two stolid Indian security men were standing close to the bottom of the stairs, but other than that, there were only a couple of officials around.

The Dalai Lama appeared at the top of the stairs, accompanied by a smiling, bald, elderly monk who was carrying a notepad. Behind the Dalai Lama walked a Tibetan bodyguard. The Dalai Lama raised his right hand as the sunlight streamed down on him. He announced to me, 'Mornings, I am always fresh. Late afternoons . . .' grinning and then added, 'morning, morning', to me and everyone else. The two burly Indian security guards bowed to him and kissed his hand.

'Will you show me your favourite flowers?' I asked.

'Favourite?' he asked.

'Yes.'

'Delphinium.'

'Which ones are delphiniums?'

He waves to my right. 'Cannot grow here. Too hot, too wet. In Lhasa, delphiniums grew very well.'

The Indian bodyguard listened carefully to our conversation, intrigued by the Dalai Lama. I found a couple of beautiful flowers. The Dalai Lama looked at a red one I had chosen and tenderly held one of the flowers from it.

'This also is good, very good,' he said.

Suddenly, he remembered something and stopped. 'Oh, orchid!'

He stepped away from the pathway, causing his entourage to veer rapidly to the left and stand back to give us both space. None of us knew what he was going to do. Like an excited child on a mission, he went to a small concrete greenhouse and found an orchid in a hanging basket. 'This orchid—1959. Har Mander Singh.' He touched the orchid in the hanging steel bowl and said, 'I received it at Tezpur, then I brought it in my train up to Mussoorie,' he continued, as he kept looking at the orchid. 'After one year, I shifted here.' He took his hand away from the flower, and indicated moving to McLeod Ganj. He then pointed back to the flower. 'I carried this. Then somehow, after one year, it stopped growing. Some of the people who took care of this flower, they thought it was dead. So, then I brought it back and it's now over fifty-six years. Each year, it grows very well.'[12]

It's clearly a flower[13] that took him back to a significant time in his life, reminding him of Har Mander Singh. He picked it up just after he left Bomdila, while the political officer was still with him. It seemed to remind him of a special time, an incubation period when he was adjusting to his new home.

*

The next day, in his late mother's drawing room at Kashmir Cottage, Tenzin Choegyal asked me how the interview with his brother went.

I told him about the walk we took from the Dalai Lama's garden to his office, and about the fifty-six-year old story of the orchid.

Tenzin looked interested. 'I think that's a local orchid,' he said.

'Yes, that's right. Replacing one that he got from around the time he met Har Mander,' I replied.

'I see. You mean from Arunachal? Oh, I didn't know.'

I realized I'd uncovered a hitherto unknown golden nugget for my story. Apparently even the Dalai Lama's own brother had not been aware of it.

*

Thousands of Tibetan refugees have settled in Dharamsala to be near their leader. On the day of my second meeting with him, I saw several gathered in front of his offices to seek his blessings.

To the right of those offices were his living quarters and beloved garden. In the Dalai Lama's garden, there was a path leading upwards, past flowers either side, past a greenhouse, past a border guard, winding around the front of his offices and finally leading to the steps at the front where he meets his visitors. It leads upwards from his home, steadily, until it rises so steeply that when I was there I saw he needed a little support to climb the slope. A Tibetan bodyguard gently took his hand and helped him onto the path.

'Then until now,' said the holy man, referring to when he entered India, 'not only myself, but I think now about 150,000 of the Tibetan refugee community are quite well settled in this country.'

He was slightly out of breath by then. 'And I think about twenty to thirty thousand students are carrying on studying.'

The Dalai Lama had reached the steepest incline of the path. 'And for them, the Government of India created one society and at the beginning the Union Education Minister was the chairperson of that committee.'

We suddenly arrived at a sentry post, and I jumped, startled, as a soldier clicked his rifle, stood at attention and stamped his feet.

'The Government of India created a special school for Tibetan students.'

The Indian Officer attached to the Office of the Dalai Lama, who was clearly used to this walk with the Dalai Lama, guided him by taking his hand briefly. At that point I rather nervously proffered my hand too, even though he had swarthy bodyguards following him, watching us all, and the Indian official[14] with us who met him practically every other day.

The Dalai Lama had been carrying his prayer beads in his left hand.

'And then meantime, in '59, when we escaped, I think about 5000 monk students, including top scholars, came too. So we asked the Indian government: "We need some special arrangement for these people in order that they carry on studying continuously." Then the Government of India provided the facility at Baxa at the border, very close to Bhutan. They settled there then shifted to south India where there is a settlement.'

As we turned the corner towards the main offices and open reception area, bright golden sunlight struck us and we were bathed in its warmth. I was still holding the Dalai Lama's hand.

'Now I think almost 10,000 monks are carrying on studying. And a few take the final examination that should include science,' he continued.

I asked if Har Mander Singh and his team played a role once the Dalai Lama crossed the border into India.

'Oh yes, yes, initially yes,' he said. 'Coming from Tibet. That's right. Okay?'[15]

Those last three words were a sign that my time with him was over for now.

He let go of my hand, climbed the five steps to his office rooms, and stepped inside.

A year after the episode we had discussed above, in 1960, on India's eleventh Republic Day, the country's president, Dr Rajendra Prasad, awarded Har Mander Singh a Padma Shri. The award was for the service Har Mander had rendered during this assignment with the Dalai Lama. The ceremony was held in the grand Durbar Hall of the presidential palace, Rashtrapati Bhavan. Prime Minister Nehru, cabinet members and the speaker of the lower house were present.

The Statesman reported that the award had been presented to Har Mander for his duties as political officer of the Kameng frontier division, as Singh 'was responsible for looking after the Tibetan refugees who crossed into India last year'.[16] The honour was widely reported in the press, with the handling of the several thousand refugees who had crossed over being cited as the reason.

The Padma Shri award is now in Singh's drawing room at his New Delhi residence, and the citation reads: 'I, the President of India,

Rajendra Prasad, for distinguished services am pleased to confer upon you the Padma Shri.'

By 1960, Singh had been promoted and was a deputy secretary in the MEA. On 10 March 1960, the Dalai Lama made a public statement on the importance of caring for other refugees and of preserving Tibetan culture. He also said that it was likely that with truth, justice and courage, 'Tibetans would eventually prevail in regaining freedom for Tibet.'

21

AIR DROPS

Diary Extract, 6 April 1959, (continuation):

Have written a separate report on this.

The word 'this' in the line above refers to the first part of this diary entry explained in the previous chapter. This was when Har Mander Singh had an audience with the Dalai Lama on 5 April at 9 a.m. In that conversation, the Dalai Lama explained to Singh what had caused his departure from Tibet. In the same discussion, the young visitor had also told him about his future plans.

Diary Extract, 6 April 1959, (continuation):

I sought the Dalai Lama's permission to read the Prime Minister's message of greetings to him. He called in the Shapes and I did so in their presence.

The telegram read:

'My colleagues and I welcome and send greetings on your safe arrival in India. We shall be happy to afford the necessary facilities to you, your family and your entourage to reside India. The people of India, who hold you in great veneration, will no doubt accord their traditional respect to your personage. Kind regards to you.

Yours sincerely
Jawaharlal Nehru.[1]

'During the first days he called in his entire cabinet ministers, the shapes, and talked in protocol language to me. He said, "We are indebted to Government of India that you have given me refuge,"' said Har Mander.

'So how did you respond?' I asked.

'Your Holiness, we feel privileged that you have chosen our country to seek refuge. I'm sure that the prime minister is looking forward to your arrival and to your peaceful stay in our country,' he replied. 'That's how we made conversation.'[2]

Diary Extract, 6 April 1959 (continuation):

Gompatse Rimpoche and ex-abbot Ngawang Sonam came over to see me. Gompatse Rimpoche said that he had finally decided to settle down in India. Ex-Abbot Ngawang Sonam said that he would be taking over charge of the Sengedzong Monastery within three months.[3]

The Dalai Lama held special blessing ceremony for Government servants in Tawang. Members of all faiths received blessings from him.

Prepared special despatch for the Administration and sent it with Yonzone at 11.30 p.m.[4]

Singh explained that former abbots had no executive authority, and that Abbot Ngawang Sonam had been the head of a monastery. His main job then was to conduct prayers.[5]

Yonzone was a junior official who knew Tibetan.

*

When the Dalai Lama visited Tawang in 2017, local government official Koncho Gyatso carefully put together an afternoon event for non-Buddhists and government officials on 'Secular Ethics and Happiness' for 1000 professional people of all faiths. It was held after the last day of teachings, on 10 April, at the Kalawangpo Convention Centre, not far from a main market area. I had also been invited.

The room was packed, with raked seating. I scrambled down as close as I could to the front, just a few rows in.

On the vast stage was the Dalai Lama, his interpreter sitting next to him, and at far corners of each side behind him were his permanent security guards. They were almost hidden by flower displays arranged by Koncho Gyatso's team. The Horticultural Development Officer (HDO) and his men had been up most of the night putting arrangements in place. We had to go through airport-level security. This level of protection is present wherever the Dalai Lama goes. Armed security personnel with AK-47s stood by the walls all around the room. Historian and broadcaster Nawang Choidak, master of ceremonies for the afternoon, stood to the left of the stage.

The Dalai Lama gave a short talk. When he finished, Nawang invited questions. I shot up out of my seat. By now I had asked the Dalai Lama most of the questions I had wanted to, so I decided to make my last one of the week more personal. I told him he had had a profound effect on Har Mander Singh so that he too followed a kind of Buddhist outlook on life now. How could I keep a balanced perspective on life and not let stresses and strains bring me down and paralyze me? How could I become a better person? I asked him.

'If sadness comes from the brain, remove that part,' responded the Dalai Lama to me. 'When a person is in a dying state, there is no pervasive mind energy. I am older than you,' he laughed, teasing me. 'Read more, study the texts. Everything is interdependent. It is important to become acquainted with a map of the emotions.'

The questions that followed mine were very long and he showed little patience for these. Afterwards, I took a keepsake of a fresh orchid (with permission) from among the many that Koncho had placed in the beautiful floral display.

*

Diary Extract, 7 April 1959 (continuation):

The Shapes send word that they wanted to have a meeting with me.
We decided to meet in Additional Political Officer's office at 1 p.m.

The Shapes, or ministers, were of a very high rank, Singh told me, and though they may have talked to him easily, he never took them for granted. 'One wouldn't ever forget one's position in life,' he said.[6]

During the 1959 Tawang visit, the Dalai Lama granted the request of some government officials to give them a blessing after he had rested. He was also, according to local research, given an official reception. The 5th Assam Rifles provided a Guard of Honour. Thousands then, as they have done for all seven visits since, thronged to see him.[7]

We were served the same sweet rice and butter salt tea that he'd had back then. Grainy photos from back in the day show how the Dalai Lama had to climb the steep slopes on his pony, literally held on and supported by a couple of people walking right beside him, level with the saddle's rear. The auspicious symbols painted on the pathways looked as though they were created with care, all the more endearing for the steep roads and primitive conditions of that environment.

The central courtyard of Tawang Monastery is reasonably large, with buildings and balconies leading off it. But it was flooded with people on 7 April 1959, almost to the day that we arrived, fifty-eight years later. This is apparent from a photograph unearthed by the Losel Nyinje Charitable Society.

At the 1959 event, the Dalai Lama gave a teaching to his devotees, along with religious sessions on 'Essential Attributes' and the Six Syllable Mantra.

As the Empowerment session finished, a hailstone shower began and soon Tawang was covered in snow. This was regarded as a good omen. The Dalai Lama presented ten silver coins to each of the monastery's monks and the meal too was served on his behalf, the Losel Nyinje Charitable Society reported.

Diary Extract, 7 April 1959 (continuation):

Called on the Dalai Lama and escorted him to the Tawang Monastery at 9.30a.m. The entire route was lined with crowds of people, and there was still larger gathering inside the Monastery. The Dalai Lama conducted the prayers and visited the various buildings. Returned at mid-day.

The midday return by the party was to the Deputy Commissioner's residence. That evening, the same Tawang historians tell us that the Dalai Lama revealed that he chose not to wear the robes of a monk—his normal attire—while he gave the teachings. 'I was uncomfortable in front of the monks.' The Dalai Lama explained that the Tsona Rinpoche of Tsona Monastery was among those receiving the teachings, a lama who had 'all kinds of transmissions and empowerments and had read many scriptures'.

It appeared the Dalai Lama was transported and impressed by the devotion, faith and commitment of many of those present, whom the historians describe as 'mentally pure and sincere'.[8]

During his time at the guest house of the Deputy Commissioner's residence in Tawang, the Dalai Lama was asked by the Tsona Rinpoche to grant an audience to the Abbott of Tawang and some other noteworthy local individuals. The abbots from Tibet were all granted an audience and were asked by the Dalai Lama about the latest news from his homeland.[9]

Singh said that there was a 'tremendous fervour amongst the villagers. It was like one of us was going to see Jesus Christ once in our lifetime. And you can imagine people who are believers, how would they feel if this happens,' he said.[10]

The worry was ever present though. Singh describes the fear as: 'of a fifth columnist joining. And in villages everyone knows everyone else, so if there was somebody to mix in a group of villagers, he would be noticed. My fear was always counteracted by the feeling that this was not possible in these areas, yet to the extent possible we took precautions about his food, about his accommodation with the limited resources that we had.'[11]

Diary Extract, 7 April, (continuation):

The meeting with the Shapes was held at 1.p.m. Murty [sic] was also present. Have recorded separate note on my discussions with them. Prepared another special despatch and sent it to Shillong with Wangchu of SIB[12]

Singh and his team were constantly on alert. Apart from handling messages from other areas and dealing with the arriving dignitaries, Har Mander saw things that have stayed with him, decades later.

'Tibetan people are very resilient. I can't forget one occasion when I, in the evening after dark, went out of my room to get some fresh air. And I found a group of Tibetans praying and chanting, in fact. And I noticed that a lot of them had wounds on their back just below the neck. And any ordinary person, like me, would shriek with pain at that kind of injury but these people—the injuries had, of course, been attended to—were intent on saying their prayers rather than thinking of their injuries. So, the Tibetans are extraordinary people that way. And I don't think anybody in the world can ultimately subdue them,' he said.[13]

Singh's comment about the Tibetans shows that underneath that tough, cool exterior, he was impressed by the character of his guests.

Tenzin noticed a sensitivity about him at that time. I asked him to recall what he remembered about the Political Officer's temperament, to which he said, 'He's very soft spoken. I think his main characteristic is dominated by gentleness. It must be coming from a person who is at peace, otherwise you won't find gentleness. He was the first government official, the first Indian who had much to do in the area who gave us all that's required for us to be in good shape. So, he took good care of us, yes.'[14]

During that interview, Tenzin suddenly became animated as he remembered something that had happened on the way, either close to Tawang or near Bomdila. From Tenzin's account, it seemed more likely to have been on the way to Bomdila, because it was likely that it had happened somewhere in the lonely mountains.

He said, 'I remember something Har Mander did. He called in a lot of supplies and they were flown in and dropped by parachute. Hats, underwear, shirts, trousers, shoes, and then food, oil, rice, pulses, all those things. They used to come in, I think, flown from Tezpur, and I knew it was about eleven days to come and I used to go to the place [the pleasure of this shows in his face] and watch from a hilltop. A small hilltop. You know the parachute how it opens, and some don't open, and with the oil tin if the parachute doesn't open it really hits the ground and there's a tremendous splash,' he told me, laughing.[15]

22

SELA PASS

Har Mander Singh breathed a little easier once the Dalai Lama and his party got through Tawang, but there was still a long way to go before they could enjoy the relative safety of Bomdila.

Diary Extract, 8 April 1959 (handwritten from here):

The Dalai Lama left Tawang at 0700 hours and was seen off by a large gathering of people and civil officials.

Almost the entire route was lined with devotees from the surrounding villages who burnt incense and paid their obeisance to the dignitary.

In Tawang, and in other monasteries around India, the Dalai Lama has his own quarters that cannot be used by anyone else. His Tawang quarters are discreetly opened for a few hours on certain days of the year so that visitors, devotees and monks can visit and pay their respects.

When I visited Tawang Monastery to have a look around, I entered through a large gateway above which sits the library. I walked into a courtyard with buildings all around. The actual monastery is on the right, past a few other buildings.

The monastery is set on a steep mountainside and its buildings are on three levels. It was, after all, first built as a religious fort that might need defending at some point. This is obvious from the stone walls that surround the compound form the outside.

Inside the outer walls, all is bright, open, and cheerful. The monks sleep in rooms in this building. Sections of the compound are divided into smaller buildings that provide a set of rooms for junior monks. I saw boys in their robes and maroon hooded sweatshirts playing in mini gardens by their quarters. Piles of logs are placed just below their dorms. Often, windows are open, and boys can be seen sitting or leaning out.

The actual monastery is richly decorated in maroon and gold, beautifully lit and with long carpets for monks to sit on during prayer time. The magnificent Buddha statue is dressed in a yellow robe, leaving one shoulder bare. Pale green cloths cover some shelves and pillars are draped in red.

When I was there in April 2017, I observed many young monks carrying cloth shoulder bags.

I was surprised to hear the theme tune of BBC television news emanating from one of these bags. I asked the bag's owner what this was about. He said, 'I like to listen to international news and find out what China and other countries are doing.' I listened, fascinated, as he told me about the news stories that he was following. We had quite a discussion about this.

By this stage the Dalai Lama had left. I met with the Abbot of Tawang Monastery and asked him if I could be shown the holy leader's special quarters. He agreed.

A senior monk escorted me upstairs to the Dalai Lama's chambers and unlocked the door.

Bright daylight was shining through the windows. In front of me was what seemed like a reception room. It was big, with a throne next to a table. The green carpet was patterned with beautiful hand-sewn flowers. Decorated cupboards sat to the throne's left. On the table by the throne, there was a picture of the Dalai Lama.

Next door was the Dalai Lama's bedroom. The bed had an open wooden cupboard at its head and a large wooden rounded side by the wall. The room was adorned with a table lamp with a white tasselled shade. The bed had silken cream and white bed linen.

The window looking out over the mountainside onto Tawang town was beautifully carved. The pervasive atmosphere of these rooms was one of peace and calm.

Even though he was not around, the Dalai Lama's presence filled the place. A visiting monk prostrated and prayed to the various beds and thrones in the suite.

Seeing the Dalai Lama's quarters was an intimate experience. It brought me a sense of tranquillity.

*

Going back to 1959, we need to place ourselves further down the mountainside, not too far from Tawang.

Near Thrimu village, there is a white-walled shrine with a sloping roof at a place called Lhau village. Legend has it that the shrine's deity had personally invited the Dalai Lama there. Locals observed that as he got nearer, he dismounted and walked the fairly long distance. The shrine's lady caretaker was not expecting the leader of the Tibetan Buddhists to be visiting at that time, as he was rumoured to be at another location. The story goes that the Dalai Lama gently asked the lady caretaker to open the door, after which he entered and offered prostrations. On leaving, he expressed a desire to revisit the place—a wish that was fulfilled in 1983.[1]

After descending the slope from Lhau village, the Dalai Lame rode to Jang. The narration is picked up in Har Mander Singh's diary.

Diary Extract, 8 April 1959 (continuation):

His Holiness rested for a while in a road-side shrine in THRIMU village and reached Jang at 12 noon.

At 3p.m. a ceremony was held where His Holiness gave his blessings individually to the people. His Holiness was accommodated in the village Community Hall.

This was rough terrain. Here one settlement straddles a fast-flowing river and is located on two large rocks. Horses and ponies got stuck in the mud and struggled to cross the freezing, perilous waters. Har Mander Singh had to take particular care of his precious passengers at this dangerous point.

At other river crossings, there were pulley bridges. But anyone caught in the current here would have been swept downstream. Once Singh had ensured that everyone had crossed safely, the party would continue.

White and red woollen cloths along the route had been placed there by locals as a gesture of respect towards their leader.

That afternoon, an empowerment ceremony was organized. It was on a smaller scale, but similar to the one I had experienced in Tawang.

The Dalai Lama slept that night in a nearby village.[2]

Meanwhile, Prime Minister Nehru had to deal diplomatically with his neighbours. India's adjoining countries were worried about the Dalai Lama's safety but were also concerned that certain decisions that might be taken concerning the Tibetan leader could impact their own relations with China. The uncertainty troubled the smaller Buddhist kingdom of Sikkim. Here's a letter the Indian prime minister wrote to its Maharajah. It was titled: 'Tibet a Sensitive Matter'. It read:

My dear Maharajah Sahib,

I received your letter of March 24 some days ago from our Political Officer in Sikkim. We can well appreciate your concern and that of the people of Sikkim about the current events in Tibet. I have made a number of statements on the subject in our Parliament during the last two weeks. I also dealt with it in a Press Conference on the 5th April. We are all thankful that His Holiness the Dalai Lama has safely reached our territory. As I have said before, we shall treat him with the respect and regard due to his position as the spiritual leader of a large number of persons not only in his country but in India. We have not yet been able to ascertain what his wishes are, but it is our intention to arrange for him to stay in one of our hill stations in North India. You can rest assured that we shall look after him well.

As regards the happenings in Tibet, our position is a difficult and delicate one. Any direct intervention by us would be resented by the Chinese and would not do the Tibetans any good. Feelings are apparently running high on both sides and I do not therefore wish to make a direct approach to Premier Chou En-Lai even informally at this stage. Such an approach would not produce any results. However, you can rest assured that the interests of the Tibetans are very much in my mind, although what we can do is not yet clear to me.

Yours sincerely,
Jawaharlal Nehru.[3]

Diary Extract, 9 April 1959:

Left Jang at 0600 hours. The entire village and the people from surrounding areas had turned out to see the Dalai Lama.

From here on, the path twisted and turned in a ridiculously labyrinthine fashion so that it went back and forth over a very short distance. The mountain sides were so steep that an endlessly twisting route was the only way to move forward, even though it was at an agonizingly slow pace.

The Dalai Lama observed the flowers along the way, and this was where Har Mander Singh was entertained by his charge's delight at being able to identify them by the use of the English noun, 'flower'.

Diary Extract, 9 April 1959 (continuation):

His Holiness halted for a while in Nuranang and took His lunch. We met contingents of people from Tawang who went to work on the Foothills-Bomdi La road returning to their home, during our journey.

As I have described in earlier chapters that one of the actions Har Mander Singh took as Political Officer during the months prior to March 1959, was to have a road built from Bomdila, his Division HQ. The road went to Rupa, lower down in the mountains and was built with voluntary labour.

There had been no coercion, he said. People had agreed to make the road freely, with their own effort. It made them happy and gave them a sense of ownership. While it was being built, he had arranged to give the workers tools and a place to stay so that they would not be out of pocket.

But now came the tricky part of the journey. Up here, between Tawang and Dirang in Kameng, there was no road. The toughest part of the journey through the Indian Himalayas was fast approaching. It was the Sela Pass, which is located at 13,764 feet.

In preparation, historians recollect, roughly twenty people travelled in advance of the party. The treacherous Sela Pass today is feared by many, as heavy snow can make the route impossible to cross.

Back in 1959, trudging through the dazzling snow, the group's progress was completely dependent on the weather. With no road, it was vital to climb the freezing slope as quickly as possible to avoid getting stuck. Getting caught in the middle of the pass could prove fatal. The advance party from Jang constructed tents to protect the visitors and fed them tea and snacks at a place then called White Camp, now known as R13 Camp.[4]

Diary Extract, 9 April 1959 (continuation):

Reached Sengedzong at 2pm. The entire village had turned out on the outskirts to receive His Holiness. The elders came forward as far as Se La top.

On the way to Lumla, Har Mander had been on his own. Now he had a whole Tibetan entourage which had swollen from eighty to around 100, as well as his own staff which would cross Sela Pass. In addition, there were villagers with incense on horseback escorting the party.

Diary Extract, 9 April 1959 (continuation):

Dr Sen who has been accompanying the party as its Medical Officer up to top and Dr Roy of Dirang Dzong took over there.

A message has been received that Menon[5] will be reaching Bomdi La tomorrow. Got information from Tawang that few more Tibetan Officers had reached the Frontier. Murty said that he would be deciding this morning whether they should be allowed to come in. At Sengedzong I received the minutes of the meeting held in Bomdi La on the 6th April to discuss arrangements for the reception of the Dalai Lama.

I sent my instructions on the points raised in the minutes, through special messenger.

Historians note that the Dalai Lama slept that night at a monastery near Sela pass called the Nas Gonpa. They record that he was offered gifts, but he only accepted some ghee.[6]

The same day, on 9 April 1959, Prime Minister Nehru told the Congress Parliamentary Party that though India supported the idea of Tibetan autonomy, the country would also try to maintain an amicable relationship with China. Nehru stated in no uncertain terms that he did not want to create a hostile situation with China nor with any other neighbour on account of the Dalai Lama having entered India. He declared that China and India had had cordial relations for centuries, and this must not be disturbed. He said that his policy on the newly arrived Tibetans was being guided by Mahatma Gandhi's concept of India being friends with everyone while resolutely sticking to its own ideals.[7]

Diary Extract, 10 April 1959:

The Dalai Lama gave blessings to the people of Sengedzong before leaving at 0700 hours. He reached Nyutamadong at 08.30 hours and halted there for half an hour.

While resting there he mentioned that as a rule he doesn't listen to the Lhasa Radio but he had done so last evening and had learnt that the Chinese had created a new enlarged National Assembly under the Chairmanship of the Panchan Lama.

Har Mander Singh interpreted the Dalai Lama's meaning here to be one of distaste for Radio Lhasa, interpreting perhaps that it might be considered by some to be a propaganda machine.[8]

At Nyutamadong, the village arranged tea for the Dalai Lama's group. The Tibetan leader rested for a little bit and then travelled to a place called Melongkang. The next day, the residents of Melongkang immediately constructed a Buddhist stupa to mark the place.

Everywhere the Dalai Lama travelled, it left an impact his followers want to mark.

Diary Extract, 10 April 1959 (continuation):

There were now four Vice-Presidents under him. One of these was Shape . . ., [gap left here in diary] Minister Incharge [sic] of the Armed Forces, who had been left behind in Lhasa as he was considered pro-Chinese.

When asked how the Chinese were arranging affairs after the Dalai Lama's escape, Har Mander Singh told me, 'There was some kind of regime for internal affairs functioning under His Holiness and afterwards. The Chinese had always wanted to build up the Panchen Lama who ranks next to His Holiness and this was their opportunity; they didn't want to leave a vacuum and had to make arrangements to fill the vacuum. The Chinese were showing that they did not care that the Dalai Lama had gone.'[9]

Diary Extract, 10 April 1959 (continuation):

One of the other three is Gen. Chiang Ko Ho who was also a Vice Chairman in the previous National Assembly and two incarnate

Lamas. The second Shape who had been left behind had also been included in the new National Assembly.

The Panchan Lama himself condemned the Rebel Forces and had said that those who were indulging in rebel activities should be severely dealt with.

I asked Har Mander if the Panchen Lama was referring to the Khampas or those who escaped with the Dalai Lama when he was commenting on the rebel forces. Har Mander felt that he must be referring to the Khampas. 'He couldn't have been thinking of anyone else.'[10]

Diary Extract, 10 April 1959 (continuation):

Before leaving Nyutamadong the Dalai Lama held a brief prayer meeting for the villagers.

After leaving Nyutamadong the Dalai Lama asked questions again about the number of schools and hospital and about other welfare activities in the Division.

I took the opportunity to point out the work being done under the NES scheme[11] in Nyutamadong, such as paving of village paths.

Diary Extract, 10 April, 1959 (continuation):

The Dalai Lama appreciated the work being done and said that good thing about Communism was that they too did a great deal for the welfare of the people but that in doing so they did not pay regard to the freedom of the individual.

This led him to ask questions about the policies of the Communist, the Socialist and the Hindu Maha Sabha of India. I had to be non-commital and say that I didn't know very much about . . . [gap left in diary] Except that the Communist Party had Communist programme, the Socialist Party had socialist programme not much different to that of the Congress Party and

the Hindu Maha Sabha party was basically a communal party of
Hindus in the same way as Akali Party was a party of Sikhs and
Muslim League was a party of Muslims.

Singh noted at the time that the Dalai Lama knew all the names of the
Indian political parties.

Diary Extract, 10 April 1959 (continuation):

The villagers of Lish held a reception for the Dalai Lama and
[gap][12]
       He reached Dirang Dzong at about 2 p.m. and was received by
a large gathering of almost 4,000. They were accommodated in the
Government Township.
       He held a blessing ceremony for the people of the area in the
evening. He also expressed special appreciation for work done by the
Assam Rifles who were returning from Dirang Dzong to Tawang,
for escorting him and also called the NCO incharge and thanked
him. He expressed desire to give some cash gift to them but I said
that this was not the (the word 'formal' crossed out) *normal*
practice and that a word of appreciation from him was as valuable
for us all as any gift.

The Dalai Lama spent this night in the Dirang Inspection Bungalow.
Locals noted that now the group was descending the mountain, the
temperature was warmer than it had been in Tawang.[13]

Diary Extract, 11 April 1959:

The Dalai Lama and party left Dirang Dzong at 0600 hours.
The Namshu people had made arrangements to receive the Dalai
Lama half way between Dirang Dzong and Rahung near the
bridge where he rested for a while. The party reached Rahung at
1215 hours.[14]

The people of Rahung were animists, which means that they often sacrificed animals to the gods they worshipped. There were still, in 2017, some animist tribes in the area. Locals remember that the Dalai Lama asked the animists to refrain from killing animals.

By now, the hardest part of the journey was almost over.

That night, on 11 April 1959, the Dalai Lama stayed at the Inspection Bungalow in Rahung.

Here again the Dalai Lama's appearance caused some confusion among his devotees, say local researchers. Eyewitnesses recalled that the Dalai Lama was not dressed in his normal formal regalia. He needed to appear inconspicuous so as not to attract attention from those who would harm him. Because of this, worshippers along the way often did not spot him and instead prostrated in front of another monk whom they mistook for their leader.

This happened many times during his journey. Once people knew who he was and confirmed his identity, they prostrated and paid their respects, but His Holiness had to be pointed out to them. Not only were his movements not always known to locals; when the group entered a village, the Dalai Lama was often hidden among his entourage.[15]

Diary Extract, 11 April 1959 (continuation):

Major Gurung and Shri Debnath had arrived from Bomdi La in accordance with my instructions to apprise me of the arrangements for accommodating the party and the reception of the Dalai Lama. They obtained my final instructions and left after about an hour.

Har Mander Singh had left Major Gurung and Shri Debnath behind at Bomdila. Major Gurung was in charge at the time. These were men Singh trusted, as he was worried about whether the Dalai Lama would be properly received and where he would be met. The Tibetan leader's reception at Singh's Divisional HQ needed to have pomp and formality as that would be the main resting and halting place. Bomdila was going to be the recuperative and familiarization centre for the Tibetans who were still sealed off and protected from the outside world.

Diary Extract, 11 April 1959 (continuation):

Several messages from Adviser were decoded and sent down for me. I have been asked to hand over Dalai Lama's letter for Kushuk Bakula to Menon for disposal. The mail and telegrams meant for Dalai Lama will be sent to me from Lokra and I shall be handing them over to Menon again for disposal. Ragasha La is to stay on in Bomdi La and Menon would tell us when he should be allowed to leave.[16]

The group was now about to enter Bomdila. It was going to be an important period for Singh, the Dalai Lama, Tenzin Choegyal, and the rest of Singh's family. Singh's wife and younger son would be meeting the holy leader for the first time. Those in Bomdila could not wait for this historic moment. The Dalai Lama was coming to Kameng's Division HQ; it would be a proper stay for him and the first real halt where extended administrative, government and civil formalities could take place. It would be the time for Singh to help familiarize the Dalai Lama with his new habitat, with new procedures too but in a more secure environment with more facilities and more of Singh's team around.

Har Mander Singh was bringing the Dalai Lama to his home.

23

THE BOMDILA CLUB

Har Mander Singh and his team had successfully negotiated the perilous zig-zag narrow paths along the mountains. These paths were never designed for a travelling caravan of Tibetan aristocrats and religious royals. Rough-hewn, the trails were only used by local tribesmen, and that too, once in a blue moon.

But now, the party was nearly at Bomdila. The first part of the mission for Singh and his team—to place protection around him (even with meagre resources) and to bring him safely away from the border—was nearly complete. There was, however, no reason to let their guard down yet.

Bruce Riedel of the Brookings Institution explains the dilemma for the Dalai Lama and for the primary representatives of his new home. He says that the biggest concern for India at this point was to prevent any attempt at a kidnapping of their newest VIP arrival.

'Clearly he [the Dalai Lama] wanted to be close enough to the border to be a credible spokesman to the people inside. But I think he also knew from the Indians that they didn't want him in a place where he could be snatched by Chinese forces.'[1]

At Bomdila, a large arch had been constructed, prepared and decorated. A welcoming party was ready with flowers, flags and scarves. Indian officials wore formal suits, the Tibetans wore long warm jackets, some of them even donning hats.[2]

There was an *Assam Tribune* reporter posted in Shillong in the lowlands. He must have got word through a local about the arrival of the Tibetans. The story appeared in the paper on 13 April 1959. He described the welcoming party for the Dalai Lama and the location where the Dalai Lama would be staying.[3]

By now the Indian Deputy Foreign Secretary, P.N. Menon, had also arrived in Bomdila. Part of the MEA, he had been India's Consul General in Lhasa. The Sikkimese translator for the Dalai Lama, Kazi Sonam Topgyal was present. There was also an Indian Intelligence Bureau (IB) official, Babu Atruk Tsering, along with some bodyguards. The 5th Assam Rifles formed a guard of honour for the Dalai Lama. Among them was Major Garung, who walked at the Dalai Lama's side, while Har Mander Singh and the newly arrived Menon walked just behind him.

Har Mander Singh's photographs from the time show locals and government officials standing in a line to greet the arriving dignitary. Singh introduced them one by one to the Dalai Lama.

Diary Extract, 12 April 1959 (typed from here):

The Dalai Lama left Rahung at 0600 hours and rached [sic] *outskirts of Bomdi La at 0945 hours.*

He was received by Shri PN Menon of the External Affairs Ministry and was given a Guard of Honour commanded by xx Major Gurung.[4] *He was then introduced to Mr Dave,*[5] *DD SIB, Pandit*[6] *of SIB, Atuk Tsering*[7] *of IB, Sarin of Survey of India, Samdup of IB and Arur of Survey of India, Mitra of HQ IGAR* [Inspector General Assam Rifles] *and local officers. Menon and Dave are putting up with us.*

The party was nearing Bomdila. Har Mander Singh, going through the diary with me, noted that the route was 'jeepable' for the Dalai Lama from this point. The vehicle transported them to Har Mander's house.

Har Mander Singh told Rinchin Norbu from the Losel Charitable Society that though the Indian IB people were 'hanging around' and had nominal responsibility for security, 'they were not really "capable" of providing any security. The security came mainly from the Assam Rifle troops that were travelling with him and also a few of his [the Dalai Lama's] own people'.[8]

One of the documents given to me by Har Mander Singh that has never been read by anyone outside the family was titled: 'Escape route of his holiness the XIVTH the Dalai Lama and Tibetan followers in Mon area from Khenzamani (Chutangmu) in Tawang Arunachal Pradesh to Tezpur in Assam.'

This document details the stops and the halting places along the way in order. There had been eleven listed stages to the journey so far. They were Chuthangmu, Gorsham, Shakti, Lumla, Thongleng village, Tawang, Jang village, Senge Dzong village, Dirang village, Rahung village, and finally Bomdila. The Dalai Lama and Har Mander Singh recalled the Bomdila stay as being roughly seven to ten days, including the approach and departure. Others place it closer to seven, including arrival and departures at posts just by Bomdila. The document provided by Har Mander Singh motions towards the latter theory.

Dairy Extract, 12 April 1959 (continuation):

A large crowd had lined up along the route up to our residence. On reaching the house my wife received the Dalai Lama. He and the senior members of his xxxxxx entourage were then served tea. The Dalai Lama very kindly consented to have all his meals with us. He was accommodated in our Guest House.

Neena Kaur served tea and sweet rice to the party on their arrival.

Tenzin remembered the reception tea too.

He said, 'You know the Indians living from the plains who come up, not the locals, they have an association community, right? They gave us a very nice high tea. I remember eating the most delicious rasgulla on that occasion. It must have been done by the ladies.' His eyes light up with the memory.[9]

As the Dalai Lama settled in, he was asked to bless a new throne that the political officer had had built for him.

I asked Har Mander Singh if this throne was based on the peacock throne or any of the Dalai Lama's historic thrones from his palaces in Tibet. Har Mander explained that the throne was intended to provide an honoured seat for the Tibetan god-king, and its design was created by the lamas around Bomdila. The concept for a suitable throne for their leader came from their devoted collective imagination, he explained. The Bomdila throne bore little resemblance or relation, he added, to any of the various ceremonial chairs for the Dalai Lama in and around Lhasa.

Har Mander Singh said that the idea was that the throne would enable the Dalai Lama to sit a little higher than everyone else. He later told an interviewer that the throne remained intact at least until the Chinese entered Tawang District during the War of 1962. Thereafter, Singh felt that the throne may have been destroyed, as he did not know what became of his Bomdila residence.[10]

'For seven days, a lot of people wanted to receive blessings. I organized for the people to come and receive blessings from him. I arranged a place for him, a sort of throne for him to sit down on and allowed people to enter the drawing room and seek his blessings. Several thousand people came in and sought his blessings and went away,' Har Mander Singh told me.[11]

In homage and respect, Singh also presented a long scarf to his guest.

Once the initial welcome formalities were over, Har Mander Singh had daily audiences with the Dalai Lama; in the mornings and the evenings. P.M. Menon and Kazi Sonam Topgyal conveyed to the Dalai Lama that he and his retinue would be treated as guests for as long as the Tibetans chose to live in India, and that everything they needed would be provided to them. The Dalai Lama would be given the same respect that he had been given on his last visit in 1956. Most importantly, they promised that the Government of India would take responsibility for the Dalai Lama's safety.[12]

The Dalai Lama expressed his gratitude for the messages from the Indian government and asked his team to reply formally on paper.

The Dalai Lama and his retinue were being placed in various appropriate buildings in what was then the main Indian administrative hub of the division. Singh drew a diagram for me of how he arranged the accommodation for his guests. In the main house lived Har Mander Singh, Neena, and his younger son Harsh Mander. (The elder boy, Raj Mander, was away at boarding school and, as stated before, only returned for vacations). To the left of the main house were the official guest quarters where the Dalai Lama was accommodated. To the right of the main residence were two buildings. In one of them, Menon and Dave were housed.

Now that the Dalai Lama was in a more settled environment, protocols kicked in and he had time to reflect on how he was feeling. The official Indian group had swollen to include extra bureaucrats and officials. The previously intimate world of the Dalai Lama and Har Mander Singh had expanded.

During the first few days of his stay in Bomdila, the Dalai Lama told Har Mander Singh and the group, 'Freedom is really very important.'

He said that he had been worried and anxious since he had left Tibet. He now felt joy to be in a free country, but he also felt pain and desperation. He was hurting, he said, knowing that most of his people were 'suffering brutal torture and suppression under the Chinese'.

'When I think about this, I feel very sad and worried from the depth of my heart . . . Since we arrived in a free country now, we must work hard with dauntless courage and do everything at our best level for the freedom of Tibet.'[13]

These impassioned sentiments from a young Dalai Lama, using words like 'freedom', may have been the reason why the Chinese now see him as a 'splittist' and a 'separatist'.

Having made such an effort to bring Tibet more closely under the control of Peking, it was, and still remains, vital for the Chinese to exert control over every corner of the country. That is why, today, Tibet has been populated with some Han Chinese industry and Han Chinese people.

The Dalai Lama, however, has softened his stance since those days, expressing his desire for a 'Middle Way' I mentioned in my preamble. His current suggestion is that Tibet remains part of China, but at the same time has autonomy.

*

About security, Singh told me that because many people were appearing on the scene at that time, there was a 'very remote possibility' that among the border people there might be someone with sinister intent.

Reading the diary, I was intrigued to know why a team from the Survey of India suddenly turned up.

Har Mander Singh explained, 'The Chinese at that time were raising a question as to whether, even though the border had been crossed, the Dalai Lama was still actually in Tibetan territory. The party that came to receive the Dalai Lama and make arrangements for his journey onward included a couple of people from the Survey of India because, I'm only guessing, the government felt that if the Dalai Lama or anyone else wanted any clarification on anything within the jurisdiction of the Survey of India, they would provide that clarification.'

I asked Har Mander who 'anyone else' could be.

'Even the people from the external affairs ministry or the Intelligence Bureau who came to meet the Dalai Lama might have needed some clarification. I think they were there to help our own people,' he replied.[14]

In fending off the question, Singh avoided a sensitive topic. Parts of NEFA were, and still is, a hotly contested area that the Chinese laid claim to.

Singh continued to touch on the subject, but only lightly, in his interviews.

'This was to be optimally cautious—during his escape the boundary questions or any such thing were not going to be discussed. But I'm only guessing, I don't know, I'm too small a fry to know why these people were sent. There were a couple of people from Delhi, but you require a much bigger platform to discuss such matters,' he said.[15]

Har Mander told me that in the same conversation that included talk about the officials from the Survey of India, that the Dalai Lama had also said, 'I'm giving up, my [old] government [not] left anymore… Giving up my trust, in my [old] government.'[16]

*

During the discussions, the Dalai Lama spoke to Har Mander Singh and the other senior Indians about what was going on in Tibet. The Dalai Lama said that he had no choice but to ask India to work to stop what was happening to Tibetans in China. Menon apparently did send a telegram to the capital regarding this matter. But the reply did not address the Dalai Lama's request, the Tibetan spiritual leader said.

Delhi felt it was important to contain and control the Dalai Lama's exposure to the rest of the world. Already, there was a multitude of pressmen gathered just outside the Inner Line. The capital was jittery about what the Dalai Lama might say in public. Now that he was on the brink of meeting the whole planet, it sought to manage him through thinly veiled instructions.

On 12 April, what is described as a 'note message',[17] arrived from Prime Minister Nehru. It was titled, 'Meeting the Press.' It read:

I thank your Holiness for the message which you have sent me through our Political Officer, Shri Har Mander Singh. I am myself anxious to meet you at the earliest opportunity. As you must have been informed, we are arranging for Your Holiness and the members of your family and your entourage to stay at Mussourie [sic].

Delhi is getting warm now and Your Holiness need not take the trouble of coming here to meet me in accordance with an earlier engagement, I am due to visit on Mussorie [sic] on the 24th and I propose to call on you the same afternoon. I have seen the report of the talk which you had with our Political Officer on the 6th April. There are a number of matters which you and I might discuss personally and I am, therefore, not giving you a detailed reply at this stage. We have certainly no objection to your brother, Gyalo Dhondup, meeting you, and we are arranging facilities for him to do so as early as possible. He can travel back with you to Mussoorie, if you so wish. I understand that some other important Tibetan personalities, who have been residing in India for some time, are also anxious to meet you. We feel these persons should not trouble you en route, but we shall certainly afford them facilities to call on you later in Mussoorie. May I draw Your Holiness's attention to one particular matter. I am informed that a large number of press correspondents: from all over the world are now gathered in Tezpur and its vicinity awaiting Your Holiness's arrival. It would be difficult for you to avoid saying something to them, and I am inclined to the view that Your Holiness might release a brief statement.[18]

Diary Extract, 12 April 1959 (continuation):

Menon, Dave and I had two meetings with the Dalai Lama, one soon after his arrival at 1300 hours and one in the evening. A meeting was also held with members of the Kashag. The meeting with the members of the Kashag turned out to be rather routine as they did not say very much.[19]

Diary continuation, 12 April

The fresh points made by His Holiness were as follows; [This sentence and the text following the four letters have all been crossed out in the diary]

a)
b)
c)
d)

Pandit came over for dinner in the evening but His Holiness sent
for his meals in his room.

Gaps in the diary reveal as much as the entries. Why would the very points the Dalai Lama made be left out? Was it just an oversight—which was unusual considering Har Mander's meticulous record keeping—or was the material too sensitive?

Now, because of the passage of time, this mystery is unlikely to be solved.

The diary does, however, refer to food. This is possibly because Singh was closely involved in the meal arrangements. He told me that the food was made by the Tibetan's entourage and supervised by the Dalai Lama's tutors. 'My wife told them she would still like to supervise the cooking as a matter of responsibility and so my wife remained in the kitchen to keep a watchful eye for added security. The cooks tasted the food. My wife helped in the cooking and His Holiness enjoyed his food. We were not so worried about details like it being too spicy,' he said.[20]

Diary Extract, 13 April 1959:

Menon, Dave and I met in my office and we discussed administrative
arrangements for moving the party to Foothills.

'Foothills' was a small staging post, and as the name suggests, was at a lower altitude. It had a few houses in it and would be a suitable stopover place for the party on its way to Mussoorie. Another common way to spell it is 'Foot Hills'.

Diary Extract, 13 April 1959 (continuation):

The family of His Holiness and his two tutors arrived at 1100 hours accompanied by Murty. All of us gathered outside my residence to receive them and they were served tea and refreshments.

In the afternoon His Holiness and his senior officers met Menon, Dave and myself. Menon has recorded a separate report on the discussion. The meeting lasted for almost six hours from 2 p.m. to 8 p.m.

It was at this meeting, most likely, that another telegram from Prime Minister Nehru for His Holiness was given to him. It read:

Perhaps, you might defer a detailed statement on the political situation in Tibet and your future intentions until you have settled down in Mussoorie and have had time to reflect on the recent developments in your country. We are making arrangements at Tezpur so that you might give darshan and blessings to people gathered here and also allow pressmen to take photographs before you leave. May I also suggest that in order to prevent embarrassment to you or distorted versions being published, it would be best if members of your party desisted from seeing the press correspondents individually and making statements to them. I am looking forward to meeting Your Holiness.

With kind regards,
Jawaharlal Nehru[21]

Diary Extract, 13 April 1959 (continuation):

After the meeting His Holiness attended a reception in his honour in the Bomdi La Club. I delivered a brief speech welcoming him to which he replied and gave a brief religious sermon.

When I interviewed Tenzin Choegyal at his home, I asked him to recall his stay in Bomdila.

It was the biggest civilian settlement that the Dalai Lama, his family and entourage had seen since they left Tibet. And being Singh's division base, his staff had made it as habitable as possible. Tenzin Choegyal noticed this and described the other stopping places along the way before and after the border as 'makeshift camps'.

He reminded us that the Dalai Lama had been in a weakened state when he crossed the Indian border.

'The journey from the Tibetan border had been arduous and long, I think from the first place up to Bomdila it must have taken at least twelve days, no? His Holiness still had not recovered fully so in Bomdila he was able to fully recover,' said Tenzin.

Diary Extract, 14 April 1959:

His Holiness gave blessings individually to the officers, members of staff and their families, the Assam Rifles personnel and the local people and people who had come to receive his blessings from surrounding villages in my residence from 0900 hours to 1045 hours. We had prepared a special throne for him in my drawing room where he gave the blessings.

Har Mander Singh and I looked at a photo of Neena serving food to the Dalai Lama and a small gathering of people. Singh is bowing to the young Tibetan who is sitting on the throne.

'He's giving me his blessings with his hands. I collected all the villagers to come and take blessings from the Dalai Lama on his throne, and I also took his blessings. I felt very happy. I considered him at that time, and I consider him now, a very holy person. The other people are his cabinet and other officials like his brother-in-law, who was his commander in chief.'[22]

*

While grand and formal gestures went on, the Dalai Lama also experienced a little frontier home entertainment. His Bomdila host explains: 'My township was at a height of 12,000-odd feet. I found, going through the township from time to time, that there was no electricity, no entertainment, and people were confined to their homes. I thought that that was bad for morale. I had an empty house in the colony and I converted it into a club.'[23]

In lonely Bomdila, Singh introduced singing to stoke enthusiasm and bring some lightness into the community. He got his Private Secretary to adapt well-known film songs, compile booklets of them and distribute these among the officers and their wives. He gave each song a number so he could summon a sing-song simply by saying, for instance, 'number 10'! These songs would be sung together by all those assembled at the club.

Singh and I looked at one of his photographs in which Indian officials and women are sitting around on the floor and chairs, facing the camera, with the Dalai Lama among them. There seems to be a happy, party atmosphere.

'They would sit together and from that book they would sing recent film songs. I felt that with that, the blues went away and people became more lively. I also laid down that on club days people will bring one dish. Everyone would bring one dish each and we would share it amongst ourselves. That again created a lot of interest,' Singh remembered.

'That's where I took the Dalai Lama,' he looked at the photograph. 'This is a scene where the girls are seated. I am seated along with the girls and we are singing these film songs to create interest. The men folk are there, His Holiness is there, all the officials and their wives. We are enjoying ourselves. I thought, after all, in one way His Holiness is holy, great, but in some ways he's also a human being and the things that please us, like singing, will also please him. So I took him to the club that I'd created.'

I asked Har Mander if he remembered any of the songs.

'There was one song we called the Bomdila anthem,' he laughed. 'We had an officer called Gill. So we always teased him by saying, "Eh Gill!" At that time, there was a film song that we modified.' He sang:

Ah Gill, hey mushkil, ji na yaha,
Zara hatke zara wadke
Yeh Bomdi La meri jaan.
Zara hatke zara bachke
Yeh Bomdi La meri jaan

I asked him to translate.

'Oh Gill, It's difficult to live here. Go Back Save yourself. This is Bomdila. This is Bomdila, my love,' he finished singing and smiled beatifically.

Singh continued describing how they entertained the Dalai Lama.

'Sitting here, we sang the song for him. He clapped. My idea was not to be a strict protocol official but to make him relax. My mind told me that definitely a thing like singing, would touch some chord in his heart [hit his heart] and relax his mind from the worries that he carries with him and which lie ahead of him.'[24]

*

During his stay in Bomdila in 1959, the Dalai Lama conducted another empowerment ceremony at a monastery for his followers. This monastery had been consecrated by a Rinpoche[25] the previous year in 1958. After 14 April, when the Dalai Lama conducted the empowerment procedures, the monastery was called Nehru Gonpa, which means a monastery in honour of the person who gave permission for the Tibetan leader to take sanctuary in his country. A many-sided wooden building painted blue, red and yellow, with a blue sign above the red wooden doorway, it still exists today.

Diary Extract, 14 April 1959, (continuation):

My estimate is that almost 4000 people received blessings from him. From 1100 hours to 1300 hours he was taken round the township and visited the Women's Welfare Centre, the Co-operative Stores, the School, the CITPC,[26] the Offices and the Hospital. He appreciated the welfare activities undertaken by the Government. A bag woven in local design which was presented to him was very much liked by him.

In the evening His Holiness attended a Cinema Show in my residence. Following films were exhibited:

a) *A documentary film on Gandhiji.*
b) *A documentary film on the Prime Minister.*
c) *A documentary film on the Himalayas.*
d) *A News-Reel on the Republic Day 1958 celebrations in New Delhi.*
e) *A NEFA documentary on the Kameng division.*

His Holiness was particularly impressed with the scenes dealing with the struggle for independence in India and the documentary on Gandhiji and the Prime Minister.

The Cinema Show was followed by a Dinner Party given by me in honour of the Dalai Lama and the members of his entourage.

Har Mander needed to keep his young Tibetan VIP occupied. He told me, 'The reason was twofold. First, my job. My problem was to fill up the seven days. Not just to leave him in his apartment, but to keep him busy. So, I took him to many establishments like a hospital, school and craft centre. My resources were very limited. For example, I had a film division. There were reels to be shown to tribal people, like a reel on Mahatma Gandhi. Something that perhaps would not interest the Dalai Lama, these kind of propaganda films, but I made him see them.'

He observed that when the Dalai Lama did go to the craft centres and other places, he asked questions and took an interest.

*

The 5th Assam Rifles were now guarding the entire area, and the Dalai Lama's own entourage had swelled as some senior monks from Tawang Monastery had joined the travelling Tibetans.

While music occurred within the settlement of Bomdila, there was celebration without it as well.

The *Assam Tribune* reported on 13 April 1959 that: 'Singing and dancing tribal people are moving in groups around Bomdi La.'[27]

The Dalai Lama had ridden two Tibetan horses in rotation from Lhasa as well as Tawang and then Bomdila. At Bomdila, he felt moved to give one to Har Mander Singh as a token of appreciation and one to Mr Dutt to thank the Government of India. However, Singh told a member of the Losel Nyinje Charitable Society who interviewed him, 'The horses were confiscated by the government and kept as a historical memento.'[28]

The sojourn at Bomdila was a seminal point in the development of the relationship between the Dalai Lama, Har Mander Singh and Singh's family. It cemented a friendship that has lasted roughly six decades so far.

Har Mander Singh still feels the same way about the Dalai Lama as he did when he first met him. He refers to him as a jewel that is impossible to hide. Occasionally, Har Mander meets him these days when he is invited to do so. Singh finds the Tibetan spiritual leader unchanged whether he meets with kings, presidents or the common man and describes him on one level as a very simple, wise monk, whose primary asset is a hearty laugh when he finds something funny.[29]

The heady days of March and April 1959 were a time when the two men could cement their relationship. This is signified by the fact that the Dalai Lama still refers to Har Mander Singh as his elder brother, in public, sometimes. It happened, for instance, in Delhi, on 7 December 2013, on a visit to meet street children.

Singh, on the other hand, refutes the honour of that title, instead calling himself 'a servant of the Dalai Lama.' That said, the affection that the Dalai Lama shows him means a lot to him. He says that the words that the Dalai Lama has said to him that stick in his mind best are, 'You're my friend.'[30]

I was curious to know how Har Mander felt once they had reached some sort of safe ground in Bomdila. He said, 'There again my feeling was that he should be safe and that was uppermost. Of course, by then his spirituality had also rubbed off on me and I was beginning to feel that there is something in this personality that is not in ordinary people like me.'

'What do you mean by his spirituality rubbing off on you?' I asked.

'I think there is something in his face. I have seen him on several occasions in India in meetings, gatherings. There is something in his face, something about him that just rubs off on you and you genuinely feel that there's something in this person . . . I'm not an agnostic or any such thing. I say my prayers occasionally, but there was this, spirituality is difficult to describe. It sort of overpowers you and makes you feel that there is someone higher than you who is taking care of things. One may believe it or one may not believe it, but I think there is somebody. Otherwise you think of a human being, how the human machinery works from the time it is fed, like a motorcar is fed petrol, to the time it leaves fumes or the exhausted part leaves. I think human machinery is the perfect machinery. Much better than machineries that human beings have created,' he said.[31]

24

TIBETANS IN DEHRADUN

The Dalai Lama has been able to institute reforms regarding the status of Tibetan women. As his pioneering sister-in-law Namgyal Lhamo Taklha explained, it was much needed. He probably could have done this in Tibet too, but the effect in Dharamsala, at any rate, has been noted.

'We are very fortunate now because in the olden days in Tibet, women were not allowed to join the government and we didn't have many options in life. It was either you get married or you go into a nunnery, and that's all the role models you know in Tibet. His Holiness the Dalai Lama feels that there should be gender equality. And even as early as 1960 when they elected, when the [Tibetan government in exile] had a parliament system and we were stepping into democracy, he said 'You must have women.' And we had the three provinces, and there was a seat left for three women.'[1]

Wherever I visit Dharamsala, the officials I meet are often male. But females are in evidence. Rinchen Khando Choegyal, wife of Tenzin, who has successfully turned Kashmir Cottage into a guest house, is also the founder and director of the Tibetan Nuns Project in that town.

This flourishing community of nuns housed in the modern, spacious Dolma Ling nunnery in Dharamsala produced some of the first batch of nuns graduating in the high Geshe-ma degree of Buddhism. The Tibetan Nuns Project, based at the Dolma Ling Nunnery and Institute, is pioneering because it set the stage for other nuns to follow and organized for the nuns to be able to take the exams and get the degree, as explained to me by an authority involved with the project at a senior level. [2,3]

The Dalai Lama's sister-in-law, Namgyal Taklha, who lives in Dehradun, is also a prime example of a successful Tibetan woman.

It was not always so, she told me. In fact, according to Namgyal, the Tibetan government in exile is probably more diverse than it might have been in Tibet.

'When we finished school, they needed interpreters, translators and also people who could read and write English—and there were a few of us girls; men too. So we were employed and became government servants. There were no female ministers before 1991. There were a couple of secretaries and, His Holiness the Dalai Lama said, you must have a woman minister, so the people's parliament elected his sister Jetsun Pema.'[4]

Nuns are now allowed to do the studies and take a Geshe-ma degree. Namgyal said that civilian women have always had more advantages than nuns, which is a contrast to monks enjoying a higher status than civilian men. Namgyal explained and added some surprising information.

'Without His Holiness I don't think the nuns would have come this far. We had more rights and more freedom than the nuns. So, His Holiness said the nuns should have the same education as the monks. So now we have all the Geshe-mas coming out. Geshe-ma is after [twenty] years of study, like a PhD degree but this Geshe-ma is only in the Gelugpa school of Tibetan Buddhism.[5] We have different schools of Buddhism. the Gelugpa nuns get the Geshe-ma degree. Other schools have other degrees like Lopon.

'Because of his outlook that we should have gender equality. Other religious heads also followed because in the Himalayan communities they didn't want to see the women go too far. But now it's open and we're getting the same education, and we have the same rights.'[6]

While monks as well as nuns often came from poor families, it seemed that the motivation for girls becoming clerics sometimes differed from boys turning to monkhood. In the case of the boys, as I have said in an early chapter, joining the priesthood was an expectation and usually happened with full family consent. On the other hand, I am told, 'A lot of the girls joined the nunneries on their own, running away from their homes. I discovered from interviewing the nuns that some of them just had sponsors for tea or a little supper and otherwise there was no money if they were from a poor family.

'If you're from more wealthy families, I'm talking about Lhasa and the nunneries there, from business homes or from aristocratic homes, they had sufficient food sent from their homes. But ones who came from the nomad families from very far or from Kham, they had nobody sending things and it was not easy, it took days and days you know to bring things from home too. So, they had to work and maybe some of the nuns had to beg, and there was no proper education like the monks had.'[7]

For many years, Namgyal was a Director of the Drikung Samtenling Nunnery in Dehradun.

'I've been educating the nuns and seeing that they get a proper education as well as a lot of workshops to make them, to empower them so they can run their own nunnery rather than having monks and people like me look after the nunnery. This year we had seven girls who graduated as *Acharya*s. I'm satisfied because now the nunnery is administered solely by nuns.'[8]

Different people have different opinions on the future of the Tibetans. I found that most of the senior Tibetans I spoke to felt that the international Tibetan diaspora needed to adapt, but at the same time respect its traditions and culture. Where this did happen, I found it was largely due to the Dalai Lama's presence.

Namgyal was from the reformation school of thought. 'We cannot be the same Tibetans that we were in Tibet, there are going to be changes. So, I think it's important for our younger generation to keep our culture and tradition. It's like wearing Tibetan dress, it's very important to wear our dress on ceremonies but then in everyday life you don't have to, you have to be comfortable too. Like I wear trouser pants in the monsoon period because I sometimes take the bus down and then you know with the umbrella, the shopping and the dress— you have to pull it up and so you have to be practical too. Tibetans are spread all over the world but it's very important for them to keep their identity, otherwise we can be lost. Like you say in America—you're in the melting pot, you really can be melted in the pot, right?'[9]

Namgyal Lhamo Taklha told me that she believed India's absorption of Tibetan refugees, though still issue-ridden, could be deemed to be successful compared to the current refugee crises emanating from the Middle East and from South-East Asia.

So, what are the lessons that the Tibetan refugee settlement programme in India can give to refugee programmes in other parts of the world?

Namgyal worked for the Central Tibetan Administration, the Tibetan government in exile for twenty-eight years.

'The Tibetan refugee programme, the resettlement programme here in India is successful. [Because] we have such a wonderful leader like His Holiness Dalai Lama who is very concerned for the welfare of the people and he keeps everybody together, united. And then another thing is we are in a country where we had a lot of support from the government and the people of India. When we first came as refugees, we had people from countries and organizations from all over the world who came to help us. And then we, the Tibetan people worked hard to make our lives successful. So [there's] all this inter-dependency of everybody, pulling together, everybody working together. That's why the Tibetan refugee settlement has been very successful, and many people come and learn from how we have managed.'[10]

'But with the other refugees in other parts of the world at the moment, the big movements that are happening, many of them are leaderless, they have no resources and they have very little backup, very little host government support if at all. What would you say to those refugees?' I asked.

Namgyal replied, 'Most important is give and take. And you have to give. You just can't say "Oh like now the Rohingya, Rohingya refugees, they've been thrown out, nobody wants them." How come some wealthy governments cannot take some? Because you just cannot leave them to die. We've become very materialistic, it's a consumer world so we don't have much kindness and compassion. Because of that we're having all these problems because we ourselves are making all these problems. If we understand that we need to create a more peaceful and a more compassionate world, as His Holiness teaches, I don't think all these problems would come.'[11]

She concluded by saying that if people shared more, there would be less violence.

*

About half an hour's drive and 12 kilometres from central Dehradun up onto the lower slopes of the Shivalak Hills sits the town's Tibetan settlement, Dekyiling. The initial population of 720 has more than doubled to around 2000. The ages of the residents, now extending to the third generation, range from new-borns to over ninety.

The settlement is not too far from the Songtsen library, founded by Namgyal Lhamo Taklha's brother, His Holiness Drikung Chetsang Rinpoche. Dekyiling is well run and properly administered. It has an aura of calm and content. The Dalai Lama's sister-in-law personally conducted me there.

On arrival, Namgyal Lhamo Taklha first took me into the administrator's office, where I met the affable thirty-one-year-old Ngawang Choedhen. I asked him about his work and his status here. Ngawang didn't have an Indian passport, he said.

'Tibetans exiles living in India, we have to go through this Foreigner Registration Act, it's called RC; Registration Certificate. Every five years we have to renew it. From the nearest foreigner registration office, it's under the Senior Superintendent Police's office. The thousands of Tibetans in various settlements, they all have this documentation, as it's mandatory. On it is our name, place of birth and our validity.'[12]

He then showed me a small, green book.

'It's a national voluntary, national contribution green book. Here all is written in Tibetan. We have to pay only 58 rupees for it annually as a contribution towards our Tibetan exile government.'[13]

When I asked how many Tibetans get Indian passports, he said the number was 'negligible'. 'It depends on our political background. We, the Tibetans never set our mind to continue in India, we would like to go back or we always hope to return to our Tibet country. That's one of the reasons why we are living here in India with a temporary registration certificate.'[14]

We completed our interview and I asked to see the settlement.

Outside the office, Ngawang Choedhen took me to a set of thirty-two neat retirement houses divided into small sets that each back onto a stupa in the middle. These were homes for former Central Tibetan Administration officers who were sixty or above and who were no longer in active service. Some of these officials were executive secretaries and themselves managed settlements. The thirty-two who live here had their homes allocated to them by the Central Tibetan Administration in Dharamsala. The average age of these residents was seventy.

Apart from free accommodation and medical treatment, they also received pensions. My guide told me that each pension arrived at and was paid once a quarter through the Tibetan Settlement office in Dehradun. It came from the department of finance in the Central Tibetan Administration, Dharamsala.

After this, I was taken to the dispensary and the medical centre. Eleven men staff this medical centre, which is bright and airy. Like the medical and dispensing staff in the fifty-six Tibetan medical centres all over India, the staff here have also been trained at Dharamsala Medical College. Tibetan doctors train for five years and intern for one year.

The centres did not have too many people sitting in the waiting area as there was a quick and efficient outpatient turnaround.

Tibetan medicine is widely considered to be authentic and successful, so I found many Indians too in the waiting area. I was told that this phenomenon repeats itself at the other Tibetan medical centres all over India.

I found that even in Delhi's Tibetan medical centres, the majority of patients are non-Tibetans. The treatment is 'pay as you go' and modestly priced. There are three different sizes of round, brown pills and powders. Medicines are dispensed from jars in the pharmacy area, which the dispensers say are made from herbs, minerals, purified metal and some animal extracts.

The health care staff in Dehradun told me that they could often cure heart and backbone problems without the need for surgery. The most common ailments that people came in with were rheumatoid arthritis, indigestion and cancer, they reported.

*

The main source of income for members of the settlement is traditional handicrafts and this includes carpet weaving. But Exile Creations Pvt Ltd run by its Tibetan directors, Ngawang Tsultrim and Kalden Chophel, aimed to provide something extra. It was a special glass blowing factory, and Ngawang took me there on the last evening of my visit to the Dekyiling settlement.

The factory had a creative and industrious feel to it. There were benches with burners and eye protection glasses at each place. Delicate, sometimes elaborate artistic glass creations of different sizes and colours were in front of each seat. It felt like an arts laboratory; brightly lit; like a fantasy set from a film maker's imagination.

The manager showed me round and told me that roughly thirty-two young people were employed here. Some of them were school dropouts. At Exile, they were taught how to blow glass beads from highly valued Italian Maroni glass. They used gas torches to heat the glass and integrate it with silver or other coloured material to create unique, beautiful items—beads for bracelets and necklaces.

At a separate bench beads were laid out. This was for the staff to inspect for damaged items. It took just 10 minutes to fashion a bead, the manager told me. And it took the directors six months to fashion a trained glass blower, he added.

The team had also created a way to work on recycled glass. On a table I saw a portrait of the Dalai Lama created from this recycled glass.

The next day, I meet with director Ngawang Tsultrim in the factory. He told me that six years ago a contract for high quality glass beads was offered to him and a glass artist friend of his. They started a company in the Dekyiling settlement to provide employment for unemployed young Tibetans who have low job prospects. Today, some of the youngsters who started six years ago are still with Exile.

The company that commissioned Exile is Danish, and they produce high end necklaces and bracelets, so they expect high quality work. The Danish firm sells onto Europe and America.

Ngawang is a former settlement resident from south India. He's an Indian citizen because he married an Indian Tibetan Sherpa. He also got an education and became a successful businessman. That is why he wants to give back to his community.

The workforce contained an equal number of boys and girls. Ngawang and Kalden also employed disabled people. They paid them higher salaries than was the norm for Dehradun.

Above every seat there was a photo of the Dalai Lama, donated by a photographer who met him in Dharamshala.

Ngawang Tsultrim felt that Indian Tibetan settlement dwellers are mostly hardworking and do well, since they inherited a similar work ethic from their parents and grandparents.

'I believe that I'm more fortunate in that I have a little more than the others so I'm trying to give this back to my own community. Though it's a sustainable business we try to give them the best of the salaries as well as helping them to improve their lives. Most of them are young boys and girls so after a period of some time they may start their own small company. This is how we wanted to have our community develop: because everybody should not be just a job seeker.'[15]

In the Tibetan settlements that I have visited, I found that the Tibetan communities all have reverence for the Dalai Lama. He cares very much for all his people and for the rest of humanity too. As evidence of this, he is responsible for making sure that Tibetans who are in need are all given some funds regularly. They often depend on this money. There seemed to be a direct link back to Dharamsala, and those who are needy are given money from there. Refugees in Nepal told me that they receive money from the Tibetan headquarters, as did pensioners in the Dehradun settlement.

The Dalai Lama is pastoral, and cares for his flock, literally.

At the regular morning sessions when he has visitors to his official residence, there are often the infirm and the elderly among them. I am told that he likes to meet each and every refugee that he can, so that he can hear their stories for himself.

They feel a palpable connection to the Dalai Lama, and he feels the same towards all of them.

25

THE DALAI LAMA
AND THE SINGH FAMILY

On 17 May 2015, I prepped for the next day's first interview with the Dalai Lama.

The hilltop hotel where the interview would be conducted had an open top floor. Looking out, the setting sun could be glimpsed to the west behind six snowcapped mountain tops. Prayer flags—yellow, blue, green, red and white—fluttered in front of them. Training my eyes east, looking across the rich green tops of the trees, I glimpsed a large complex. Two levels above that were monk residences. One level above that was the temple, and higher up the hill was a sitting area for audiences just by the Dalai Lama's residence, reception rooms and offices.

I knew the Dalai Lama was in his residence. I got excited as I looked across the trees, having waited years for this moment. At that point, I didn't know I'd be fortunate to meet him not just once, but a few more times.

*

The day of my primary meeting with His Holiness arrived. I worked on questions in my McLeod Ganj hotel room and got ready.

There was a narrow roadway up to the temple which was accessible to visitors.

Beyond the temple was a covered courtyard designed by architect Munishwar Nath Ashish Ganju, with white umbrella-like structures above the wide walking areas on the hillside. This forecourt was a short walk from the entrance to the road leading to the Dalai Lama's official rooms. The forecourt was partially covered with a tensile membrane roof.

To one side of the walkways were areas of dry grass where trainee monks sat at times with senior boys who ritualistically argued and debated with them, testing their abilities to concentrate.

Walking further beyond the courtyard to the iron gates at the entrance of the Dalai Lama's complex, there was a holding building. Here security checks took place and we were fully searched after presenting our credentials. When it came to my personal belongings, Tibetan women in traditional dress extracted every item from my large handbag and even checked the perfume by spraying it. They also checked my lipstick by asking me to use it.

There were swarthy, serious-looking security men everywhere— from India's IB and other agencies, as well as many Tibetans.

His Holiness is reportedly classified as someone who needs Z-list security protection; the highest level in the land, accorded to prime ministers and other top-ranking individuals.

The influence that the Dalai Lama exerts can be seen by the constant flow of visitors to the buildings.

A winding path surrounded by beautiful plants and flowers led to a round structure just by the entrance to his official rooms. Tenzin Taklha, secretary to the Office of His Holiness and the Dalai Lama's nephew, emerged dressed in a traditional dark robe over his smart trousers, wearing glasses, looking busy with a pad of paper under his arm.

When the Dalai Lama appeared in the doorway, there was gentle scurrying around him by the Tibetan visitors. He motioned to them to give him space. They parted and he went up the steps.

An assorted group of people lined up to pay obeisance and receive his blessings; Tibetans old and young, Indians too.

I stood opposite him by the round structure and he pointed to me, asking his nephew in Tibetan who I was.

Tenzin answered that I was related to Har Mander Singh.

His Holiness came and slapped me on the back, and then we posed for a photo with his arm around me.

He said, 'Har Mander Singh is my very, very close friend.'

'I'm his niece,' I tell him.

He slapped me on the back again and held my shoulders. Then he laughed and pointed to his head. 'His son . . . I was in Bomdila, 1959. Beginning April. I think, his son,' he mimed toddling, 'he dressed in Tibetan clothes.' He gestured as if to mime the height of a small child. 'Very young. Now he has become bald.' He laughed and slapped my shoulder one more time.

'Thank you,' I said as he turned and walked up into his complex.

I stood, smiling but gobsmacked. It was not what I expected from my first meeting with the Spiritual Leader of the Buddhist Himalaya Belt.

Later, when we were seated next to each other in the Dalai Lama's formal room, the Dalai Lama said thoughtfully, 'Now, except me, all are gone. Now he [my cousin Harsh Mander] has also become quite a smart, gentle person.'

He asked me about Har Mander, 'Is he still alive?' When I responded in the affirmative, he told me, 'A few years ago, I met him in Delhi. He looks quite old. Oh, then I must meet him on occasion, yes.'

'Mr Menon?' he continued.

I told him that he was no more, as were so many other officials who had been involved in the mission at that time.

I then asked him, 'Now you're here, leading the community. What part did he play in getting you to here?

He said, 'When I reached Bomdila, mentally, physically, some difficulties. Mentally, the last nine years [before leaving Tibet] were a difficult life. Then, finally, there's no other choice except to escape with great risk. Then, we reached this country. And then physically, when I was in southern Tibet somewhere and dysentery developed, then my body became very weak, very weak. But, because of the danger I had to go like that. Then, when I reached Tawang, my physical condition day by day improved. Then, finally, when I reached Bomdila. I spent maybe, I think, ten, I don't know. Ten days, more than ten days, I think, with Har Mander. So, he took full care of me with his wife. My meals and everything, he took care. Then his son, with Monpa dress, you could see him running here and there. Monpa dress, like Tibetan dress. I remember.

'So, tremendous relief. Physically, mentally some difficulties, weak, and then such persons, Har Mander Singh, his wife. Full of warm feelings and smiles, and they took care. So, there's one major experience when I reached India. The first, tremendous relief, feeling of tremendous relief when I reach Khenzimane, the border. Translator, Sonam Kazi, and bodyguard Atuk Babu. Then another one. When I saw from a few hundred metres, and I saw it in their faces. I immediately recognised and say, "Oh, old friend." And, besides that, official of government of India who are receiving me. And I feel tremendous relief, or happy. Personally, something like reunion. The officials of Government of India now taking care of me, like that.'[1]

The time when the Dalai Lama was with Har Mander Singh and his family in Bomdila seemed to have made a strong impression on the Dalai Lama. He referred to it when we first met, he referred to it in the interview, and he referred to it twice on 8 April 2017 in Tawang, when I asked him about his memories of 1959.

Continuing the narration, the Dalai Lama told me how he had met Har Mander Singh a couple of years earlier in New Delhi, when he had gone to visit a home for street children that Harsh Mander ran in the capital. He also repeated his favourite observation—about Har Mander Singh and his son both being bald now.

The Dalai Lama enjoys being around children and they seem to enjoy being with him. Here I should explain that the visit to the street children the Dalai Lama was speaking of on 8 April 2017 were the street children he visited on 7 December 2013, at a care home in Mehrauli, Delhi, that Harsh Mander has established. Harsh Mander welcomed the Dalai Lama along with his own father, Har Mander Singh.

In his welcome speech, Harsh Mander said that the care home was built on a sense of love and compassion, and that the Dalai Lama also represents these values. This is shown, said Harsh Mander, by the fact that the Dalai Lama displays no anger or bitterness about what happened to him. Harsh Mander added that although the Tibetan is a Buddhist leader, he did not exclusively promote Buddhism, preferring instead to praise the attributes of other faiths.[2]

When the Dalai Lama spoke, he referred to Har Mander Singh first.

'My dear elder brother was very helpful to me at the end of March 1959. I spent days resting with him when Harsh Mander was very small.' Then came his favourite joke about the men of the Singh family. 'Now look, his head is shiny like mine and his father's!

'And my young brothers and sisters, I'm extremely happy to be here to meet you in this home you have found, where you get food, shelter and education . . . yesterday I was moved by beggars I saw on the street. Their faces looked poor and weak, their eyes hollow; completely demoralized . . . yesterday, I saw sadness, today I've seen hope . . . there is a candour and straightforwardness about poor people I don't see elsewhere. In a soup kitchen in Los Angeles I've participated in, I noticed more joy among those eating than I see at the formal dinners of the better off.'

He added that there needed to be more of a sense that seven billion human beings are actually one family. 'If that's what we stress there'll be no basis for war, bullying or cheating each other. If we see others as part of 'us' there'll be no room to neglect them.

'Children don't feel hopeless or helpless. You must study seriously and eventually go on to higher education. Remember, you're not alone. You can study and work, build up your lives. Develop self-confidence. Feeling demoralized is a source of failure. You must not lose hope. In late March and early April 1959, when I and many Tibetans reached

India, we kept up our self-confidence and determination; you must do the same.

'If you give up, you make no progress. If you work hard, keep up your confidence and determination, you'll be successful in whatever you do. If others show you affection now, when you grow up and help others, without exploiting, deceiving or bullying them, you'll find yourself surrounded by friends. Please keep this in mind. I'm with you, please believe me.'[3]

In November 2017, I too went to this care home with my sons. On the outskirts of Delhi, it has a calm and peaceful atmosphere, spacious facilities, and is well run. A lot of time and care is taken to bring the children here to a state where they can be confident in themselves. They have psychologists and therapeutic care where needed, because some of them have suffered trauma. Some of the children have nightmares and display other symptoms of silent suffering.

Harsh Mander works hard to establish links with colleges and companies so that these children have a future after they leave the home, but it is an uphill struggle.

*

Har Mander Singh's son Harsh Mander was present on a few occasions when I met with his father at his home. I also interviewed him to hear his side of the story.

'I was just a child of four [when the Dalai Lama stayed for around a week in Bomdila], so I have very few memories but lots of received memories,' said Harsh Mander. 'The most striking thing my parents speak about when they recall those days is the extraordinary equanimity and calmness with which the Dalai Lama dealt with that moment in his life.

'He had lost his kingdom, he had lost his home forever. He'd been uprooted. He'd almost lost his life. There were tens of thousands of refugees rendered homeless with him. But they said that he never lost his dignity, his grace and his calmness. That was perhaps the beginning of his adult journey to becoming a world statesman. That turning point was important.

'With my parents, the Dalai Lama spent his first days in exile. They had to take care of his food make sure he wasn't poisoned, that there was no sabotage. It built a relationship of grace and friendship which extended and has lasted a lifetime with my parents.

'I think it must have been difficult also because—one cannot imagine the absence of communication in the world but more so in that area. You had to trek for four days to reach Bomdila. We as children used to be carried on muleback. There were no shops. Our rations had to be dropped every ten to fifteen days. So, in the middle of that, a figure like the Dalai Lama being brought across, with tens of thousands of dispossessed, angry refugees, uncertain about their future, that's why the story is important.

'There are many problems with India but the welcome that it gave to an unlimited number of refugees to make India their home also began from there. And at great political cost to the country. Nehru had a very close relationship with the Chinese leadership which converted into a humiliating war a few years later. All of these consequences were born for the sake of giving a home to an unarmed, gentle set of people. So, I think the world has a lot to learn from this story. It is a story that should be told.

'My mother is no longer alive, but she and my father recalled that they were afraid that he [the Dalai Lama] would be poisoned. Therefore, it was necessary to take every precaution. His food had to be prepared by my mother's own hand. She didn't know his eating habits. The Dalai Lama's mother taught her basic Tibetan cooking and I'm told he's probably one of the first Dalai Lamas who ate from a homemaker's hand.[4]

'I was a small child of four, and apparently I used to keep going and playing on his lap. People used to stop me and he used to say, "No, he gives me happiness and solace." Therefore, even now when he meets me all these sixty-odd years later, he still remembers me as a small child and laughs as if time should have stopped.

'The Indian government, of which my father was the frontline representative, opened their country and their heart and their homeland to him, and my father was the instrument by which that was accomplished.

'The whole world knows the Dalai Lama today. Perhaps he's the most loved human being on the planet today. Mandela would probably have been the most loved but after his passing I can hardly think of somebody as widely loved and respected as His Holiness.

'There was a very graceful moment when fifty years of the [Tibetan] exile were completed. They organized a programme in Delhi called "Thank you, India." He invited my father symbolically to be the person that he thanked, publicly, on behalf of all of India. Because he was the first person who had given him hospitality ...

'The extraordinary quality of grace and dignity in the face of enormous loss, injustice and dispossession, never losing your gentleness, never losing your compassion, that's what I take away most from this story.

'My father was just in his early thirties but was given India's very high award at that young age in recognition of the fact that he accomplished both the rescue and the graceful welcome, in very difficult times, to a man who went on to represent the finest values of compassion in the world.'[5]

The remaining members of the Har Mander Singh family are grateful for the experience of having been in the close presence of the Dalai Lama for a short while in 1959, but sixty years later, there is a wider feeling that the survivors of that time are disappearing one by one. With them, their oral memories will also disappear, which is why I devoted my time to creating this book for the young people of today.

The topic of recording personal histories was raised by Namgyal Lhamo Taklha in Dehradun, when she spoke to me in November 2017.

Namgyal keeps a low profile. As I wrote this, she was not in the best of health but I hoped that when this book is published, she would be able to read it.

'Yes, I like to be quiet because I'm writing and then I do my own housework here, go shopping, and all that takes a lot of time,' said Namgyal Lhamo Taklha. 'I'm writing because it is important to preserve Tibetan culture and if I don't do this now the older people are dying and with them the story goes. And then also I'm studying Buddhism. I'm trying to practice prayers and meditations and that takes time too. And it is good, I have given up real social life because once you go here then you go there and then you're just going round and round, for what? I find it very superficial.'

'So you've broken your purdah and you're talking to me. Why did you choose to talk to me?' I asked.

'Well you see as a Tibetan I think it's very important to talk to people like you because more people will know about what's happened to our country and I think it's a duty of every Tibetan to preserve our culture, our tradition, our history and also inform others of what Tibet was like and especially for the younger people, younger Tibetans, they are all born everywhere all over the world and they don't know much about Tibet so it is good. I feel it's necessary to talk to you, so a lot of people can understand what Tibet was.'[6]

26

TO TEZPUR

Har Mander now needed to move the party from Bomdila and get it down to the village of Foot Hills. Leaving at sunrise, they had to cover roughly 97 kilometres to get to the next venue, Khelong.

Diary Extract, 15 April 1959:

The first advance party consisting of the Dalai Lama's family members and his tutors along with their attendants accompanied by Murty left this morning in six jeeps.

This is where the pages of Har Mander Singh's diary seem to end. If there was more, it is lost to the ravages of time. He was now escorting the Dalai Lama to an official showcase event for all the world to see. It was also going to be a government handover, so he may have felt that his intimate time with the Dalai Lama was coming to an end and he would no longer need to write up the events for himself. The veil was being lifted. From now on, every move the Dalai Lama made would be chronicled and tabulated by others. From now on, the Tibetan guest's every movement would be scrutinized publicly.

As mentioned above, Singh arranged for the group to stop for one night, on 15 April 1959, in Khelong, a halting post along the Chaku road, now a National Highway. It's been suggested that the stopover was arranged because the media group assembling in Tezpur, Assam, had swollen and needed extra management before the guests arrived.[1]

Khelong was the final destination within the Kameng Division, and here, the Dalai Lama planted a Bonsum tree that, as with all his plantings, immediately acquired holy status.

Nowadays, lines of religious flags are strung along to other trees from the Bonsum's lower branches.

The party left the following morning at 6.45 a.m.

The group reached Foot Hills at 7.45 a.m. on 16 April 1959. On the Dalai Lama's car fluttered the Indian and the Tibetan flags—the latter showing a rising sun with blue and red rays held up by two dragons.

Har Mander Singh remembered that the jeep convoy was in sections.

'In the first group, there were two tutors and family members of His Holiness.'

T.S. Murthy accompanied this group.

'In the second group, His Holiness was accompanied by myself, Menon and my wife. At that time, there were around twenty-five jeeps in all.'[2]

There were press reports that the convoy consisted of station wagons as well as jeeps though the total number differed.[3] The Dalai Lama's vehicle was, in Singh's words, 'better than a jeep'.[4]

The Assam Rifles was led by a captain, and two riflemen carrying Bren guns kept an eye on either side of the road for signs of trouble.

They stopped overnight at Foot Hills on 16 April 1959. Here, the Assam Rifles laid out army ground sheets to cover the boggy ground. The *Assam Tribune* reported that Nepalis and Bhutanese, known as Bhutiyas, living at Foot Hills, 'Fell at his feet and the Dalai Lama blessed them all raising his hands'.[5] The Dalai Lama was presented with scarves by the wives of officers of the Assam Rifles.

Everywhere he went, he met with service chiefs of the area. Here, he was introduced to the inspector generals of the Assam Rifles and two deputy inspector generals of police.

He had breakfast at one Commandant Major Punje's home along with seventy-five other officials. Breakfast for the Dalai Lama, the *Assam Tribune* said, tended to be 'simple Western food which included porridge, bread and butter, eggs and fruits'.[6] Despite the primitive location, the village had managed to rustle up a carpet for him to walk on.

Until then, Har Mander Singh had kept the area around the Dalai Lama sterile in terms of newsmen. So, most of the foreign and local journalists were lurking at lower altitudes, in Tezpur. There, they collected at the bar and the billiard room.

The Dalai Lama might have wished to speak to the world, but India felt that this event needed to be choreographed so as not to embarrass its government.

Meanwhile, preparations in Tezpur were underway. All public traffic between Foot Hills and Tezpur had been halted for security and for the ease of passage of the visiting convoy.

On 15 April 1959, the *Statesman* reported that a rostrum was being constructed in a 'hurried' way in the Tezpur college campus, most probably for the Dalai Lama to give a statement.[7]

*

On the morning after the Dalai Lama's party left Foot Hills in April 1959, they crossed the Inner Line. And, on the other side of the Inner Line, the world's press was waiting. Some international cameramen had posted themselves just outside Foot Hills to try to get images of the Dalai Lama as he drove away.

A double page photo spread in *Life* magazine dated 25 May 1959, showed the jeep caravan emerging through a forest into a flat field with a rock-edged stream, complete with a flock of sheep and lamb scampering ahead of the vehicles in the foreground. The caption reads that the convoy is approaching Assam's state boundary. 'Jeeps sent by India had penetrated 60 miles into wild frontier to pick up Dalai Lama after his 300-mile trek.'[8]

Many newspapers excitedly published the first picture of the Dalai Lama taken at Foot Hills. An image of him arriving at Tezpur shows him flanked by Menon and F.C. Phuken, Deputy Commissioner of Darrang. As he arrived at the border, pressmen who had taken up positions waved and ran after the vehicle.

The party arrived at Tezpur on 17 April 1959. A four-seater Victor Moth had been flown into NEFA in case it was needed.

The Dalai Lama stepped out of his vehicle at Tezpur and onto the stage at Darrang College Grounds. There was a crowd of around 10,000 people according to an article in the *Assam Tribune* that is dated 19 April 1959.[9] Two decoratively painted live elephants raised their trunks in salute to the Tibetan leader.

He is said to have smiled at the crowd as the throng cheered and clapped, eager to hear him despite it being a hot day. He folded his hands and symbolically blessed the audience by scattering a bunch of flowers over them. The reception lasted around fifteen minutes and the paper noted that the Dalai Lama's mother was present, along with Gyayum Chemo and other high Tibetan officials. Another reporter noted the arrival of his mother Diki Tsering, younger brother and sister; three former cabinet ministers, lord chamberlains, attendants, officials and personal aides. After an opening welcome speech, the Dalai Lama said, 'May religion, which is the only means of achieving lasting peace for humanity, flourish forever.' He thanked the people for the reception and blessed them by saying, 'For your spiritual advancement'. His words were translated from Tibetan into English by his brother-in-law.

Har Mander Singh conducted the Dalai Lama down to Circuit House, Tezpur. Soon, he would be handing charge of the young spiritual leader over to his colleagues in government. His charge was about to be revealed to the world via the international media.

At Circuit House, the Dalai Lama was delighted to be finally reunited with his elder brother, Gyalo Thondup. The requests made via Har Mander Singh and his team had been met.

Officials, non-officials and ladies welcomed the Dalai Lama at Circuit House, reported the *Assam Tribune*.[10] There was also a mountain of telegrams, messages and letters waiting for him. Another minister from Assam formally welcomed the Dalai Lama on behalf of his state government.

In addition to the pressmen, just as before, Buddhists flocked to the town by foot, mule and cart to catch a glimpse of the Dalai Lama.

Now it was time for the Tibetan god-king to speak to the world for the first time since his arrival in India.

Har Mander Singh said that there was an internal discussion between the Dalai Lama and his close advisers, before he chose two Tibetan officials to go on stage and to speak.[11]

The statement was likely to have been approved by Delhi and referred to the Dalai Lama in the third person.

The statement said that the Dalai Lama had come to India of his own free will and not under duress. He added that he had left Lhasa due to the strained relations between Tibet and China. He also expressed gratitude to the Indian government and to Prime Minister Nehru for granting him sanctuary.

The early part of the statement referred to a view that Tibetans are different to the Han Chinese, and that Tibetans had 'always' desired independence. Then it spoke of the existence of Tibetan independence and autonomy despite occasions of the 'imposition' of Chinese 'suzerainty,' even after the Seventeen-Point Agreement was signed.

It said that the Chinese government was supposed to look after external affairs and defence for Tibet, but to still allow the freedom of religion and traditional customs.

Historical ties between India and Tibet were also mentioned, especially because India was where Buddha gained enlightenment. Finally, the statement explained that the Dalai Lama would be proceeding to Mussoorie, where he would rest and reflect on what he would be doing next.

Sen was supervising the seventy-five or so media personnel that had gathered. This practice of supervision has continued today. Visiting media is normally carefully controlled and corralled at the Dalai Lama's public events.

In Bomdila, on the 14 April 1959, Indian Foreign Secretary S. Dutt had made a statement saying that Prime Minister Nehru would be in Mussoorie to meet the Dalai Lama on the 24 April 1959. The authorities felt that Mussoorie was the most neutral place for the Dalai Lama to be while a permanent home could be found for him. India perhaps wanted the Dalai Lama to live in a hill station as it was a compromise between the mountains of the home he had just left and the often-scorching plains of India. The hills are also harder to access than the capital, so security and protection is easier to manage in a satellite location that can be isolated if needs be. Therefore, the Indian government made temporary arrangements in Mussoorie for the whole of the Tibetan party to stay for an extended period. Mr S. Dutt also stated that Government Joint Secretary Mr S. Sen would receive the Dalai Lama at Tezpur once he left Bomdila and escort him to Mussoorie.

The statement from the Dalai Lama can be read in full, courtesy of Claude Arpi.[12] I quote below some extracts.

'. . . On 29th March 1959 . . . Dalai Lama sent two emissaries across . . . Indo-Tibetan border requesting Government of India's permission to enter India and seek asylum there . . . the Dalai Lama . . . has experienced . . . respect and hospitality . . . by the people of the Kameng Frontier Division of the North East Frontier Agency . . . the Government of India's officers posted there . . . spared no efforts in making his stay and journey through this extremely well administered part of India as comfortable as possible . . . As the Dalai Lama . . . spiritual head of all . . . Buddhists in Tibet, his . . . concern is . . . perpetual flourishing of his . . . religion and freedom of his country . . .'[13]

The Chinese, who had been watching closely, swiftly issued an official rebuttal to the Dalai Lama's version of events and an interpretation of history to reinforce their argument. They had been reporting that the Dalai Lama had been abducted and had not left Tibet of his own free will. This was repeated in the statement.

In the Chinese statement, the premise for the Dalai Lama's testimonial was also denied, with supporting reasons given. One of these reasons was said to be that the document issued on behalf of the Dalai Lama talked of him in the third person, in a 'European or quasi-European' way whereas Tibetans, they said, tended to write in the first person. Therefore, the Chinese statement said, he could not have written it himself.

The overall tenor of the statement was that outside influences were exerting pressure on the Dalai Lama and the Tibetan elite to disrupt the unity of Tibet. For instance, again on the subject of language, the statement said that 'Suzerainty' was not a term commonly found in documents either from the Chinese Central People's Government, or from the Tibet local government.

It referred to the Dalai Lama and a 'gang of Tibetan rebels' 'fostered' by 'British Indian expansionist elements'.[14] The Chinese found the document full of 'constrained arguments, fraught with lies and loopholes'.

It rejected the idea of Tibetan autonomy, saying that China was a unified country, formed by the Han and other nationalities. This concept was corroborated by saying that the 'political and religious systems' of Tibet had been 'instituted successively' by the central government in Peking.

The statement said that the Dalai Lama and his officials had always been able to perform their work and function normally, with religion, customs and habits respected. As if by way of evidence, it said that Tibetan currency had been in circulation.

As a reason for any disruption of the above, the statement said that there had been an agreement that the Tibetan local government should carry out reforms on its own. The statement also said that the

Tibetan army was supposed to have been systematically and gradually merged with the PLA, and that neither of these had taken place.

Further, it said that the Tibet local government had been informed at the end of 1956 that democratic reforms were needed to be in place before 1962, and that these had not occurred.

An 'independent Tibet', the Chinese statement read, had only been promoted by 'imperialists', which resulted in the armed rebellion of 10 March 1959.

While the Chinese admitted that, as a result of dealing with the Khampa rebellion, there had been some damage to buildings and some casualties had occurred, they denied that lamas had been killed and that monasteries had been damaged.

The statement also said that the Dalai Lama had attended the dance performance voluntarily. They called the description of the mortar shell attack on the Norbulingka palace a 'fabrication', saying that the reason for the Dalai Lama's departure from his palace was an abduction by his advisers. For evidence, the Chinese said that if they had wished to attack and destroy a target, their shells would not have fallen short and only landed in the Norbulingka palace pond.

On 19 April 1959, the official Chinese rebuttal was broadcast via Peking Radio. It was later distributed by the New China News Agency.

In reply, Nehru later gave an elaborate statement to the Lok Sabha on 27 April 1959. Referring to the Chinese, he said that they were using language reminiscent of the Cold War, whether it was true or not. He said it was 'distressing' that a 'great nation' was making 'fantastic' charges against India.[15] Dealing with each one in turn, he said that it would be impossible to keep the Dalai Lama in India under duress. He stated that the Dalai Lama was free to go anywhere he wished.

Nehru also wrote that since the Panchen Lama had pronounced on the subject at hand, he would welcome him to India and have him meet with the Dalai Lama there. The same applied to the Chinese ambassador 'or any other emissary of the Chinese government. Each would be able to meet the Dalai Lama and would be treated with courtesy, whatever his views were'.[16]

Ongoing diplomatic manoeuvring aside, there was a mood of celebration in Tezpur that day. Newspapers reported that the Dalai Lama rode in a Land Rover with Har Mander Singh seated in the rear and Menon in the front. The reported number of excited pressmen assembled in Tezpur that day varied from fifty-two to 200. Singh remembered them yelling questions at the Dalai Lama without giving each other space and time.

Har Mander Singh's special days with the Dalai Lama and his entourage of family, cabinet and retinue ended at Tezpur.

That part of the journey, the final farewells, must have contained a degree of emotion. The Dalai Lama left an impact on Singh, one that the latter remembers to this day. One that made him consider his own beliefs and have a finer appreciation for the teachings of Buddhism.

Singh remembered, 'When we crossed NEFA area and reached Assam, Assam Planning Minister K.P. Tripathi arrived there to receive His Holiness and the group. Now my responsibility of escorting His Holiness was over. Fortunately, before His Holiness left [for] Mussoorie, he joyfully granted a special and final audience to my wife and me in a small room in the train arranged for him. This is the end of the account about His Holiness arrival in India which is jotted in my diary.'[17]

That final audience must have contained a degree of unspoken emotion as the two friends and families were separating, not knowing when they would be meeting again.

From that time on, however, the Dalai Lama kept a place in his heart for his Indian companion. For Har Mander, the Dalai Lama left a lasting impression that had moved his soul.

It was time to think about policy and the Tibetans left behind who might be in disarray without the Dalai Lama in their midst. It was important for the sake of the Tibetan people that the Dalai Lama send out the right messages to them and to China. It was felt vital that a government in exile be established.

Meanwhile, in Tezpur, after lunch, a special train had been arranged to take the Dalai Lama and his party from Tezpur to Mussoorie. It left Tezpur around 1 p.m.

The platform was packed with well-wishers and devotees. The train made a few stops along the way, and each time, the holy man's carriage was surrounded by people hoping to catch a glimpse of him or obtain his blessings.

The first halt was at Ragiva that evening at 8.15 p.m. The train was heading for Mussoorie via Siliguri in West Bengal, where it was due the following morning. There, the Tibetan leader was due to attend a reception arranged where he would meet followers from Bhutan, Sikkim and Darjeeling.

The Dalai Lama arrived in Mussoorie on 20 April 1959.

At Mussoorie, he met Prime Minister Nehru and they talked about the rehabilitation of the thousands of Tibetan refugees who had started to follow their leader into exile.

By May 1959, 7000 refugees had arrived at Tezpur and were housed in a thatched bamboo camp. Later, the number of Tibetan refugees in India scattered all over the country from north to south was to settle eventually at around 150,000. That is more refugees than many Western countries could ever imagine absorbing during the Middle East refugee crisis of the late 2000s.

Meanwhile, the Dalai Lama's thoughts were back in Kameng Division and what was happening there. He was so concerned that he directed his cabinet to send Singh a letter from Mussoorie. To the best of my knowledge, this letter has never been seen in public before, and is reproduced here.

Dear Shri Har Mander Singh,

We would like to thank you for all the services you have offered with much eagerness and interest to His Holiness and party when passing through your jurisdiction. We have thus been able to reach your Mussoorie safely and have had the great opportunity of meeting the Prime Minister.

Owing to the unbearable oppression by the Chinese Communists in Tibet, it is expected that there will be large number of refugees coming into India through all the Indo Tibetan frontiers. We believe that some five thousand refugees have already reached Tawang so far and feel extremely grateful to your Government for granting asylum and for undertaking measures for their relief. Although such kind facilities are being extended by your Government, we feel it is most important that there be no pro-Chinese of spies coming through among the refugees, who would, no doubt, cause much internal disturbance. In view of this, we have been directed by His Holiness to depute Kalon Surkhang, Kunling Dzasa, Phala Dronyerchemo, Khenchung Losang Gyaltsen and Kusung Depon Taklha Sey to assist you in checking such happenings and guide the refugees to respect Indian rules and regulations. We would therefore, request you to recognise the above mentioned Officials as Assisting Commissioners in control of the Tibetan refugees. Moreover, we would be thankful if you would kindly consult them in matters concerning the refugees for whom your kind help would also be greatly appreciated.

Thanking,
Yours Sincerely,
KASHAG.

Much of the Tibetan refugee population was moved to road camps in the hills of northern and southern India, where they remain today.

Shortly after this letter was sent to Singh, the Dalai Lama and the eighty people who had left Lhasa with him moved to Dharamsala and settled there.

The Dalai Lama was worried about the preservation of a Tibetan education for those youngsters following him, and he raised the issue with Nehru.

Following this, the Central Tibetan School Administration was formed within the Indian Ministry of Human Resource Development in 1961, and the Indian government set up schools for Tibetan children. This initiative began with just one Indian teacher educating Tibetan children in a tent. Today, there are seventy-one schools across India, with over 500 teaching and over 200 non-teaching staff. Around 10,000 students are currently being educated through this programme.[18]

In a press conference on 20 June 1959, the Dalai Lama rejected the Seventeen-Point Agreement that the Chinese had got him to concede. Setting up Tibetan administrative departments, he created the departments of Information, Education, Home, Security, Religious Affairs and Economic Affairs.

27

REASONS FOR WAR

It is natural for countries in south Asia to be strongly influenced by territorialism. Having been through so many eras of conquering emperors and invading nations, they feel protective towards their own terrain but at the same time, acquisitional. China and India, at the time of the story recounted here, both desired the crown of Asia, and China had built an army that far outnumbered and outgunned India's.

The situation in the late fifties and early sixties was muddied by the fact that borders, whether respected or violated, were not always well defined.

To India's north-west there was—and still is—the Line of Control (LoC) that came into being after 1971. It runs along parts of Jammu and Kashmir separating India from Pakistan.

To India's northeast, however, there was—and is—an oddly titled Line of Actual Control (LAC) that in some places is neither actual nor a line. In hilly or steep mountain slopes, often there is little more than a stone post in the grass and some loose stones nearby. The historic border, originally known as the McMahon Line, was perhaps not always clearly defined at ground level.

Nehru, in his time, was wary of using the term because of its imperial connotations. However, that does not alter the fact that it is still the longest disputed border in the world. Shashank Joshi, who used to be senior research fellow at the Royal United Services Institute in London and is now defence editor at *The Economist*, explained the reasons behind the problem.

'The basic dispute was twofold: One problem was that India wanted to go by the McMahon Line, while China stated that the line was agreed upon between Britain and Tibet at the 1914 Shimla Convention, and that it could not therefore be binding on China itself. The second problem was that each side differed on how the McMahon Line ran in practice. For tens of kilometres, the line did not follow the watershed exactly—the general principle of borders in mountainous areas—but went south of a key ridge, called Thag La. India unilaterally decided that its control should run north of the line, but when it did this, China pushed back strongly. As in modern India-China disputes, part of the disagreement is over the principle of the border and its very basis, and the other part is over the application of that principle on the ground, in very tricky terrain.'[1]

China had once before marched south to the Thag La Bridge, claiming that territory as theirs, and laid strong claims on much of NEFA.

Tawang, in particular, was considered by China as Sino property due to its close connection to Tsona situated across its own border in Tibet. India occupied Tawang properly in 1951, when an Indian officer, Bob Kathing, and sixty members of the Assam Rifles were sent to the town. This led to some tension between the Tibetan authorities and India. China portrayed this as a forcible annexation.

Tawang is also important because it was a crucial staging point for the Dalai Lama on his flight from Tibet in 1959.

Since the 1980s, China has been re-raising its claim on Tawang, and there is tension every time the Dalai Lama or senior Indian officials visit there.

China's sensitivity over the Indo-Tibetan border in NEFA influenced Har Mander Singh's actions, as he did not at any point wish to trigger a physical conflict. Not only was he in charge of precious passengers, he and his team were also the guardians of part of an important frontier. The frontier of a country that did not match the might of the Dragon.

At the time, Chinese air power was five times that of India, and its troop numbers had a Medusa-like quality. India's soldiers seemed like a handful in comparison with the waves of PLA men who could appear as if by magic and with terrifying discipline.

Though the adventure passed without an immediate all-out conflagration over the Dalai Lama or over territory, the Chinese were smarting. Peking was furious that the Dalai Lama, along with the thousands of Tibetans who followed him, had been given a home.

China had been unable to control or to coerce him into accepting its manipulation of Tibet. The best it could do was to verbally condemn him and build the status of another figure, a Panchen Lama, in his place.

Immediately following April 1959, despite the above factors, Prime Minister Nehru followed a 'Forward Policy' of putting Indian troops and military posts by, on and over the LAC. He ordered the army's Fourth Division to be placed just by the point where the actual LoC abutted the tiny kingdom of Bhutan. In a dangerous display of foolhardiness, an instruction was given for the division to move ahead to the Thag La ridge. This was an area that the Chinese had several years before been populating and administering without opposition.[2]

Shashank Joshi said, 'India's decision was also based on genuine tension between the letter of the McMahon Line, which put India south of the ridge, and its spirit, which was more generous to India.'[3]

*

When I interviewed Har Mander Singh in Delhi, I asked if the granting sanctuary to the Dalai Lama was the prime reason for the Chinese actions of 1962. He replied, 'It must have provoked the Chinese very much because they thought that they had taken all the precautions to prevent His Holiness from escaping from Lhasa.'

Shashank Joshi commented, 'It's important to note that over this period China felt that India was supporting US-backed action to subvert its control of Tibet, including sponsoring unrest. India did in fact allow and work with US intelligence efforts to work with Tibetans, but after—not before—the conflict. In large part, China was paranoid. India did not have designs on Tibet and was not working to overthrow Chinese control there.'[4]

Singh indicated that it was the Tibetans who ensured that the Dalai Lama got to the Tibetan border safely because of their devotion to their spiritual leader. Singh felt that the Tibetan people would have taken risks on behalf of their leader rather than have him come to any harm.[5]

By September 1962, China had had enough of India's Forward Policy and the gilded throne on which the Dalai Lama seemed to have been installed. The country launched a two-pronged attack on India's border to the west and to the east on 20 October. The attack was to result in the capture of the very places that Har Mander Singh was so familiar with—his home and headquarters at Bomdila, the Sela Pass, Kameng; indeed, much of NEFA.

Joshi says that it was also to 'teach India a lesson'. In other words, to establish the fact of Chinese dominance, and to make India think twice about pressing its claims in the future. This general psychological motivation was as important as any specific appetite for territory.

We should bear in mind here the domestic political dynamics around China's decision. After the Great Leap Forward, there had been real tension among China's elite. Mao wanted to consolidate his power and push his own, radical line. But he had rivals like Liu Shaoqi and future leader Deng Xioping. In this way, Mao's success in 1962 was probably also connected to the Cultural Revolution later. This is an argument made to me by Dr Shashank Joshi.[6]

In the west, the Chinese routed Indian soldiers from Aksai Chin. In the east, they moved fearlessly to the LAC.

Two days later, the Cuban missile crisis erupted, distracting Washington. The US asked its Ambassador to India, John Kenneth Galbraith, to handle the Indo-Sino situation, given that for President John F. Kennedy, both confrontations were of concern. I reached out to Bruce Riedel to learn about his investigation into this turbulent period. His knowledge and expertise were gained from many fields of research and work. Bruce served as senior adviser on south Asia and the Middle East to four consecutive American presidents, culminating with Barack Obama.

He told me that the decision to launch these attacks on India at vulnerable, undermanned and under-defended positions points happened for many reasons.

'We have to begin by saying that Chinese decision making in the early 1960s was all about Mao Tse Tung. It was not a collective decision-making process. This was a dictatorship with a very unique dictator at the top. Much has been written about his lifestyle. So, anybody trying to figure out the causes of Chinese behaviour is really trying to look inside the mind of Mao Tse Tung and that's of course difficult to do. He's long since dead, [and] he was never interviewed in any disciplined fashion but I think if you try to put yourself in Mao's head, there were a variety of reasons why he'd come to despise Nehru and to want to weaken India. One was the presence of the Dalai Lama and the threat that the Tibetan resistance movement, symbolized by the Dalai Lama, posed to Chinese control of Tibet. I think that's a fundamental reason. There were other reasons as well. I think that there was rivalry with Nehru for control and influence on the non-aligned movement. There was rivalry between India and China for being the exemplar for development in the decolonized world. How much each of those factors played in Mao's decision-making is very hard to weigh. I think in some ways, it's a fruitless exercise to try to say which is number one and which is number two, because I think that at any one time Mao's priorities may have been shifting. But I don't think there is any question that Mao went to war in 1962 to consolidate and defend China's takeover of Tibet and to implicitly teach the Indians a lesson that interference, as Mao would see it, in Chinese internal affairs would have a heavy price. And I think in that sense he succeeded.'[7]

The Chinese troops now outnumbered the Indians three to one, and quickly gained control of the border area in NEFA. Indian troops also suffered from grave shortcomings like a lack of proper infrastructure such as airfields and roads. So, it was hard for the Indians to get equipment and ammunition to the troops at the border.[8]

The Chinese consolidated their hold on Aksai Chin in the west. They had controlled much of it before 1962, which is why they were able to build a road across it in the 1950s. It is under their command to this day. They demolished all the posts set up under India's Forward Policy.

One of India's responses was to consider supporting the Tibetan guerrilla resistance movement.

The US decided to fully back India in the conflict with China for obvious reasons—to stop the Communist advance. Canada and the UK, too, provided military aid.

Riedel describes in his book *JFK'S Forgotten Crisis* how US Air Force Boeing 707s flew from Europe and Thailand with weapons and ammunition. By early November, he says, there were eight flights a day into Calcutta.

US Air Force aircraft took the arms and infantry equipment to the Indian front line. Britain's Royal Air Force was soon doing the same.

For three weeks at the end of October, there was a lull in the fighting and the Indians took advantage of this. They built a protective line for themselves due south of Thag La Ridge, where the McMahon Line ran. They constructed it at Sela Pass, which Har Mander had helped the Dalai Lama and his party cross just three years earlier.

But feeding supplies to high altitude regions is never easy for the Indians, and Sela Pass was no exception. Access here is limited due to the harsh terrain and sudden snowfalls. Even today, roads can be blocked for hours. The Chinese still managed to dominate the Indians here. They had been building up their troops and supplies through a sophisticated network of roads and supply depots near the front line.

Furthermore, by focusing on the Thag La Ridge region, Tawang—one of China's most prized targets—was left exposed.

In the middle of November 1962, the Chinese launched a second, all-out attack on India. They again expanded their hold over Aksai Chin, and took the western section of NEFA, including the part that had been under Har Mander Singh. Soon they had the eastern portion in their grip as well.

Indian's specially constructed Fourth Division had been decimated by 20 November. The Chinese army had control of Sela Pass, the entire route to Bomdila and Singh's former HQ.

By now, Nehru had sent several appeals to President Kennedy for help. He was hoping to attack the Chinese army's supply lines in Tibet, but with limited air power, India needed US air assistance to mount a defence of India's own infrastructure, support systems and metropolitan areas.

Simultaneously, Nehru was also asking for help from the British and wrote to Harold Macmillan. He wanted the assistance of around 350 combat aircraft and twelve squadrons of fighter aircraft.

Both countries responded. Dr Joshi comments:

'It's worth noting that the Americans did not give Nehru everything he wanted. They certainly were not willing to give him the level of air support that he was seeking. India's grave concern was that introducing the Indian Air Force against China, without proper US or British air defence of Indian cities, would lead to devastating retaliatory airstrikes. One of the most common complaints in Indian military circles to this day is that India should have used its aircraft and erred greatly in not doing so. This is debateable, but it is a widely held belief.'[9]

In addition, on the advice of the American Ambassador to Delhi, John Kenneth Galbraith, Riedel says, an American Navy carrier battle group was commissioned from the US Marine base in Honolulu. Underlining his favourable response, Kennedy gave his word that the supplies airlifts would increase, and that the US Navy would sail to the Bay of Bengal.

Suddenly, though, the Chinese announced a ceasefire and a withdrawal of the PLA to its side of the McMahon Line (which it refused to accept as legal).

Ceasefire notwithstanding, the Chinese remained in Aksai Chin but withdrew from NEFA while maintaining their claim on the territory.

China told India that the withdrawal was what it was and there was nothing more to be read into it. If India tried to seize an advantage, then the ceasefire would not hold.

The Chinese continued to withdraw PLA forces through December 1962.

Bruce Riedel says that China's cessation of hostilities was strategic. 'Mao had accomplished his goal of humiliating Nehru: China had prevailed over its Asian rival.'[10] Joshi adds that certainly India was humiliated in the eyes of many of its regional partners, and countries like Nepal had to think carefully about how they balanced their future relations between Beijing and New Delhi. They would be a little more cautious about siding with a defeated power.[11]

Riedel states that American and British support for India also played into Mao's decision. He knew that these countries would not stop their aid to India, and the Korea conflict had taught him that there were serious opponents who could inflict damage on his country. India fighting alone was manageable; the Allies working together gave him pause for thought.

The US had a few reasons for tilting towards India. It wanted India to support its covert pro-Tibetan operations in Tibet in order to build resistance to the march of Communism. It also wanted to work with the British to reduce tension over Kashmir, which both Pakistan and India wrestled over. The resulting proposal included working with the British to help India create an air defence plan.

The plan took effect in November 1963, when the Royal Air Force and the US Air Force each provided a fighter jet squadron for the purpose of exercises. Australia and Canada pitched in. Riedel says that the exercise showed that the US, the UK and the Commonwealth were prepared to come to the defence of India's skies.

For Shashank Joshi, the exercises, code-named *Shiksha*, which means 'learning', was a double-edged sword. He says that India wanted it to serve as a deterrent for China but on the other hand, India was embarrassed about its reliance on a series of pro-US, NATO countries. India's own claim to be 'non-aligned' was at serious risk and the delicate balancing of priorities would be an exercise for Nehru in the years after 1962. He needed Western support, but he did not wish to be seen as 'aligned' in the Cold War.[12]

In 1963, India agreed to work with the CIA to help the resistance movement the Tibetans were fighting to develop. The Indians created the Tibetan fighting group they called the Special Frontier Force (SFF), which would be supported by the CIA with a secret air force. The American planes were stationed in the east coast state of Odisha and would be co-ordinated by India's IB wing, the Aviation Research Centre.

Once Tibetans had been trained in Colorado and other CIA complexes, they needed to be parachuted into Tibet. India thought such drops would be too much of an incitement to the Chinese, so agreed instead to smuggle the Tibetans across the LAC. There were plenty of airdrops into Tibet too. Most of these were from sites outside India, such as East Pakistan (now Bangladesh).

The cooperation between India's IB and the CIA was eventually abandoned in the 1960s as the US changed its priorities.

NEFA, now the state of Arunachal Pradesh, remains highly militarized. Most Chinese soldiers are well to the rear of the border, in the inner, more distant parts of Tibet. China relies on transport links to 'surge' troops to the border, rather than keeping them close to it (like India). India holds the territory as best it can. Incursions by the Chinese occur frequently.

Since Indian Prime Minister Narendra Modi came to power, a nationalistic tone has crept into debates. India has been upgrading its defence capability at the border since the Manmohan Singh administration in the 2000s, before Modi came to power. It still does not match the mighty Dragon, but it aspires to do so.

Permission for the Dalai Lama to visit Tawang Monastery in April 2017 was described by China as a provocative act, which is why there was extra vigilance during the visit.

China still considers the territory its own. Bruce Riedel predicts the continuation of an uneasy truce but that a possible event outside the region may throw a grenade into the mix.

Joshi says that the Doklam stand-off over summer 2017 shows that the border remains a major flashpoint. The skirmish was the worst India–China crisis in thirty years, involving Chinese threats of war and serious tension. As both sides have differing perceptions of the LAC, such incidents are likely to recur, especially as they are used by the Chinese to intimidate India during key political moments, such as major bilateral political visits.[13] As for another visit to Arunachal Pradesh by a figure such as the Dalai Lama, the Chinese would not be happy.

Bruce Riedel comments, 'I think there would be pretty strong protests by the Chinese. I doubt that they will interfere on the ground. I think that's too risky. I think that Sino-Indian relations have evolved now to the point where there is mutual deterrence, because they both have nuclear weapons and a great deal of cooperation on economic and trade issues. I think there is another factor too, which wouldn't have been there a month ago, which is the Chinese are worried or anxious about the behaviour of the new Trump administration. I think they will have to be cautious. What the Chinese do not want is to push countries like India and Japan and Vietnam and others closer towards to the United States. So, I suspect they will be vociferous in their protest. The worst case for the Indians would be if the Trump administration now begins to treat the Dalai Lama with more importance than previous administrations have. The Dalai Lama has always visited the White House, but it's always been very low-key and informal. It's conceivable to me, I don't know, I don't talk to the Trump people for the most part but having taken a phone call of the president of Taiwan, I wouldn't be shocked at all to see the Dalai Lama get a more formal reception at the White House. Sometime in the future the Chinese would be very much irritated by something like that.'[14]

The border skirmishes between China and India have continued over the years. Generally, at any given time, one side's troops can be found on the other side of the notional boundary.

The problem is that with a demarcation that is so hotly contested, the border between China and its neighbours remains open to interpretation according to a country's mood on any given day.

*

In 2017, Indo-Sino relations were still in a poor state of health. China resents the fact that India, as it had done so many times before, allowed the Dalai Lama to visit the Tawang region in April 2017. China claims it as its own and the country still smarts from the Dalai Lama being given sanctuary in India.

But then for a couple of months at the border, things became very dicey.

It started with a standoff in Doklam there on 16 June 2017.

International attention focussed on the problem, fearing an escalation. This was justified as both sides reinforced their troops at a certain part of the approximately 3500-kilometre shared border.

The issue blew up when India objected to an attempt by China to lengthen a border road in an area that is known in India as Doklam and in China as Donglang. The road itself was being extended to the Jam Pheri ridge, according to Bhutan.

This plateau sits at the intersection of the tiny kingdom of Bhutan, the north-eastern Indian state of Sikkim, and China. The high, flat territory is an area of dispute between Bhutan and China. India and Bhutan have a Friendship Treaty that dates to the 1950s and was renewed in 2007.

Bhutan, according to Shashank Joshi, is probably the closest thing that India has to an ally in the subcontinent.[15] That's why, with China extending its border road, India became alarmed.

'This is because India and China also agreed in 2012 that the tri-junction would be determined through mutual consultations. China's road building violated that agreement, because it would have resulted in the tri-junction being pushed to the south,' says Joshi.

India's seven North-East states, of which Assam and Arunachal Pradesh form two, are only linked to the rest of India by a 19-kilometre wide corridor. An extended Chinese border road nearby would give that country increased access to this corridor, which is so thin it is commonly referred to as a 'chicken's neck'.

At Doklam, when Indians formed human 'walls', China immediately took umbrage, saying that India was stopping its 'normal activities' and demanded an immediate withdrawal.

While both sides rushed extra troops to the border, China responded to India's action by preventing around fifty-seven Hindu Indian pilgrims from travelling to the Mansarovar lake in Tibet. This lake is considered holy by Hindus and is a place of pilgrimage.

There is an agreement in place between the neighbours allowing devotees access to this lake under normal conditions. The route is usually through the freezing Nathu La Pass in Sikkim.

Bhutan, too, asked China to cease building the road. Meanwhile, tactics and strategy became a focal point of discussion on the fairly shouty Indian television news panels. 'What if' debates rose to a fever's pitch.

Indian military analysts talked about how India could go on the offensive against China. The country's annexation of Sikkim years earlier proved useful to India because that little former Himalayan kingdom was about the only part of the border where Indian soldiers had a strategic and land advantage. Indian posts in eastern Sikkim are at a higher altitude, able to look down on Chinese troops who are narrowly sandwiched in the Chumbi Valley between Bhutan and India.

The Indian foreign ministry stated that the action by the Chinese to build the road 'would represent a significant change of status quo with serious security implications for India'.[16]

The then Indian Defence and Finance Minister Arun Jaitley issued the warning that things were different this time round; this was not 1962 and India would protect its territory.

China, on the other hand, said that it had every right to build the road as the area was within its own territory and that Indian soldiers had been 'trespassing'. Further, it said that it was many times mightier than it had been in 1962. It also reminded India of the neighbour's defeat at its hands. It said that the border India spoke of in Sikkim had been fixed with the British in 1890, so it considered the breach by India as 'very serious'.[17]

Joshi explains: 'The border was broadly defined by the 1890 treaty, but it was not delimited in detail, and parts of the treaty clash in important ways: the border follows the watershed but is meant to start at Mount Gipmochi—which is not on the watershed. So, there are basic problems with the text itself. On top of that, China had agreed with Bhutan that it wouldn't unilaterally change the status quo and had agreed with India that it wouldn't change the tri-junction unilaterally— yet did just this. So, the issue is wider than the treaty itself.'[18]

Back door channels between India and China went into frenetic overdrive. Some minor skirmishes took place elsewhere on at the border at Ladakh. The border issue felt as though it was about to explode at any moment.

Bhutan's ambassador to India, Vetsop Namgyel, described China's road construction as being 'in violation of an agreement between the two countries'.[19] Bhutan and China do not have formal relations, but they do have contact through their channels in Delhi.

Perhaps China's reasons for the behaviour over Doklam suggested one analyst to a news organization,[20] were to get Bhutan to interact directly with China and become receptive to it in the manner that Nepal has done in recent decades.

So far, though, Bhutan has refused to accept closer relations with China, and, says this news organization, maintained its position as India's closest friend on the subcontinent.[21]

After 1962, there was friction at the Indo-Sino border in 1967, and in 1986–87 in the Sumdorong Chu crisis. But the 2017 flare-up was at another level and threatened the possibility of war, which had been absent on the previous two occasions.

With the Dalai Lama's continued presence in India and visit to Arunachal Pradesh, China's hackles were raised.

China eventually allowed the previously barred fifty-seven or so Hindu pilgrims to visit the holy lake, which was likely an indication that China was not wishing to escalate matters right along the whole border—just that part where China nudged Sikkim and Bhutan.

India pulled back its troops, and the Chinese did the same.

Just a week before Prime Minister Narendra Modi was due to visit his counterpart in China, the situation calmed down.

By the afternoon of Monday, 28 August 2017, the situation had de-escalated. China claimed victory, while a senior Indian government official called it an 'honourable draw'.[22] The fact that the two countries were about to attend a BRICS[23] summit together probably played a role in this.

China had warned India of 'serious consequences'[24] should the situation be allowed to escalate, and the fact remains that China's military might over that of India's is as supreme as it ever was. India had, in the beginning, declared that it would not back down, but seemed to have changed its mind later. I wonder if this had anything to do with its need for its trade with China.

But there is a larger reason behind the incident that led to this skirmish.

China is pursuing something it calls the Belt and Road Initiative (BRI). It's a twenty-first-century version of the old Silk land and sea routes to make an economic two-way super-highway between China and the rest of the world. Announced in 2013, it is a masterplan like no other and demonstrates the Chinese capacity for forward thinking while the world order changes and traditional power structures crumble. On the one hand, the BRI is a land route based on the Silk Route connecting China and Europe that includes trade and infrastructure projects. On the other hand, it's a modern maritime shipping pathway; an ocean-based interlinked system of port developments and shipping routes through the Pacific and Asia.

At the time of writing this manuscript it involves sixty-eight countries.[25]

This giant infrastructure project sits alongside China's assertive stance in the South China Sea over recent years; island-building and claiming territory there.

By building a road on the Doklam Plateau and creating a permanent, tangible presence the way it has in Nepal and Bangladesh, say analysts,[26] China is encircling India and strengthening its position.

Pakistan, for instance, gets the second largest amount on infrastructural investment in the world from China. Those new roads, as I have seen for myself in Nepal and Bangladesh, are wide enough for tanks to roll down, if needed. The plan is a pet project of President Xi Jinping and his country is spending billions of dollars across Africa, Asia, the Middle East and Europe on it.

The US and North Korea have taken an ambivalent position towards the BRI. The UK, the US Germany and France have attended meetings in Beijing to listen to the proposal, the most recent one of which at the time of writing was May 2017.

India was notably absent. It is boycotting the plan. It takes issue with a proposed corridor from China into Pakistan that would run through Pakistan-controlled portions of the historic state of Jammu and Kashmir, a state that both India and Pakistan lay claim to in its entirety. This corridor is said to have investments upwards of $ 46 billion. Also, in the proposal is a high-speed railway running from China to Singapore over 3000 kilometres.

There is a plan for a pipeline across Asia. New Zealand, the UK and the Arctic are also supposed to be in the mix at the concept stage. The BRI is something India fears but cannot stop if, and when, it goes ahead. Some construction is already underway.

The Doklam incident aside, analysts like Shashank Joshi feel that all-out war as it happened in 1962 is unlikely. Neither side is interested in war, says Bruce Riedel too, because China and India are 'competitors, not enemies, with a booming bilateral trade relationship'.[27]

28

TIBETAN TRAIL

Tibetans who have escaped and who live in India—and their ensuing progeny—do not always have an easy time, whether they are aristocrats or not. Challenges present themselves across class and generations. Tibetans in India may form a community that revolves around one charismatic spiritual leader in his eighties, but they still face the issue of being a minority that has had a traumatic history. I found the fascinating story of Tenzin Choegyal, the Dalai Lama's youngest brother, an example of the above.

Tenzin, also identified as an incarnation, enjoyed playing soldier as a young man and was later able to fulfil his dream of becoming a military man. Irreverent, with a face that easily breaks into an ironic smile, he is capable of being serious and humorous in one go. The Dalai Lama likes to have him accompany him when he travels, so he is often in the background on visits round India or elsewhere in the world.

(In recent years, though, the Dalai Lama has reduced his international travel on medical advice).

After answering my questions during our interview, Tenzin told me how talking about 1959 and the years after reminded him of something his famous elder brother said to him about his life. Tenzin had, after all, been put into monastic Buddhist training since he had been recognized as a reincarnation. He told me, 'I'll tell you something that's very, very hilarious. Whenever we talk about escaping in 1959 His Holiness teases me, saying that,' he laughed as he said this, 'there are many people who escaped that year, but most people felt sad.' Then he added, 'You should be feeling happy because you don't have to go back to the monastery.

'I think in a way it's true, because firstly I don't have to wear a monk's robe, and second I could go to a school, which I always wanted to do. Yes, for me I lost my country, but I think that opened up a lot of things for me individually.'[1]

Thus, Tenzin appears to look on the escape of March 1959 as an event that allowed him to pursue his ambitions for a mainstream childhood, away from strict monastic confines in draughty temples where he apparently did not feel too free. He seemed to long to be like other children; those who weren't training to be monks.

'In what way did your life change when you came to India?' I asked him.

'If I'd stayed in the monastery I wouldn't know. I might know the scriptures, but my interpretation of the scripture will be different because I don't know the other side. I think it's okay to say that for me I think it [coming to India] became a very lucky break in life,' he replied.

I continued, 'So what did you get a chance to do?'

Tenzin paused before answering, 'I went to school. I enjoyed school. I became a college dropout. Then I had my hippy days.'[2]

In 2008, Tenzin gave an interview to a magazine, *Lion's Roar*, that covers Buddhism-related matters.

It says that once the family had been found a place to stay in India, Tenzin Choegyal attended St Joseph's Jesuit boarding school in Darjeeling. He was thirteen.

The establishment had been a popular choice for rich Tibetan families for a couple of decades. At St Joseph's, Tenzin needed to learn English pretty much from scratch. He apparently found math a challenge and tried his best to fit in. But it seems he did not want to study very hard. 'I was very lazy; slothful is the word,' he told *Lion's Roar*.[3]

The article says that Tenzin then, and now, was popular, so he had lots of friends with whom to while away his time. After nine years he graduated and enrolled at a Darjeeling College. Then he won a scholarship to a community college in Washington state. Here, writes the magazine, he managed to maintain an average B plus in his studies. Then, suddenly, he apparently grew homesick.

He told the magazine that he had had a case of 'culture shock'.[4] Abandoning his US college, he returned to Dharamsala. His sister Jetsun Pema had founded a hostel and school for refugee children from Tibet. Tenzin started teaching there.

A beautiful Tibetan, Rinchen Khando, was a secretary in the administrator's office.[5] Tenzin married her and by the time he was twenty-eight, was father to both a daughter and a son. Later, Tenzin Choegyal's wife, Rinchen Khando, would go on to become the Tibetan government in exile's minster of education and found the Tibetan Nuns project mentioned in an earlier chapter.

I had the good fortune of spending time with Rinchen Khando later on during a visit to the Tibetan Nuns project. I was shown round the airy, light, modern yet traditional ecclesiastical building and saw the canteen and a butter sculpting room. I met with ladies who had chosen to remain within a Buddhist study environment while not training to become nuns creating handicrafts for sale in the nunnery shop.

With a quiet strength, she spoke candidly of her life and work, what she is doing, and the plans to allow lay ladies to attend workshops at the project.

We sat talking on the steps in a stone courtyard that is open to the sky. She is planning to extend the building to create more facilities with the help of its architect Munishwar Nath Ashish Ganju, the same architect who worked on the courtyard roof of the temple by the Dalai Lama's residence. The few hours I spent in the company of Mrs Rinchen Khando will stay with me.

I could see what may have drawn Tenzin to her.

Mrs Khando's husband had been telling me about his earlier years. 'Then I rediscovered the values of Buddhist philosophy, I enjoyed studying. I'm still studying, and then I was able to go and be a soldier for a while, which I used to dream about.' His voice rose as he said the next part, 'I think I did a lot of things that I really enjoyed, yes. I joined the Special Frontier Force, which is composed of Tibetan men, and this was first started by, I think it's the continuation of what the CIA did with Tibetan recruits. Later on, they had an understanding with the Government of India, particularly after '62. Then, both the Government of India and the USA, they joined hand in hand and raised this unit as crack troops. Now this came into being in October 1962. I joined in August '75, so it's peace time, but during that time young Tibetans were encouraged to do National Service. Actually, I was going there for six months, but then I got stuck for two and a half years.'

After the Indo-Sino war, the newly formed SFF that Tenzin later joined became a part of the Indian army. The *Lion's Roar* piece describes it as: 'A covert unit in charge of gathering intelligence and fighting terrorism at the country's porous borders. When Choegyal joined the SFF, it was comprised almost entirely of Tibetans. (Today the SFF ranks are more diversified, but there are still an estimated 10,000 Tibetans serving in the force.)'[6]

I asked Tenzin if he enjoyed being a soldier, to which he said, 'I enjoyed the army life, but I didn't like the higher up state . . . As a matter of fact, I left the force by accusing the Inspector General of corruption!'[7]

Tenzin Choegyal took early retirement, at thirty-six. He returned to Dharamsala. The magazine article says that after a short while Tenzin felt able to work again, first in the Dalai Lama's security department, then as his Private Secretary for a while. This post is now held by Tenzin Taklha, Namgyal Lhamo Taklha's son and nephew both of Tenzin as well as of the Dalai Lama.

The Private Secretary post is the first and final port of call for all those seeking the Dalai Lama's time. There are six secretaries in separate departments. It involves managing the Dalai Lama's diary—all his communications and travel arrangements.

The Dalai Lama still values Tenzin's presence. For Tenzin, his revered brother is a god-hero whom he loves serving. He seems to have found contentment even while being able to retain a surprising outspokenness and an endearing, searing frankness that cuts through anything woolly.

He is deeply spiritual and thoughtful, a very calm Rinpoche who takes his religion seriously.

*

While Tenzin leads a quiet, well-organized life, setting aside time for contemplation, his brother, the Dalai Lama has an extremely disciplined routine; rising early and retiring to bed early.

The Dalai Lama's day begins at 3 a.m., when he showers after waking up. After this, until 5 a.m., he prays, meditates and performs prostrations. At 5 a.m., the Dalai Lama walks for half an hour around his garden, the one he allowed me into. If rain prevents the outdoor exercise, the leader of the Tibetan Buddhists walks barefoot on a treadmill in his quarters.

A typical breakfast consists of hot porridge, a barley powder known as *tsampa,* bread with jam or marmalade, and tea, taking place at 5.30 a.m. for half an hour. During breakfast, the Dalai Lama listens to the BBC's World Service News, joining the biggest English-speaking radio audience on the planet.

At 6 a.m., he picks up his morning meditation and prayers for another three hours. That's five hours in total so far. At 9 a.m., the Dalai Lama uses the next two and a half hours in the study of Buddhist texts and commentaries. The Dalai Lama's lunch is served at 11.30 a.m. In Dharamsala, the spiritual leader eats vegetarian food.[8] However, his website states that he does not always maintain a vegetarian diet when he is travelling outside Dharamsala.

This is the Dalai Lama's routine. It sets a marker for young monks and nuns to try to follow in their respective monasteries and nunneries.

*

Besides Tenzin, there's another, younger ex-monk who found he could not handle the strictures of monastic training. But the Buddhist faith is broad and welcomes such individuals whether they choose to become monks or not.

Jampa Phende's name means someone who is caring, helpful and happy. I found that he reflects his name because he is always jolly and content. Like countless others, he rebelled against a strict monastic upbringing simply because his non-theological interests were forbidden at that time.

As I sat in my room at the Gakyi Khang Zhang hotel, Jampa told me about his curriculum. It provided a useful insight into what Tenzin Choegyal might have studied had he continued his formal monk learning.

'We had all modern education. Mathematics, geography, world history, Indian history, science, Tibetan writing, reading all the grammar, English.' The inhibiting factor for Jampa was the rigidity.

Movies and sport were forbidden pastimes. 'As a huge fan of movies and sports, I had to break many rules. Now when I look back those were such interesting, wonderful days of my life.'

Tibetan monks and nuns are not secretive. Much of their learning processes are on display to the public. Their strict code of discipline for self-training is called the *Vinaya*, and was set down by the Buddha.

This is what Jampa's schedule looked like.

'We had to get up around 5 a.m., then we had morning prayers followed by breakfast.' Then came the learning of scriptures, for which Jampa has invented a verb—'by hearting'.

School classes ran from 9 a.m. to 12 p.m. After a break for lunch, there were more classes from 2 to 5 p.m. Then, 5 to 6 p.m. was for a dinner break, after which the teenagers studied once again from 6 p.m. to 8.30 p.m. Vinaya rules state that dinner is forbidden. This is where the young monk Jampa suffered acutely, as he and his fellow monks got hungry in the evenings and the light snack of a loaf of bread was never enough for the growing, energetic young men. Jampa told me he and his friends would share any extra food saved between them.

'We had to by heart many scriptures. After 8.30 p.m. we had to go back to our residential places and then again, there we have teachers, we have to again learn scriptures and we have to again recite what we had learnt in the morning and evening in school. Then until 11 p.m. we have to study and after 11 p.m. we can sleep. During that time, it felt that the days were hard, but now I can say it's worth it.'

Today, Jampa Phende leads a more relaxed lifestyle, enjoying a lie in on Sundays and watching his favourite football team, Real Madrid, play when there is an electricity supply in the monastery.

However, Jampa's monastic learning taught him a great deal.

Jampa explained that in his Buddhist training days he had little knowledge of 'the whole world, and about scriptures'. 'I don't harm people because of all those lessons I got. I'm no more a monk but the things I learnt in the monastery help me here in Tawang. I'm happy for all those lessons.'

He said that apart from a few key things there was also a way of thinking that has stayed with him. 'From the age of ten, we were taught to respect other people. We are taught to pray, to think about good things, to do only that which is good for other people. Modern languages, modern studies like mathematics and English are also very helpful. If I didn't study then, I wouldn't be an English teacher now. I would be doing a much harder job.

'But now I love what I do and how I live, teaching around 100 students in this small monastery. I was a monk and I studied in the monk community. Now it is time for me to pay back.'

When I asked him if he would like to do this work for the rest of his life, Jampa reflected.

'Maybe. It's nice to be in the monk community. You need not worry about the haste of society. In the monk community the way of thinking is different to the people outside, in the city.'

But growing up in the monastery wasn't a bed of roses, Jampa said. The discipline was harsh, and punishment was often meted out. 'You got slashes, you got beaten up, you have to prostrate thousands of times in the prayer hall. One of the hardest things was by hearting the scriptures. You have to mug up piles of scriptures, piles of books. It was too difficult for me; keeping in mind the scriptures. Getting up early in the morning, staying up late, by hearting.'

By fifteen, the football and cricket loving boy monk would frequently run away from the monastery to play in the forest. Back then, he often thought: 'They could have given us permission for us to play sport on our birthdays or to learn by watching television programmes instead of banning it.'

He would abscond at night to a nearby town to watch movies.

He received severe punishments each time on his return after absconding. He found it all hard to take, and coupled with the scripture learning, he got disillusioned. One of Jampa's biggest challenges during the daily curriculum was debate time (I have described what happens in debating sessions in an earlier chapter), when trainee monks have to use learnt scriptures to reinforce their arguments against a challenger. The stress of trying to focus on what he had learnt so that he could recite the words rapidly to his interlocutors was all too much for him.

Thousands of monk students around the world probably mirror Jampa Phende's experiences, some choosing to stick with the course while others decide to leave their orders. But I have observed that even those who step away from monastic life remain in close contact with their former schoolfellows and teachers, always showing them respect. They seem to have a stillness and peace about them, even now. Many of them, without a doubt, revere the Dalai Lama.

Jampa Phende described to me how it was for him during the Dalai Lama's 2017 Tawang visit. 'During all the teachings, when the Dalai Lama came here recently, he advised us to keep our minds calm.

"When we get any trouble, any problem, be happy, and think it's due to karma!" These words help me so much.'

As a Monpa of ethnic Tibetan heritage who lived in India, and someone who revered the Dalai Lama, I asked Jampa if he felt Indian. He replied, 'More like a Tibetan. I have an Indian passport and am an Indian citizen, but I was brought up in the Tibetan community. I am part of Tibetan society, I was educated in Tibetan, I eat my food the Tibetan way. Not that I don't like India. Here, all the world's major religions live together. India is a good place with good people in it.'[9]

One refrain I heard from every Tibetan I met is that they want to go to Tibet. And Jampa is no exception. 'Of course, I want to go Lhasa once in this life. I used to tell my friends, "One day I'll go to Lhasa and I'll take one picture in front of Potala. There's a very famous statue of the future Buddha, and I want to see that."'

Jampa had strong feelings about what it is like to live by the Indo-Sino border. 'The Chinese see Arunachal as their part, Tawang as their part, so whenever people from Arunachal go to get visas to go to Tibet, the Chinese embassy tells us, "You are our own people. Why do you need visas to go to your own home place?" The Chinese government gives us some special papers.'

Jampa did not feel secure with these. 'What will happen if we come back?' In other words, perhaps he was not sure if he would be allowed to leave China in the first instance and re-enter India in the second.

'We don't want to be under China or Tibet our whole lives. I want to spend my life in Tawang. If we take what they give us; special papers, a special pass to go to Tibet, there will be problems when we come back. We won't be allowed back or maybe at the airport the Indian police would question us because we have Indian passports but something different instead of visas. I want to come back—one week is enough to be in Tibet.'[10]

People broadly know about the story of the Tibetans who fled China following the Dalai Lama's escape in 1959, but they know little about what happens to them once they manage to get across the border.

There are Tibetan communities scattered all over the world—in Canada, the US, Europe—but the largest number of refugees live in India. Countries like Canada have periodic special refugee intake programmes. In many cities in India there are Tibetan centres where the culture is promoted, where the Dalai Lama's birthday is celebrated, and where you will frequently find an office with large rectangular photos of him on the walls. There will often be an official or three coordinating Tibet related activity or regional visits from the Dalai Lama.

The 150,000 refugees India took in have settled across the country, some still in camps, or, as in Dharamsala, in integrated communities.

In McLeod Ganj and beyond, nestling in the mountains, steep pathways and half constructed new buildings, is a busy and bustling little township. There are cheap and expensive restaurants, hostels and meditation centres.

Walking downhill from McLeod Ganj, one can go to the Library of Tibetan Works and Archives buildings, where audio visual, photographic and documentary records are kept. The archive is manned by a helpful Tibetan called Tashi, who, when I visited, patiently studied all his lists and brought out anything he could think of that might contain evidence related to the story being narrated here.

Throughout my trip to look for records of the March 1959 escape, I found very little apart from some of Har Mander Singh's own photographs reproduced in books and albums. It was as though I was finding mirror images of my research as I hunted for new information.

In McLeod Ganj, there was an atmosphere of healthy Indo-Tibetan culture. From my small hotel, the walk down to the main bazaar passed an expensive two-floor hotel with fashionable Indo-Tibetan tones reflected in the furniture and decor. The bazaar was nearly like any other hill station in India, with small cafés, *dhabas,* bookshops, clothes shops and souvenir stalls. The difference here was that you could see a mainly Tibetan population, descendants of those who fled in 1959 along with their families.

Each stallholder and shop owner may have a hidden story to tell. Ask them to talk and you may make intriguing discoveries. Dotted around are souvenir shops selling handbound notebooks, Tibetan prayer flags, books and writing materials. There was even a Tibetan tailor displaying Tibetan tops, chubas, striped aprons and similar items. I got talking to her and she told me: 'I had to leave my son and family behind.' She shook her head wistfully. 'I would love to go back some day and see them.'

It is difficult to understand why Tibetans would take such life-threatening journeys and run the risk of never seeing their families again, but those that worship the Dalai Lama and look to him as their teacher want to follow their religion peacefully.

In China, it is forbidden to keep images of the Dalai Lama at home or anywhere else. He is seen as a 'splittist, a separatist' whose main aim is to divide China and disrupt its 'One China' policy.

The One China policy states that the whole of China is united, even though the country has regions with their own cultures, languages, and religions. Two prominent areas are the Tibetan plateau and the territory where mainly Muslim Uighurs live. China has sought to merge these two communities more with mainstream society.

Many Tibetans fleeing China have found they can get to the country's border via a route that takes them through blinding snow and dangerous terrain. This journey has them passing the base of Mount Everest to the Nepalese border, and many refugees have perished. Some of them suffer snow blindness, frostbite and other disease, that is, if they ever get to the border. In recent years, even this escape route has become more perilous with an increase in Chinese vigilance at the border.

Out of the trickle of Tibetans, some do make it to the Nepalese border, but they face a tough time once they get across. Those that choose to or those that get caught go to a processing centre in Kathmandu where procedures can take weeks or months. This centre, set back from the main road and not easily accessible to general visitors, is like a sorting post for those who want to get to India—to go to Dharamsala or settle somewhere else in a land that they see as full of hope and opportunity. Some may fail the several levels of interviews and form filling. If they escape being sent back, they disappear into the Nepalese black economy.

Between 1959 and 1989, many were given refugee cards after they had been 'processed' via a refugee centre not open to the general public or the media. Since 1989, these cards are rarely handed out.

Undocumented Nepali Tibetans who do not have refugee cards are unable to own property, businesses or even a vehicle. The aim for many is to get processed and pass through Nepal to get to India, where they can disappear or travel to Dharamsala to be close to the Dalai Lama.

In Nepal, unable to officially work, drive or get a formal education, they resort to illegal work and are susceptible to addictions such as drugs and alcohol. Mostly, they settle in the capital.

With every year that China extends financial support to Nepal, it strengthens its hold on the country. Joint military and security agreements have been designed to secure the Chinese border from escaping Tibetans. Chinese security works very tightly with Nepali forces nowadays. The operation has been so successful that the number of Tibetans making the precarious journey around Mount Everest to Nepal, often wearing ordinary cotton day clothes, has shrunk to less than 200 a year when once it was in the thousands. In Nepal, to be a Tibetan is to be a second-class citizen.

When I raised the issue on behalf of BBC News with a Nepali home ministry government official, he yelled at me and got cross. He told me to go and discuss the subject with the ministry of foreign affairs. So, I asked a Nepali government Joint Secretary on Foreign Affairs, Arjun Thapa, about the topic. He went on the record for me and said, tellingly, 'When they [Tibetans] come here, we are not happy. The Government of Nepal is not happy because we don't want to carry out any activities which may be detrimental to the interests of our neighbour, China.'[11]

In April 2013, when I was in Nepal, President Jimmy Carter was in Kathmandu visiting his Carter Centre[12] in the country. I asked him about the plight of Tibetans in Nepal.

He told me, 'The Tibetan refugees should be welcomed. There has, as you know, been a tacit agreement in the past that the refugees coming out of Tibet would not be abused when they arrived here but lately I understand that at the border, there has been some harassment of people coming from Tibet. The Chinese government is putting pressure on officials in Nepal to interrupt this movement of people. I think they should have a right to go where they wish.'[13]

This answer, which was reproduced in national newspapers the very next day, drew, according to the Director of the Carter Centre, an irate response from a Chinese official in Kathmandu. The Director himself told me that he was not very pleased that I had asked the former American President this question.

Thapa said that Nepal likes its inhabitants to be sensitive to its 'China Policy' and not carry out 'anti-China activity'.[14]

Before my BBC report,[15] it had, according to Nepal watchers, not been at all clear about what 'anti-China activity' was.

Then Arjun Thapa elucidated it in his interview with me. 'According to our own China policy we are not supposed to allow any anti-China activities in Nepal. For example, they [the Tibetans] sometimes stage a huge demo in front of the Chinese embassy and sometimes, for example, they chant anti-Chinese slogans.'[16]

It was a rare and revelatory on the record explanation by a Nepali government official.

Away from Kathmandu, in the mountains, Tibetans from remote villages in Nepal by the Tibetan border are now producing their second and third generations. But the younger Tibetans mostly leave their rural homes and drift down to the capital, where there is more activity and excitement. But just as in India, they have no citizenship or official status, which leads to a feeling of disconnection and being in limbo.

To witness this for myself, I journeyed up to the Tibetan village of Bridim by the Tibetan border. Here, original Tibetan clothes, handicrafts, culture and the language are lovingly retained.

When I visited, there was a set of shacks to one side of Bridim village, where elderly relatives live in poverty and ill health.

One woman, who could barely walk, was only a few hundred feet from the village health centre but was unable to get to it and no one from the health centre would come up to see to her. She sadly passed away in a major earthquake in the area in 2015.

In Dhunche, Langtang, there is a Special Education Academy for Disabled Children. I've been there.

Here, the ethnic locals are the Tamang people from Tibet, who were said to be the king's mountain cavaliers. They speak a Tibetan dialect and practise Buddhism or their original Shamanic Bon religion.

Over 90 per cent of disabled Nepalese children never attend school. In the Academy for Disabled children are a few albino children too. The one carer supposed to be in charge of this place was not even in attendance the day I visited. Apparently, he often goes missing, leaving the children as I found them—silent, forlorn, not even playing, looking lost and alien. This is their home, but sadly in the outside world, they are pariahs, and considered to have a contagious disease. They tend to die young, so are not considered worth educating. The Dolma Development Fund tries to have these children placed in well-equipped schools, but for the ethnic Tibetan young, life is set against them. Middle class educators are too scared to accept the children for fear of parents removing current students from school.

But not everything is bleak for people living in this area.

Travel tour and trekking organizer, Tsering Lama, and former banker, Tim Gocher, set up a non-profit organisation bringing eco-tourism and scholarships to ethnic Tibetans in the area. The Dolma Foundation has educated scores of impoverished children in the Langtang mountains of Nepal, and recently rebuilt the whole village after it was devastated in the 2015 earthquake.

On the trek up to Bridim from the main road, there is a Tibetan refugee settlement. Here I found a young couple whose baby girl had just been born.

Every so often the Dalai Lama's local representative team visits them to provide some modest financial support. This is the only means the couple has to survive, but like most other Tibetans in south Asia, they have no residential status. They told me that they see no hope of a secure future for their little daughter either. Their plight is mirrored by thousands of Tibetan refugees in south Asia, young and old, caught in limbo with nowhere to go.

29

THE TIBETAN STATE

After the Dalai Lama fled Tibet, there was so much that had been left behind suddenly; so many loved ones who were unable to escape and so much the Tibetans in exile wanted to know, that a fact-finding mission to Tibet was deemed essential. In 1980, one was granted permission by the Chinese.

Lobsang Samten, the Dalai Lama's late older brother, was one of the people who was allowed to be a part of this mission. His widow, Namgyal Lhamo Taklha, told me, 'From 1959, a few refugees were coming out and we knew nothing about what was happening. Then the Chinese permitted the Tibetans to come and see what was happening there.

'It's very complicated, how it was opened up. I heard that the higher leaders of the Chinese in Peking, they didn't think the situation was that bad in Tibet because the officials in Tibet were saying: "Everything's good, fine." When the delegation came in 1980, a fact-finding delegation, people came running to see them and it was very emotional and then the delegations saw how poor Tibet was, how much suffering the people had gone through.'

Lobsang Samten was a part of the first delegation, and his visit home was to have disastrous consequences, as Namgyal explained. 'He came back very sad and very upset and very stressed and I think it was due to that that he passed away in 1985.'[1]

Since that time, more and more stringent rules and controls have been applied in Tibet.

Still, the Dalai Lama advocates a peaceful existence without violence.

Some Tibetans protest Chinese control to the extreme by killing themselves, often setting themselves on fire. They turn in on themselves to remonstrate against their restricted lives. They have used self-immolation in various countries—China, Nepal, India. Sometimes, they do this at significant public places.

I visited the Boudha stupa in Kathmandu where one such suicide took place. A thirty-eight-year-old monk set fire to himself in 2013 in front of devotees at this famous religious and tourist shrine.

As a result, in places like the Boudha stupa in Kathmandu there is a web of CCTV cameras, a high level of police and security presence— the men patrol with wooden sticks and stand on guard outside monasteries.

In Nepal, there is a ban on public celebrations of the Dalai Lama's birthday, and the Dalai Lama's representative in Nepal refuses to meet visitors in the open. He feels more secure talking inside closed premises like a hotel room.

Tibetans here sometimes live in fear and second-generation men and women talk wistfully as they look across the mountains, longing to visit the land of their forefathers.

In contrast, McLeod Ganj in India feels as though it is a much freer Tibet, where the religion, culture and languages are easily practised.

At the top of the winding path that leads to the bazaar there is a museum displaying modern Tibetan art. It is a bright space with white walls and large windows. The place feels open, symbolizing the lack of restriction.

Here, there are also annual film festivals, mostly showing movies with a Himalayan or Tibetan theme. At the approach to the grand temple there is a tall, black statue of a male Tibetan on fire; it stands imposing and proud, a symbol of the Tibetan spirit of resistance.

Further along the right, there is a first wall commemorating those who have committed suicide. Some are as young as fifteen, and they lived in different parts of China. Under each photo is a name, age, where they lived, where they killed themselves and how. It's a sobering sight.

Around the hill that houses the grand temple and past the hillside rocks are Tibetan inscriptions. Some of them are simple Buddhist texts, others are messages to the Dalai Lama.

After climbing for twenty minutes, I arrived at a large flat area with a platform. Looking out to the horizon and there is another wall of photographs; here are more suicide victims who chose to control their own destinies by dying as opposed to living in an environment where they were controlled by others.

While to date authorities report suicides climbing to over 150, there may be more that go unreported. And with extra vigilance now, there are many who attempt to kill themselves but fail. Authorities want to prevent another embarrassing addition to the statistics. For this reason, when would-be self-immolators are identified in the act, they are immediately scooped up and rushed to hospital. Often, they die, but if they survive, they may disappear into the system.

*

I wanted to know Har Mander's views on the topic.

On a visit to New Delhi, I asked him to join me for a short walk. We found a bench to sit on in a grassy area in the colony.

He said, 'My personal feeling, is that the Tibetans are very different from the Chinese people. But that's big politics and I'm a very small man but I always pray that Tibetans should get their homeland. Meanwhile it makes me very happy that these settlements made for Tibetans in our country are prospering and Tibetans are doing very important jobs all over India.'

'But how does it make you feel when they kill themselves?' I asked him.

'This kind of thing happens all over the world when people get very emotional. The ultimate sacrifice is to give your own life. It shows the devotion of the people to the Dalai Lama and their country,' he replied. 'It doesn't mean that I support it.'

I then asked Har Mander what his views were on the countries that are involved in this matter, to which he said, 'China is becoming a great power. The difficult part of China is wearing away . . . Becoming more a money state and people are getting used to some kind of democracy like America. In the future, it will certainly be one of the greatest countries of the world. With America, with the European Union.'

'And what is the future for the Dalai Lama?' I queried.

'He has himself said he is not sure whether there'll be a successor or not. He mentions there may be no Dalai Lama and that the dynasty ends with the Fourteenth.

'There are many possibilities. One possibility is that the Chinese will, following the same rituals, produce a Dalai Lama and say that this is a Fifteenth Dalai Lama. There is very little possibility that the world will be able to accept that. In this great world's struggle for supremacy by various countries, little Tibet has lots to fight for and I, who have interacted with them [Tibetans] at some point, will always pray for their happiness and good fortune,' said Har Mander.[2]

*

Tenzin Choegyal, is realistic about his own status. Like his brother, he thinks that the Tibetans often need more initiative to help themselves.

'Today we are stateless, and for travel purposes we are getting an identity certificate, but legally we are not covered at all. We are very naïve. We let things happen to us. I think we are gentle, we are very kind, but we are not made to compete. There's something wrong in our culture.'

'So, do you think it can survive, Tenzin?' I asked him.

He paused thoughtfully before replying, 'Yeah. I don't think our surviving is a problem. I think people should make it survive by realizing its value, rather than just keep it going. We keep it going for a reason, so it used to be-whatever value we have at large, I think those values should serve people, serve us, but just to save them as a tradition doesn't make sense anymore.'

'Play the game? Then you'll lose the gentleness,' I commented.

Laughingly, he responded, 'Yeah, that's true, so we have to choose. But then, you know, there is a time to die. There is a time to merge. There is a time for growth. Maybe our culture and our race, maybe we are supposed to disappear? I don't know . . . or let assimilation take place. That's a gentler way of disappearing. I don't know, but then these are large issues concerning a lot of people . . . I can't ask more. No, I always say that we are being indifferent, and my wife doesn't agree. From early morning on we go into an argument! I think we are not doing enough. We have to become more vibrant.'

I asked him how this could be done.

'Well, take an interest in life, do something to achieve results,' he replied.[3]

Tenzin added that the Dalai Lama keeps a sense of perspective and concerns himself with world peace rather than just having a narrow Tibet focus.

Tenzin remains close to the Dalai Lama and his siblings. I am told that when the family gets together, there are lots of in-jokes, much laughter and an ease of familiarity among these aristocrats from Tibet. No one takes themselves too seriously.

In the interview that Tenzin gave to Buddhist magazine the *Lion's Roar*, he described what happened when he got together with his sister and his holy elder brother. These three siblings, he told the interviewer, were the youngest of their generation of siblings. He speaks reverentially of how much the Dalai Lama has influenced him.

'He has made me into what I am today. It probably wasn't intended.'[4]

This doesn't mean that teasing between the two brothers does not happen, with Tenzin Choegyal usually being the recipient rather than the other way around.

'Sometimes, when he says something I don't agree with, His Holiness says, "Oh, look at your face! You're already making a face!"'[5]

Tenzin calls his brother 'Your Presence'.

In the *Lion's Roar* piece, the Dalai Lama echoed Tenzin Choegyal's sentiments of being close to his two youngest siblings. He said that when the three of them are together, then: 'It's like we are at the top of the world. We're quite similar too. Straightforward, openhearted. My younger brother has quite a sharp mind.'

For the rest of the family, he said, 'My oldest brother is now very sick in America. My second brother is mostly in Hong Kong; our relationship has a little bit of distance. Then his father,' he gestured towards his translator, also his nephew, sitting on his right, 'we were very, very close. When he passed away, I felt very sad. When I was born, my eldest sister actually opened one of my eyes. My mother was a very dignified, warmhearted person. She was very, very gentle—none of my brothers and sisters ever experienced her temper. My father, on the other hand, was quick to lose his.'[6]

In 1990, Tenzin Choegyal stood for election to the Tibetan parliament in exile. Each of the thirteen divisions of Tibet is represented by the Tibetan government in Dharamsala, with Tenzin representing his childhood province of Amdo. He was a representative for five years. During this time, he concerned himself with the rights and integration of refugees and the preservation of Tibetan culture.

He resigned, yet again. He explained a bit of the reason to his 2008 interlocutor, 'There's a tremendous opportunity if you look at how much sympathy we have from the free world, but I don't think we are utilizing it. We're just bogged down with solving small problems, when we can be doing much bigger things, like making sure that Tibetans in India have employment, and that nobody is living under the poverty line.'[7]

As for the monks populating the narrow hill lanes of McLeod Ganj, he said, 'We are operating in a very peculiar situation—we are in exile. I love Tibet, and I really wish success to our cause and our people, but I'm very concerned with the way we are heading. Whatever we do in life, we have to love it or leave it. If each individual realizes his or her potential and tries to transform and becomes less selfish, I think we'll have a wonderful future, a wonderful Tibet.'[8]

*

There has been a shift in the mindset of the affluent part of mainstream Chinese society over recent years. The BBC's Jon Sudworth, who was based in Beijing in 2018, filed a news report in 2015 that featured a former senior Communist party official who prayed in front of a shrine that included a picture of the Dalai Lama in his own home. This act is forbidden for many Tibetans, so for a top ex-official to allow himself to be broadcast by the BBC in this way sent out a message to the world. The filming was not even covert; the ex-official knew what he was doing. The official's name is Xiao Wunan and he is the Deputy Chairman of the Asia Pacific Exchange and Cooperation Foundation (APECF).

APECF is considered by many to be supported by and have the approval of the Chinese government—one of its softer, milder acolytes. It seems to be part of China's soft diplomacy arm, for it was involved in a multi-billion-dollar investment cultivating a Buddhist location in Nepal.

Mr Xiao is rumoured to come from a well-connected family, and certainly he has enough high-powered contacts to be able to be outspoken. He was introduced to the BBC by an intermediary.

The BBC report shows a senior Tibetan Buddhist Monk called Geshe Sonam sitting next to Mr Xiao but stated that the former did not wish to discuss the Dalai lama or politics at that time. Mr Xiao dismissed any controversy around the Tibetan spiritual leader.

'In regard to the political problems between the Dalai Lama and China . . . we hardly pay any attention,' he said. 'It's really hard for us to judge him from that angle. As Buddhists, we only pay attention to him as part of our Buddhist practice.'[9]

At this meeting, Xiao Wunan gave the BBC a video, recorded when he met the Dalai Lama in Dharamsala in 2012. In the video exchange, the Dalai Lama told Xiao Wunan that he was worried about Buddhists in China being exploited by fake monks. The former Chinese official replied, 'We are really in need of a Buddhist leader. I think Your Holiness can play such an important role.'[10]

Sudworth's report posits the theory that allowing the release of the video is significant. Either China may be signalling a softening of its anti-Dalai Lama stance and an interest in dialogue, or else it wishes to appear to be doing so perhaps.

The man who introduced Mr Xiao to the BBC was a wealthy businessman in his thirties, Sun Keijia. Mr Sun is part of a growing trend of wealthy Chinese who no longer derive complete joy from consumerism alone as they and everyone in their lives have got all the accoutrements of a high net-worth lifestyle. Since there is little more they seek to buy, they turn to spiritualism in fear of losing their new-found riches. They seek protection, and the easiest way is to turn to the Buddhism sitting on their own doorstep. Even here, though, competition kicks in. In his piece, Jon Sudworth quoted writer Ian Johnson: 'But there's still often an element of status competition in their spiritual pursuits. In the past, it was who knew the highest-level official. But now the wealthy are competing over who patronizes the most powerful monk.'[11]

Previously, there was an order to Chinese society but with certain reforms and economic growth, the rigid structures of society have loosened so much that a new anxiety and uncertainty is in the air.

Mr Sun, for instance, told Sudworth that he was once faced with big business problems that he could not solve working on his own. So, he turned to 'Buddha, ghosts and God'. Mr Sun decided that his salvation lay with Tibetan monks. The strategy seems to have worked as he is now said to be worth over $ 100 million.

Where once, and even now, monasteries had been, and are sometimes still overrun, and overt Dalai Lama followers beaten, Mr Sun owns a chain of Buddhist clubs. He personally pays for monks like Geshe Sonam to preach in them. He also gives them donations for their monasteries and religious buildings back in Tibet. The influencers who attend these clubs are looking for spiritual guidance like Mr Sun. He told Jon Sudworth, 'What I want is influence. My friends who come here are attracted to this place. I can use the resources they bring to do my other business. From that angle, it is also my contribution for spreading Buddhism. This brings good karma and so I get what I want.'[12]

Sun invited the BBC team to meet some of the rich patrons who use his club. A photograph shows Sun and two of them sitting round in a circle with their eyes closed and their hands folded. Geshe Sonam is blessing their watches, necklaces and beads. One of them, a woman, in turn presents a man she describes as an important office bearer in the National Development and Reform Commission of China. After the prayers, the camera team witness an opulent meal at a round table.

The lama professes to feeling conflicted. He feels he could use his time better and eat more quickly rather than wait to get through several lavish courses. On the other hand, he knows that going out and about among the population is a way of helping others.

Sudworth states, 'Buddhist monks need the money and dozens, perhaps hundreds, are now prospecting for funds in China's big cities.'[13]

This Chinese-Buddhist phenomenon has been gaining attention steadily since around 2013. Reuters theorized that that it may be because President Xi Jinping might have a softer side than might be expected.

While economic growth is China's mantra, President Xi apparently has concerns about the single-minded pursuit of material wealth.[14] There were reports that the Chinese President felt that his people were beginning to lose their 'moral compass' and therefore wished for more tolerance of 'traditional faiths' by Communist party chiefs. The hope, it was reported, was that these 'traditional faiths' would help to replace the 'vacuum' left by 'the country's breakneck growth and rush to get rich.' This vacuum, said sources close to the President as reported by Reuters, was also allowing corruption to breed and thrive.

Reuters also stated that sceptics viewed the policy as a way of managing dissatisfaction among the general population and a tactic by which the Communist Party could control dissent.

Those in favour of the pro-faith policy point out that, under Communism, there was less crime than when economic reforms were introduced. In effect, the idea was that more tolerance would be shown towards religion though religion would not be formally promoted.

There is a Buddhist view—highlighted by the Dalai Lama in his McLeod Ganj interview with me—that if anything bad happens, it is to do with one's own karma. Sceptics say that this is a convenient idea to promote to a Chinese who cannot afford a doctor, education or a home of their own.

In early 2013, Xi Jinping met a Taiwanese Buddhist monk along with his delegation. That year, Xi announced the need for a 'material and spiritual civilization'.[15]

Reuters also revealed the following nugget, which marries with the BBC story.

'President Xi and his family have feelings for Buddhism,' said Xiao Wunan, executive vice chairman of the Asia Pacific Exchange and Cooperation Foundation, a Beijing-backed non-governmental organization.

In 2013, the Bureau of Religious Affairs' deputy director wrote in the State organ, *The Peoples' Daily*, 'treating religions well should become a common consensus . . . and the right to practice religions should be protected'.[16]

However, the Reuters piece concluded that in China economic development would always be given priority over its moral counterpart.

Playing alongside the seeming softening of heart is a long serving family relationship. Xi Jinping's liberal-minded father, Xi Zhongxun, was once close to the current Dalai Lama.

On his 1954 visit to China, the Dalai Lama gave Xi senior a pricey watch, which the senior apparatchik wore for years to come.[17]

The Dalai Lama spent five to six months in 1954 learning about Marxism and the Chinese language and Xi Senior was one of the party officials who spent extended time with him then. Before his death in 2002, he championed the rights of the Tibetans and the Uyghurs. He even objected to the army opposition of the Tiananmen Square student protest in 1989.

Xi Junior is playing his cards close to his chest, but there are glimmers of reasons to expect a rapprochement with Tibetan Buddhists. His glamorous wife is described as having an interest in Buddhism and when Xi Jinping was in charge of one of the Chinese provinces, Zhejiang, he held a World Buddhist Forum in the region's main city.

However, in 2011, Xi Jinping went to Tibet and promised to break the 'Dalai Lama clique', adding that he would 'completely smash any plot to destroy stability in Tibet and jeopardize national unity'.[18]

The Dalai Lama, along with his family and supporters, remains hopeful but unsure if the Communist Party system will allow a digression from its previous hardline on the issue.

30

INFLUENCES

I had been worried as I stood at the entrance to Har Mander Singh's home in New Delhi before my first interview with him. The last time I'd seen him, he had been looking good, standing upright, telling anecdotes and entertaining me over dinner.

Since then he'd suffered a stroke that had laid him up for a while. His sons had warned me that he had been prey to some anxiety and that his recall was fading. So, I didn't know what condition I was going to find him in as I climbed the stone stairs of his home and rang the doorbell.

I screamed with delight when I saw him. He gave me a hug and grabbed me by the shoulders, keeping me close in a tight hold as he steered me through the dining room and into his drawing room. To my surprise, he seemed strong, his mind sharp as ever, his sense of wry, dry humour plain for anyone to see.

There, on the wall, was an array of photos. These were all new for I did not recall seeing them before. With his arm still firmly holding me around my shoulder, he stood me in front of them.

The first one he showed me was a photo of the holiest place for Sikhs, the Golden Temple. 'This is my past religion, the religion in which I was born,' he said. There is a picture of the first Sikh guru,

Guru Nanak. 'I go and read the Granth Sahib [the Sikh holy book],' he told me.

Then, he came to a photo taken with his camera of the Dalai Lama and Har Mander and his wife Neena. As he did so, he said, 'This [Buddhism] is my adopted religion. They have equal place for me. The Dalai Lama gave this to me, and this was printed but there's an inscription in his own hand.'

'When did he give it to you?' I asked.

'Amongst [sic] one of our meetings. I don't know.'

Next, he showed me another photo. 'This is Potala Palace which he left behind. This is woven with thread. This is not a painting, it's embroidery.'

He then showed me a painting. 'This is when I was in Bomdila. A great Lama painted this for me.'

I was a bit nonplussed as I did not understand the meaning behind the different elements in the painting. I asked what it was.

'It's whatever it teaches; love of animals and all birds and everything; nature. He painted it for me. He was so great a Lama, but he gave it to me, so this is my Tibetan place and that's my family.'

Then he showed me other images from his later career. 'That is the Choegyal of Sikkim. The king of Sikkim, his American wife and his children. I was number two in the Indian office, so I established very good relations with him. Your auntie, my wife, had even better relations with him because she used to tell him Punjabi jokes when he was drunk. This was the ex-king of Belgium,' he showed me a black and white photo of a royal couple he hosted.

He then moved on to another framed picture, 'Here, you know, just outside our house in Bomdila in 1959. That's His Holiness, that's Auntie Neena, and that's me, and he sent this picture to me and he inscribed it with his words, and then he got it translated.'

The Dalai Lama's signature appeared on a special message written by him on this framed image, which he gave Har Mander Singh on the fiftieth anniversary of his escape and safe passage through Kameng. It reads:

To one of my earliest friends, Mr and Mrs Har Mander Singh:
For rembersance [sic] and with my blessing and prayers for your all
time success and good health.

Buddhist Bikshu,
Dalai Lama
May 29, 2009

'I thought that as these are the new additions in the house, I'll show them to you. I had a very small camera, a box camera, with which I took pictures of his Holiness's journey. I took little pictures with the camera . . . but his Holiness and his staff spent a lot of money to convert those silly pictures into treasure.'

Later, Har Mander sat at his table and opened his photograph album. 'This is in Bomdila. This is during the journey. You see Assam Rifles people,' he pointed to a man, 'and he was the Commander in Chief, also related to him.'[1]

As I absorbed the impression that the Dalai Lama and the Tibetans left on Har Mander Singh, my thoughts went to Har Mander's views on the impact of the resettling of the Tibetans on India.

I asked him, 'What did it cost India to give the Dalai Lama sanctuary?'

'This is my personal opinion and not government opinion,' he replied. 'It cost India a lot. On humanitarian reasons, on religious reasons they gave refuge to Dalai Lama. He's one of the greatest human beings of this century so in my opinion, that was a wise decision, but it has certainly not pleased the Chinese, they are annoyed that in some way we have interfered in their internal affairs. But that was a choice that India has made and with the choice come the consequences.'[2]

Many supporters of the Dalai Lama played a role in his escape from the Tibet Autonomous Region in 1959. When I asked him how he would characterize his role in the Dalai Lama's story, he was diffident.

'I think there is something called providence and providence placed me in that position. With the grace of God, I was able to come up to the expectation and a sign of that was the conferment of the Padma Shri award only the next year. It indicated that the government was satisfied with my work and my superiors who met me, they also indicated that they were satisfied. I think what you're saying is true, that history imposed this role on me and as it is I was able to fulfil that role. I may have failed in other circumstances, but these circumstances were exclusive, and I was able to play that role. So, if not Indians, certainly the Tibetans would remember my role in this episode.'³

I then asked him a more personal question, 'What do you think the Dalai Lama made of you?'

'I don't know, but I have a feeling,' he laughed a little, 'that he thinks well of me. The other day here, Harsh, my son, invited him to talk to the street children who are in Harsh's care. He noticed me in the crowd, and he said, "Har Mander Singh, come to me", then he got hold of both my hands and I was feeling as if I should run away from here. He made me sit next to his chair and he kept holding both my hands for the entire period of that show. There must be some feeling for me somewhere.'

'People refer to the Dalai Lama as a God King. Did you see him in that light?' I wanted to know.

'He has appointed a Prime Minister, so all temporal powers are now with the Prime Minister. He has only spiritual powers, and he spends a lot of time praying, meeting people, thinking of his country, its future and so on. About God or King,' he smiled, 'I don't know, but that he was something very special, I've always felt.

'I've always felt there are three people in this century who are above all of us. One is Mahatma Gandhi, one is Nelson Mandela, and one is the Dalai Lama. If you want to count another one then that's the American president, the earliest one. Who fought those two wars; Abraham Lincoln. These are really the greatest in these centuries.'

'But did he feel like a God or did he feel like an ordinary person?'

'It's a very controversial thing,' he laughed, 'First of all my own conception of God is not very clear. I go and read the Granth Sahib.

'I don't know. The persons in my life I have lost are my daughter, my sister, my wife and my parents, and I pray for them, but I don't know who these prayers reach or don't reach,' he became emotional, and swallowed. 'It only softens me and gives me the feeling that I had done what needed to be done for them. But whether there is a God, whether he'll take cognizance of my prayers over millions and millions of others praying simultaneously, I don't know.'

Finally, Har Mander reflected on his role in the story of the Dalai Lama's escape.

To the Losel Nyinje Charitable Society he had said, 'Actually, the government had no option . . . to give responsibility to me. Because, I was the head of that area. If it would have been accessible area very big leaders would have come to seek blessings and seek recognition as it was a great thing . . . to receive such dignitaries in [a] personal way and also in [an] official way. The government had no option but to entrust this responsibility on me since there was no road beyond Rupa. I did my best and I think it was the blessings of god.'[4]

To me, he said, 'There were a lot of people on the Indian and Tibetan side who outranked me but at that point of time whenever the occasion comes to take up a job and I'm surrounded by high dignitaries I carry on, and I always think that it is my job, and I have to do it.

'Like much later on I was posted to Andaman and Nicobar Islands and the ex-king of Belgium wanted to visit that area. There was no appropriate place apart from my home for him to stay in so he stayed with us. My wife had the knack of making people comfortable. When the responsibility is placed on me, then I go ahead and try and make a success of it.'

At this point, I couldn't help but say, 'If something had happened . . .'

He replied, 'The load was very great but I was so absorbed from moment to moment, when I have to send a message, I have to encrypt it and decrypt it, so all my thinking time was taken up with these things rather than the responsibility which I thought will sort itself out by itself. I was fortunate to, yeah, to experience this.'

I asked one final question, 'During that time, things were very sensitive between India and China; how do you see relations between the two countries now?'

'The northern territories, definitely the territory we have talked about, is ours,' he said. 'Traditionally, historically, in all ways. There is no doubt about that. If a monastery on one side pays taxes to a monastery on the other side that doesn't make the territory of the monastery belong to this party or that party, so I think certain areas belong to India and certain territories belong to China or Tibet.'[5]

*

On Sunday, 19 November 2017, a private meeting I had requested took place at the Taj Mahal Hotel Delhi between the Dalai Lama and some of Har Mander Singh's family; he was there with his elder son Raj Mander and I was there with my two sons, Jai and Sukh.

We waited in the lobby and were then asked to come up to the suite. We all waited in one room.

When the Dalai Lama knew Har Mander Singh had arrived at his suite, he almost dashed out into the corridor and grabbed him hard, held him in a tight embrace and then held his head close to his for the whole meeting.

We sat around him. It was a special reunion, with no one else there save for the Dalai Lama's immediate retinue and his Delhi Representative, Tempa Tsering, joined by Ngodup Dongchung. The Dalai Lama's nephew and Namgyal Lhamo Taklha's son, Tenzin Taklha were also present.

The Dalai Lama sat on a couch next to Har Mander Singh and I sat on a separate chair to ask my first question. 'How can we all live with a more open heart, Holiness?'

He replied, 'This self-centered attitude, what value does it have? It's very harmful. An altruistic mental attitude, is of immense benefit. So, use extensively your intelligence. Analyze different kinds of emotions. What emotions are beneficial to one's own peace of mind and eventually one's health also. What kinds of emotions are very bad for our health, not only do they destroy the peace of mind but they destroy one physically also. They have a very negative effect. These are analytical meditations, so analyze. I'm a practitioner. In my own family, particularly my mother, she was very kind, very compassionate. I always describe that my first guru of compassion is my mother.

'The way to develop a more compassionate mind with compassionate feeling, is to consider everyone. Have a sense of sharing with brothers and sisters. I am totally dedicated to trying to create a sense of oneness among seven billion human beings.'

My younger son Sukh then asked the Dalai Lama a question.

'Your Holiness, you're speaking about us understanding our oneness. But there's so much in the news that we see about differences, divides, racism, men and women; all sorts of conflict. A lot of young people especially nowadays may be more confused as to what they can do. So much power rests with the politicians. What would you say for young people is one thing that we can do to be part of the solution?'

The Dalai Lama listened intently before replying to Sukh.

'I think constantly experiencing anger, stress, fear is very bad for our health. Some scientists say such a destructive emotion is actually eating our human system. You also need the practice of tolerance, forgiveness; these things. All religion teaches us that. So basically, human nature is more positive and logically human beings are one of the social animals, any social animals, they have emotion which bring us together; and that's love,' he replied.

'So therefore, my number one commitment is try to promote human love and compassion with a sense of oneness of the entire humanity. I think look at the past century, the twentieth century; we belong to that century. Now you I think most probably belong to the twenty-first century. So our century I think was full of problems: killing, violence. So, at the beginning of this twenty-first century, some of this violence is a resurgence of the past century's mentality. To always consider power is important whenever you face some opposition, to use force; that's old thinking.

'Young people now should pay more attention about ancient Indian knowledge, how to tackle our emotion and how to bring inner peace.

'Another point; this world belongs to seven billion human beings, not special leaders like the rajas. That's the olden times. Now we are in modern times, now people are the real owners of the world.'

'When you look at Har Mander Singh today, what do you feel?' I asked him.

The Dalai Lama turned to Har Mander Singh, whose head was inches from his own and looked straight at him while pausing for a few seconds. Then he said, 'It makes me feel old. Two old men. I semi-retired, then in 2011, I totally retired,' he turned to Har Mander. 'So now I also become like you. A retired person! because the Dalai Lama institution lasts for four centuries but . . . now I feel old fashioned and feel some connection with the feudal system. That is outdated and now are modern times. Democracy is very relevant so therefore, since 2001 we already achieved electorate political leadership.' He laughed.

'So now my commitment is regarding Tibet. Since political responsibility is now handed over completely to the elected political leadership. During my last thirty years' experience of meeting with scientists and many scholars, I really found ancient Indian knowledge which we study and practise is very helpful. Therefore, now in order to serve humanity, firstly within the country, this ancient knowledge must be revived. Only this country has the ability to combine modern education, modern technology, science with ancient Indian knowledge which brings inner peace.

'When I first reached India, you took full care of me,' he looked directly at Har Mander.

Finally, the Dalai Lama expressed a wish that was personal to the family he was sitting with. He felt it important that successive generations of the two families should stay connected and proceeded to give a wider example of a friendship that straddled politics.

He said, 'We are very, very close in my mind. So, the younger generation and the next generation; children, grandchildren grand grandchildren—I feel our friendship will remain. For instance, two or three years ago, there was one Chinese who is the son of one Chinese general I knew from 1957, or '58. The Chinese general eventually became a very close friend of mine. So, his son came to see me in Japan.

'He brought his own young son and he told me it was because his father was a very close friend of mine. So, now his father has passed away, he came to see me, and he wanted to keep this friendship going from generation to generation. He brought his own son. It's nice.'[6]

This wish, for the friendship between the two families to continue, is part of the Dalai Lama's wider message of spreading love and compassion to the world.

*

In writing this book, I got to know more about how the Dalai Lama came to be connected with Har Mander Singh's family.

I discovered a little bit about the Dalai Lama's world.

I found out just how much he is respected and loved by his followers. I saw the effect he can have on people. Through his message of kindness, peace and non-violence, he is a symbol of unity, and unites much of the Tibetan Buddhist world. So far, their mission has been largely peaceful.

If that situation changes, I am not sure what will happen.

This journey of discovery has taken me several years, and much sacrifice.

But it has given me great experiential riches.

The exploration took me to parts of India I had never visited before, like the North-East, Himachal Pradesh, and Uttarakhand. I met people from all walks of life, from different ethnicities, and formed relationships that have added to my existence.

I found out how closely connected the people of the eastern Himalayas are to the Dalai Lama. I learnt of the simple, primordial bond that the Monpas, the Bhutanese and others feel with him.

The memories formed over the past five years make up my own mental sojourn.

I am grateful to all those people who have helped me tell this precious narrative.

The story of *An Officer and His Holiness* is a miniscule part of a huge international network woven around the Dalai Lama; an evolving universe.

The awe-inspiring larger story of the Dalai Lama is fast-moving. I will watch with deep curiosity and wonder as it develops over the coming years.

NOTES

Preamble: How and Why I Wrote this Book

1. http://factsanddetails.com/china/cat6/sub33/item224.html
2. http://www.worldbank.org/en/country/china/overview, December 2018.
3. https://uk.reuters.com/article/uk-china-tibet-australia/australia-university-accused-of-bowing-to-china-by-barring-dalai-lama-idUKBRE93H09O20130418, April 2019.

Prologue: Giants' Dance

1. Formerly known as Bombay, Calcutta and Bangalore.
2. https://www.britishempire.co.uk/biography/gandhi.htm
3. http://www.historydiscussion.net/history-of-india/jawaharlal-nehrusforeign-policy/682
4. Thubten Samphel, Director Tibet Policy Institute, April 2018.
5. http://www.archieve.claudearpi.net/maintenance/uploaded_pics/590427_PM_Debate_LS.pdf, December 2018.
6. Mikel Dunham, *Buddha's Warriors* (Penguin Books, New York, 2004), p. 301.

1: Looking Back

1. Raj Mander, phone interviews with the author, June to October 2017.
2. G.P. Singh, *Historical Researches into Some Aspects of the Culture and Civilization of North-East India* (Gyan Publishing House, New Delhi, 2009), p. 88.
3. Julie G. Marshall, *Britain and Tibet: 1765–1947* (Routledge, USA and Canada, 2005), p. 298.
4. Har Mander Singh, interview with the author, New Delhi residence, 21–22 May 2015.
5. Ibid.
6. Ibid.

2: The Early Years

1. Mrs Namgyal Lhamo Taklha, interview with the author, Dehradun, November 2017.
2. Stephen Talty, *Escape from the Land of the Snows* (Crown Publishers, New York, 2011), p. 12.
3. Ibid.
4. *Ibid.*, p. 20.
5. Har Mander Singh, interview with the author, 21–22 May 2015.
6. Har Mander Singh, telephone interview with the author, 5 September 2015.
7. Har Mander Singh, interview with author, 21–22 May 2016.
8. Ibid.
9. Har Mander Singh, interview with the author, 21–22 May 2015.
10. Ibid.
11. Ibid.
12. Har Mander Singh, interview with the author, India International Centre, New Delhi, December 2005.
13. Har Mander Singh, interview with the author, 21–22 May 2015.
14. Huseyn Shaheed Suhrawardy was an East Pakistani politician and statesman working in the first half of the twentieth century.
15. Har Mander Singh, email interview with the author, June 2017.
16. Major General Sandhu (Retired), email interview with the author, November–December 2017.

17. Ibid.
18. Har Mander Singh, interview with the author, 21–22 May 2015.
19. Major General Sandhu (Retired), email interview with author, November–December 2017.
20. http://claudearpi.blogspot.com/2014/12/romanticism-and-hostile-borders.html
21. Verrier Elwin began his work as a Christian missionary in India. British by birth, he developed into an ethnologist, anthropologist and later became a committed activist, renowned for his studies to do with tribes of India; http://claudearpi.blogspot.com/2014/12/romanticism-and-hostileborders.html, December 2018.
22. Har Mander Singh, interview with the author, 21–22 May 2015.
23. Ibid.
24. Raj Mander, phone interview with the author, June to October 2017.

3: In the Land of the Dawn-lit Mountains

1. In later years, Har Mander Singh became a Deputy Secretary for Nagaland, Ministry of External Affairs; Deputy Secretary for Nagaland, Emergency Affairs; Financial Adviser/Counsellor, Office of Political Office, Sikkim and Bhutan; Director, Nagaland, Ministry of External Affairs. He was an Additional Political Officer, Tuensang Division, and the Director, Supply and Transport, NEFA, based in Tezpur, Assam.
2. Har Mander Singh, interview with the author, 21–22 May 2015.
3. Claude Arpi http://claudearpi.blogspot.co.uk/2014/12/romanticismand-hostile-borders.html December 2014.
4. Har Mander Singh, interview with the author, 21–22 May 2015.
5. Ibid.
6. Ibid.
7. Raj Mander, phone interview, June to October 2017.
8. Ibid.
9. Ibid.
10. Ibid.
11. Ibid.
12. Har Mander Singh, interview with the author, 21–22 May 2015.
13. Ibid.
14. Ibid.

15. Ibid.
16. Ibid.
17. Ibid.
18. Ibid.
19. Ibid.
20. Claude Arpi, http://claudearpi.blogspot.co.uk/2014/12/romanticismand-hostile-borders.html December 2018.
21. Har Mander Singh, interview with the author, 21–22 May 2015.
22. Ibid.

4: The Warriors

1. Stephen Talty, *Escape from the Land of the Snows* (Random House, New York, 2011), p. 60.
2. Bruce Riedel, *JFK'S Forgotten Crisis: Tibet, the CIA and the Sino-Indian War* (Brookings Institution, Washington D.C., 2015), p. 23. Bruce Riedel (Senior Fellow, The Saban Center for Middle East Policy, The Brookings Institution) spent thirty years in the CIA, was a senior adviser to four US presidents on South Asia and the Middle East, as a staff member of the National Security Council.
3. https://history.state.gov/historicaldocuments/frus1950-55Intel/d250
4. Mikel Dunham, *Buddha's Warriors*, (Penguin Books, New York, 2004), p. 26.
5. Tenzin Choegyal, interview with the author, Dharamsala 2015.
6. The Mongol monk was Geshe Wangyal, a Kalmuk monk who had studied at Lhasa.
7. Tenzin Choegyal, interview with the author, Dharamsala, May 2015.
8. Mikel Dunham, *Buddha's Warriors*, (Penguin Books, New York, 2004), p. 203.
9. *Ibid.* Quoting Roger E. McCarthy, *Tears of the Lotus: Accounts of Tibetan Resistance to the Chinese Invasion 1950-1962* (McFarland & Co, Jefferson, North Carolina, and London, 2006), p. 240.
10. Tenzin Choegyal, interview with the author, Dharamsala, May 2015.
11. Mikel Dunham, *Buddha's Warriors* (Penguin Books, New York, 2004), p. 254.
12. Tenzin Choegyal, interview with the author, Dharamsala, May 2015.
13. Tibet is the source of water for the entire region; https://www.forbes.com/2010/09/09/water-china-tibet-2020-opinions-contributorssteven-solomon.html#76847a240f73

5: Inside Potala Palace

1. Stephen Talty, *Escape from the Land of the Snows* (Random House, New York, 2011), p. 30.
2. *Ibid.*, p. 31.
3. *Ibid.*, p. 35.
4. Heinrich Harrer, *Seven Years in Tibet* (Harper Collins, London, 2005).
5. Stephen Talty, *Escape from the Land of the Snows* (Random House, New York, 2011), p. 36.
6. All this information comes from Thubten Samphel, Director, Tibet Policy Institute.
7. Stephen Talty, *Escape from the Land of the Snows* (Random House, New York, 2011), p. 34.
8. The Dalai Lama, interview with the author, McLeod Ganj, Dharamsala, May 2015.
9. Ibid.
10. Ibid.
11. Stephen Talty, *Escape from the Land of the Snows* (Random House, New York, 2011), p. 48.
12. The Dalai Lama, interview with the author, McLeod Ganj, Dharamsala, May 2015.
13. Ibid.
14. Ibid.
15. Ibid.
16. Ibid.
17. Ibid.
18. Ibid.
19. Ibid.
20. Ibid.
21. Ibid.
22. Information from Thubten Samphel, Director, Tibet Policy Institute, Dharamsala.
23. https://www.icj.org/summary-of-a-report-on-tibet-submitted-to-theinternational-commission-of-jurists-by-shri-purshottam-trikamdassenior-advocate-supreme-court-of-india/
24. Information from the Dalai Lama's interview with the author, official residence Mcleod Ganj, May 2015; https://www.icj.org/summaryof-

a-report-on-tibet-submitted-to-the-international-commission-
ofjurists-by-shri-purshottam-trikamdas-senior-advocate-supreme-
courtof-india/

6: Tension in Lhasa

1. Mrs Namgyal Lhamo Taklha, interview with the author, Dehradun, November 2017.
2. Ibid.
3. Ibid.
4. Ibid.
5. Mikel Dunham, *Buddha's Warriors* (Penguin Books, New York, 2004), p. 122.
6. *Ibid.*, p. 129.
7. Stephen Talty, *Escape from the Land of the Snows* (Random House, New York, 2011), p. 66.
8. Bruce Riedel, telephone interview with the author, 7 December 2016.
9. Stephen Talty, *Escape from the Land of the Snows* (Random House, New York, 2011), p. 75.
10. *Ibid.*, p. 77.
11. *Ibid.*, pp. 83–84.
12. *Ibid.*
13. *Ibid.*, p. 82. See also, Chao, Shan, *Peking Review*, vol 18, 5 May 1959.
14. The Valley of Words Literary Festival is founded and organized by Mr and Mrs Sanjeev Chopra who run the Shivalik Hills Foundation.
15. Mrs Namgyal Lhamo Takhla, interview with the author, Dehradun, November 2017.

7: The Escape

1. Stephen Talty, *Escape From the Land of the Snows* (Random House, New York, 2011), p. 72.
2. *Ibid.*, p. 96.
3. *Ibid.*, p. 264.
4. *Ibid.*, p. 101.
5. Bruce Riedel, telephone interview with the author, 7 December 2016.
6. Stephen Talty, *Escape From the Land of the Snows* (Random House, New York, 2011), p. 83. Talty states that the Chinese, most likely, never

intended to snatch the Dalai Lama to Peking or harm him in any way that spring. It would not have served their purpose.

7. *Ibid.*, p. 89.
8. The Dalai Lama, interview with the author, McLeod Ganj, Dharamsala, May 2015.
9. Mikel Dunham, *Buddha's Warriors* (Penguin Books, New York, 2004), p. 282.
10. The Dalai Lama, interview with the author, residential palace, McLeod Ganj, Dharamsala, May 2015.
11. The Dalai Lama, interview with the author, McLeod Ganj, Dharamsala, May 2018.
12. Mikel Dunham, *Buddha's Warriors* (Penguin Books, New York, 2004), p. 284.
13. The Dalai Lama, interview with the author, McLeod Ganj, Dharamsala, May 2015.
14. Stephen Talty, *Escape From the Land of the Snows* (Random House, New York, 2011), p. 163.
15. Mikel Dunham, *Buddha's Warriors* (Penguin Books, New York, 2004), p. 286.
16. Tenzin Choegyal, interview with the author, Kashmir Cottage, Dharamsala, May 2015.
17. Ibid.
18. Ibid.
19. The Dalai Lama, interview with the author, McLeod Ganj, Dharamsala, May 2015.
20. Ibid.
21. Ibid.
22. Ibid.
23. Ibid.
24. Stephen Talty, *Escape From the Land of the Snows* (Random House, New York, 2011), p. 130.
25. *Ibid.*, p. 156.
26. *Ibid.*, p. 161.
27. Tenzin Choegyal, interview with the author, McLeod Ganj, Dharamsala, May 2015.
28. The Dalai Lama, interview with the author, Palace, McLeod Ganj, Dharamsala, 20 May 2016.
29. Ibid.

8: Mission Command

1. Har Mander Singh, interview with the author, New Delhi, May 2016.
2. Ibid.
3. Ibid.
4. Ibid.
5. Ibid.
6. For the compilation of the images for this book, the author was asked to take care whenever borrowing the original photo album and to handle it personally. Now, there is only one original album in existence. It contains the small black and white images that were printed in 1959 after the journey. So Har Mander and his family, are aware of how precious the visual record is.
7. The National Highways of Arunachal Pradesh are vital to the state as they link the major towns and townships. They wind and snake through the mountains, but they are the only means by which vehicles can travel from one place to another. Should snow, landslides or flooding block any of them, vehicular travel is paralyzed for hours or days.
8. https://timesofindia.indiatimes.com/city/guwahati/Arunachalgets-first-state-disaster-management-unit/articleshow/30041353.cms?referral=PM
9. https://www.hindustantimes.com/india-news/iaf-chopper-crashthree-bodies-found-search-on-for-fourth-in-arunachal-pradesh/storyja3Xo1K7Gtt18KahRaaPhJ.Html

9: The Execution Phase

1. Extract from Har Mander Singh's historic 1959 diary of his mission to conduct the Dalai Lama from the Indian border to the plains of India.
2. Har Mander Singh, interview with the author, New Delhi, May 2016. The first Indian administrator to make contact with Tawang had been Major Khathing, a well-known person who was one of Har Mander's predecessors.
3. Har Mander Singh, interview with the author, New Delhi, 2015.
4. Har Mander Singh, interview with the author, New Delhi, May 2016.
5. Jampa Phende, interview with the author, Tawang, April 2017.

10: The Set Up

1. Har Mander Singh, interview with the author, New Delhi, 21–22 May 2015.
2. Ibid.
3. Ibid.
4. Har Mander Singh's immediate subordinates were a) an additional political officer, then b), an Assistant Political Officer, T.S. Murthy, then c) a base superintendent. T.S. Murthy played a critical role in the story. Since he was a Chinese Mandarin speaker he would have been able to identify any Chinese following the Dalai Lama who might have been pretending to be part of the Tibetan party.
5. OC Wing was the Officer Commanding the Assam Rifles. There would be around three to four OC wings, or companies, of the Assam Rifles under one Commanding Officer.
6. Har Mander Singh, interview with the author, New Delhi, 21–22 May 2015.
7. Ibid.
8. Jampa Phende, interview with the author, Tawang, April 2017.
9. This information comes from a paper written and presented by Mr Tsewang Dorjee, Visiting Fellow at the Tibetan Policy Institute, Dharamshala. The paper was called 'Tibetan Narrative on Tawang: A Historical Perspective'. The title of the event was 'Focusing the Frontiers: the Borderland, Identity, Perceptions and Imaginings of Monpas of Tawang in India China Border'. It was organized by the International Strategic Studies Programme, the National Institute for Advanced Studies, Bengaluru, India.
10. K. Lama was Katuk Lama, an Assistant Political Officer to Har Mander Singh.
11. Claude Arpi, http://claudearpi.blogspot.co.uk/2017/03/relaxing-onway-as-dalai-lama-will-soon.html

11: Getting Closer

1. Additional Political Officer T.S. Murthy.
2. Chutangmu is an Indian border police check post, about 40 miles north of Tawang.
3. Lokra was not just the headquarters of the Assam Rifles, but also the communications hub through which messages arrived from Shillong.

4. The man in charge of the Assam Rifles at Lokra HQ was called a Commandant; he was a commissioned officer. of a fairly senior rank—a lieutenant colonel.
5. A Tibetan speaking official.
6. Har Mander Singh, interview with the author, New Delhi, 21–22 May 2015.
7. Gompatse Rinpoche was a high-ranking Tibetan who, incidentally, made a gift of a painting to Har Mander Singh.
8. Har Mander Singh, interview, India International Centre, New Delhi, 2005.
9. CSO is the Chief Signals Officer.
10. Inspector General, Assam Rifles. The inspector general of the Assam Rifles was the apex officer of the force, and not the chief of many inspectors general in the Assam Rifles.
11. Bdr is the border.
12. Har Mander Singh, interview with the author, New Delhi, 21–22 May 2015.
13. Har Mander Singh, interview with the author, India International Centre, New Delhi, 2005.
14. CTM is Chutangmu.
15. Dr Sen, a qualified physician, was T.S. Murthy's second in command, and Murthy reported to Singh at the forward post of Tawang. Dr Sen was in the wireless transmission (WT) room at this time.

12: Tawang to Lumla

1. Har Mander may have had sporadic access to WT rooms during the journey.
2. An informal communication.
3. Additional Political Officer T.S. Murthy, Singh's second permanently based at Tawang.
4. Har Mander Singh, interview with the author, 21-22 May 2015.
5. Ibid.
6. The *Crossing of the Frontiers* is a work put together by a team of committed Monpa researchers living in Kameng and working under the auspices of the Losel Nyinje Charitable Society, Tawang. The book was published in Tawang in 2017 and one copy was presented to the Dalai Lama during his 2017 visit there. Another copy was given to the author by one of the

book's creators, Nawang Chodak. Losel Nyinje Charitable Society & Monyul Social Welfare Association, The Crossing of the Frontier (Losel Nyinje Charitable Society, Tawang, 2017), Chapter 1.

7. Ibid.

8. Mrs Namgyal Lhamo Taklha, interview with the author, November 2017.

9. Gorsham and Shakti are grazing places right next to the border on the Indian side.

10. Lumla is the first settlement closest to the Indian border on the Indian side.

11. DST was the Director of Supplies and Transport.

13: Meeting Tenzin Choegyal, and the Chase

1. Tenzin Choegyal, interview with the author, Dharamsala, May 2015.

2. Losel Nyinje Charitable Society & Monyul Social Welfare Association, The Crossing of the Frontier (Losel Nyinje Charitable Society, Tawang, 2017), Chapter 2.

3. Ibid.

4. https://www.hindustantimes.com/india-news/severe-bilateralconsequences-if-dalai-lama-visits-arunachal-pradesh-chinese-media/story-8OdxuJbWmwuix3YgEN0YZK.html, December 2018

5. The Dalai Lamas are sometimes referred to by their numbers.

6. Mahayana Buddhists form more than half of Buddhists in the world today. There are other forms of Buddhism practised all over the world too.

14: Dream Warriors and the Old Town

1. Mikel Dunham, *Buddha's Warriors* (Penguin Books, New York, 2004), p. 201.

2. The Dalai Lama, interview with the author, official residence, McLeod Ganj, 18 May 2015.

3. Athar Norbu, interview with author Mikel Dunham; Mikel Dunham, *Buddha's Warriors* (Penguin Books, New York, 2004), p. 300.

4. *Ibid.*

5. *Ibid.*

6. The Dalai Lama, interview with the author, McLeod Ganj, Dharamsala, May 2015.

7. Tenzin Choegyal, interview with the author, May 2015.

8. Bruce Riedel, telephone interview with the author, 7 December 2016.

9. The Dalai Lama, interview with the author, McLeod Ganj, Dharamsala, May 2015.

10. https://www.aljazeera.com/programmes/aljazeeracorrespondent/2011/10/20111017122121250153.html,December2018.

11. https://audioboom.com/posts/2491868-how-china-s-growingeconomic-influence-in-nepal-affects-the-plight-of-stateless-tibetans-there

12. The Dalai Lama, interview with the author, McLeod Ganj, Dharamsala, May 2015.

13. Thubten Samphel, Director Tibetan Policy Institute, said that a taped message was also likely to have been sent to the Khampas.

14. Sikkim in 1959 was an independent country.

15. Sikkim was an independent kingdom until 1975, when it was annexed by India and became a state.

16. The Dalai Lama, interview with the author, McLeod Ganj, Dharamsala, May 2015.

17. Ibid.

18. *Ibid.*

19. Bruce Riedel, telephone interview with the author, 7 June 2016.

15: The Miracles

1. In 2018, the current Panchen Lama, Gedhun Choekyi Nyima, who was recognized by the Dalai Lama when he was six, remains captive in China and is not allowed to interact with the outside world.

2. Stephen Talty, *Escape From the Land of the Snows* (Random House, New York, 2011), p. 302.

3. *Ibid.*, p. 163.

4. Mikel Dunham, *Buddha's Warriors* (Penguin Books, New York, 2004), p. 302.

5. The Dalai Lama, interview with the author, McLeod Ganj, Dharamsala, May 2015.

6. Ibid.

7. Tenzin Choegyal, interview with the author, Dharamsala, May 2015.

8. The Dalai Lama, interview with the author, McLeod Ganj, Dharamsala, May 2015.

9. A dzo is a mix of between a yak and a male cow. Most of the escaping Dalai Lama party were riding these stocky, short-legged animals.

10. Stephen Talty, *Escape From the Land of the Snows* (Random House, New York, 2011), p. 173.

11. *Ibid.*

12. The Dalai Lama, interview with the author, McLeod Ganj, Dharamsala, May 2015.

13. Ibid.

14. Ibid.

15. Ibid.

16. Ibid.

17. Ibid.

18. Ibid.

19. Ibid.

20. Ibid.

21. Bruce Riedel, telephone interview with the author, 7 December 2016.

22. The Dalai Lama, interview with the author, McLeod Ganj, Dharamsala, May 2015.

23. Tenzin Choegyal, interview with the author, Dharamsala, May 2015.

16: Across the Border

1. Stephen Talty, *Escape From the Land of the Snows* (Random House, New York, 2011), p. 215.

2. Tenzin Choegyal, interview with the author, Kashmir Cottage, May 2015.

3. Ibid.

4. Ibid.

5. Ibid.

6. Ibid.

7. Ibid.

8. Har Mander Singh, interview with the author, 21–22 May 2015.

9. Sub inspector Wangdi was the local representative of the India Intelligence Bureau.

10. Har Mander Singh, interview with the author, 21–22 May 2015.

11. Losel Nyinje Charitable Society and Monyul Social Welfare Association, *The Crossing of the Frontier* (Losel Nyinje Charitable Society, Tawang, 2017).

12. Claude Arpi, http://www.archieve.claudearpi.net/maintenance/ uploaded_pics/590403_Nehru_to_Dalai_Lama.pdf, December 2018.
13. http://www.archieve.claudearpi.net/maintenance/uploaded_pics/ 590403_Nehru_to_Dalai_Lama.pdf. The author has reproduced the same numbering system used by Claude Arpi found.
14. Bruce Riedel, telephone interview with the author, 7 December 2016.

17: The Encounter

1. Tsona was the last post and monastery in Tibet before the Indian border. *Dzong* means fort, *pen* means commander.
2. Gyalo Dhandup, also spelt Gyalo Thondup, is the second eldest brother of the Dalai Lama. He was his former chief of staff and unofficial envoy. He and his wife bought land on the outskirts of Kalimpong and he lived there, liaising with the CIA and many other countries on behalf of his brother.
3. This diary entry meant that Sen's messages had been passed on to Har Mander Singh, NEFA Secretariat headquarter, Shillong, as well as Singh's Division headquarter, Bomdila.
4. Mani Lung is hard to translate, but it seems to mean the transmission of Mani. Mani originates from the mantra: Om Mani Padme Hum, which means 'Oh the Jewel in Lotus'. This is the mantra of the Lord of Compassion, Avalokiteshvara (Explanation given by Thubten Samphel, Director Tibet Policy Institute).
5. Losel Nyinje Charitable Society and Monyul Social Welfare Association, *The Crossing of the Frontier* (Losel Nyinje Charitable Society, Tawang, 2017).
6. Har Mander Singh, interview with the author, 21–22 May 2015.
7. The word is pronounced 'Shahbays'.
8. Yonzone was a Tibetan-speaking local functionary for the Indian intelligence.
9. Losel Nyinje Charitable Society and Monyul Social Welfare Association, *The Crossing of the Frontier* (Losel Nyinje Charitable Society, Tawang, 2017).
10. OCPCP was the officer commanding the police check post.
11. Har Mander Singh said that the OCPCP was in touch with Bhutan, but the decision under discussion was not something that could be taken at

his level. The decision about whether or not the Dalai Lama could go through Bhutan could only be made at the highest level in the country, that is, by the King of Bhutan.

12. Har Mander Singh, telephone interview with author, August 2016.
13. Claude Arpi, http://www.claudearpi.net/wp-content/uploads/2016/12/SW-Vol-48.pdf, December 2018.
14. Losel Nyinje Charitable Society and Monyul Social Welfare Association, *The Crossing of the Frontier* (Losel Nyinje Charitable Society, Tawang, 2017).

18: Lumla to Tawang

1. Kocka was of a similar rank to T.S. Murthy, a second in command to Har Mander Singh.
2. 'The Maharajah' refers to the King of Bhutan.
3. Har Mander Singh would write a letter to the Director of Medical Services and so the matter of smallpox vaccinations would be taken up accordingly.
4. Thongleng was the next stage in the journey, a small halting station.
5. The Dalai Lama, interview with the author, McLeod Ganj, Dharamsala, May 2015.
6. Ibid.
7. Abbott of Bomdila, interview with the author, April 2017.
8. Ibid.
9. The former Archbishop of Canterbury, Lord Rowan Williams, accompanied the Dalai Lama to this performance.
10. Har Mander Singh, interview with the author, New Delhi residence, May 2015.
11. Har Mander Singh, telephone interview with the author, 8 August 2016.
12. Har Mander Singh, interview with the author, New Delhi, May 2015.
13. Ibid.
14. Ibid.
15. Ibid.
16. The Consul General was one rank below ambassador.
17. Har Mander Singh, interview with the author, 21–22 May 2015.
18. Ibid.
19. Ibid.

19: Tawang Impressions

1. Har Mander Singh, interview with the author, 21–22 May 2015.
2. The Khenpu was the person in charge of the monastery, and the Dalai Lama had a special affection for him since he was a religious being. Har Mander Singh had already been to the monastery a few times.
3. The research was done by the Losel Nyinje Charitable Society.
4. Har Mander Singh, interview with the author, 21–22 May 2015.
5. Tenzin Choegyal, interview with the author, Kashmir Cottage, May2015.
6. Ibid.
7. Har Mander Singh, interview with the author, 21–22 May 2015.
8. The Dalai Lama, interview with the author, McLeod Ganj, Dharamsala, May 2015.

20: The Orchid

1. Losel Nyinje Charitable Society & Monyul Social Welfare Association, The Crossing of the Frontier (Losel Nyinje Charitable Society, Tawang, 2017).
2. Ibid.
3. Har Mander Singh, interview with the author, 21–22 May 2015.
4. Ibid.
5. Jampa Phende, interview with author, Tawang, April 2017.
6. Ibid.
7. Koncho Gyatso, interview with the author, April 2017.
8. SSB armed forces are the local Sashastra Seema Bal forces.
9. Koncho Gyatso, interview with the author, April 2017.
10. Har Mander Singh, interview with the author, 21–22 May 2015.
11. Ibid.
12. The Dalai Lama, interview with the author, McLeod Ganj, Dharamsala, May 2015.
13. The orchid that the Dalai Lama showed me when I visited him in his garden was from a family of a different variety that abound in lower or west Kameng District. Due to the unique variety of these flowers, they have been nurtured and grown in the Tipi Orchid Sanctuary. It is home to over 500 hybrids and types, and found in colours ranging from

red, magenta and satin white to a kind of velvet purple. This is around half the total number of orchid species found in India. The Hindi for orchid is 'Pushpa'. There is a Sita Pushpa and a Draupadi pushpa, which, according to legend, are believed to have been worn by Sita and Draupadi respectively. Some types of orchids are ornamental and rare. Since these flowers grow abundantly at lower altitudes over many parts of Arunachal, there are also orchid sanctuaries at Sessa, Dirang and Jengging. Both the horticultural departments as well as the Forestry Service take an interest in these and hope that orchid-growing might develop into a cottage industry in the future.

14. Guru Sharan Singh was the chief Indian official in Dharamsala who liaised with the Dalai Lama's office.

15. The Dalai Lama, interview with the author, Dharamsala, the Dalai Lama's garden, May 2015.

16. 'President Presents Awards', *The Statesman*, 27 April 1960.

21: Air Drops

1. Losel Nyinje Charitable Society & Monyul Social Welfare Association, *The Crossing of the Frontier* (Losel Nyinje Charitable Society, Tawang, 2017), Chapter 3.

2. Har Mander Singh, interview with the author, 21–22 May 2015.

3. Sengedzong is a monastery town between Tawang and Bomdila.

4. A special despatch was a document that was highly confidential.

5. Har Mander Singh, interview with the author, 21–22 May 2015.

6. Ibid.

7. Losel Nyinje Charitable Society & Monyul Social Welfare Association, The Crossing of the Frontier (Losel Nyinje Charitable Society, Tawang, 2017), Chapter 3.

8. Ibid.

9. Ibid

10. Har Mander Singh, interview with the author, 21–22 May 2015.

11. Ibid.

12. Subsidiary Intelligence Bureau.

13. Har Mander Singh, interview with the author, 21–22 May 2015.

14. Tenzin Choegyal, interview with the author, Dharamsala, May 2015.

15. Ibid.

22: Sela Pass

1. Losel Nyinje Charitable Society & Monyul Social Welfare Association, *The Crossing of the Frontier* (Losel Nyinje Charitable Society, Tawang, 2017), Chapter 4.
2. *Ibid.*
3. *Ibid.*
4. *Ibid.*
5. Menon was the representative from the MEA.
6. Losel Nyinje Charitable Society & Monyul Social Welfare Association, *The Crossing of the Frontier* (Losel Nyinje Charitable Society, Tawang, 2017), Chapter 4.
7. *Ibid.*
8. Har Mander Singh, interview with the author, 21–22 May 2015.
9. Ibid.
10. Har Mander Singh, audio interview with author, New Delhi residence, May 2015.
11. The National Expansion Scheme (NES) was one of India's nation-wide development schemes, under which village pathways would be improved or paved. The budget for this would have come from Singh's divisional coffer.
12. Lish was a village on the road to Bomdila.
13. Losel Nyinje Charitable Society & Monyul Social Welfare Association, *The Crossing of the Frontier* (Losel Nyinje Charitable Society, Tawang, 2017), Chapter 4.
14. The Namshu people were the residents of Namshu Village.
15. Losel Nyinje Charitable Society & Monyul Social Welfare Association, *The Crossing of the Frontier* (Losel Nyinje Charitable Society, Tawang, 2017), Chapter 4.
16. Kushuk Bakula was a senior Buddhist based in Ladakh, whose presence the Dalai Lama had asked for.

23: The Bomdila Club

1. Bruce Riedel, telephone interview with author, 7 December 2016.
2. Losel Nyinje Charitable Society & Monyul Social Welfare Association, *The Crossing of the Frontier* (Losel Nyinje Charitable Society, Tawang, 2017), Chapter 4.

3. P.T.I, 'Dalai Lama Arrives at Bomdila', *Assam Tribune*, story filed from Shillong, 13 April 1959.
4. Major Gurung had been located in Bomdila.
5. Dave was the deputy director, Subsidiary IB.
6. Pandit also represented the Subsidiary IB.
7. Atuk Tsering was with the IB.
8. Losel Nyinje Charitable Society & Monyul Social Welfare Association, *The Crossing of the Frontier* (Losel Nyinje Charitable Society, Tawang, 2017), Chapter 5.
9. Tenzin Choegyal, interview with author, Kashmir Cottage, May 2015.
10. Losel Nyinje Charitable Society & Monyul Social Welfare Association, *The Crossing of the Frontier* (Losel Nyinje Charitable Society, Tawang, 2017), Chapter 5; Rinchin Norbu interview with Har Mander Singh.
11. *Ibid.*
12. *Ibid.*
13. Claude Arpi, www.archieve.claudearpi.net/maintenance/uploaded . . . / Dalai_Lama_Bio_Tawang.pdf December 2018.
14. Har Mander Singh, interview with the author, 21–22 May 2015.
15. Ibid.
16. Ibid.
17. Losel Nyinje Charitable Society & Monyul Social Welfare Association, *The Crossing of the Frontier* (Losel Nyinje Charitable Society, Tawang, 2017), Chapter 5.
18. *Ibid.*
19. Kashag people are the five members of the Dalai Lama's cabinet.
20. Har Mander Singh, interview with the author, 21–22 May 2015.
21. Losel Nyinje Charitable Society & Monyul Social Welfare Association, *The Crossing of the Frontier* (Losel Nyinje Charitable Society, Tawang, 2017), Chapter 5.
22. Har Mander Singh, interview with author, New Delhi residence, May 2015.
23. Ibid.
24. Ibid.
25. The Rinpoche who consecrated the monastery at Bomdila on 28 January 1958 whence the Dalai Lama conducted the empowerment ceremony on 14 April 1959 was called the 12th Tsona Gontse Jetsun Jamphel

Wangchuk Rinpoche. Source: *The Crossing of the Frontier* (Losel Nyinje Charitable Society, Tawang, 2017), Chapter 5.

26. CITPC was the Cottage Industries Training and Production Centre.
27. 'Dalai Lama arrives at Bomdila', *Assam Tribune*, 13 April 2019.
28. Losel Nyinje Charitable Society & Monyul Social Welfare Association, *The Crossing of the Frontier* (Losel Nyinje Charitable Society, Tawang, 2017), Chapter 5.
29. Ibid; Rinchin Norbu interview with Har Mander Singh.
30. *Ibid.*
31. *Ibid.*

24: Tibetans in Dehradun

1. Mrs Namgyal Lhamo Taklha, interview with the author, Dehradun, November 2017.
2. https://tnp.org/2013-milestone-geshema-exams-begin/. Architect Ashish Ganju designed the nunnery with Rinchen Khando Choegyal.
3. These are comments to the author from Philippa Russell, Construction Manager, Tibetan Nuns Project, Dolma Ling Nunnery. Philippa Russel's life and works cover a larger spectrum of activities from writing, managing a rural health centre, to environmental advocacy in the region.
4. Ibid.
5. The Geshe-ma confers professorship after around twenty years of studying five sacred texts. It is the highest level of training in the Gelugpa school of Tibetan Buddhism.
6. Mrs Namgyal Lhamo Taklha, interview with the author, Dehradun, November 2017.
7. Ibid.
8. Ibid; *Acharya* is a nun or priest graduate, someone who has completed the very lengthy training.
9. Ibid.
10. Ibid.
11. Ibid.
12. Ngawang Choedhen, interview with author, Dehradun, November 2017.
13. Ibid.
14. Ibid.

15. Ngawang Tsultrim, interview with author, Dekyiling Tibetan, November 2017.

25: The Dalai Lama and the Singh Family

1. The Dalai Lama, interview with the author, McLeod Ganj, Dharamsala, May 2015.
2. Harsh Mander, interview with the author, May 2015.
3. https://www.dalailama.com/ December 2018.
4. Har Mander Singh, interview with the author, 21–22 May 2015.
5. Harsh Mander, interview with the author, New Delhi, May 2015.
6. Namgyal Lhamo Taklha, interview with the author, Dehradun, November 2017.

26: To Tezpur

1. Losel Nyinje Charitable Society & Monyul Social Welfare Association, *The Crossing of the Frontier* (Losel Nyinje Charitable Society, Tawang, 2017), Chapter 6.
2. Ibid.
3. 'The Dalai Lama arrives at Foot Hills', *Assam Tribune*, 18 April 1959.
4. Har Mander Singh, interview with the author, New Delhi, May 2015.
5. 'The Dalai Lama arrives at Foot Hills', *Assam Tribune*, 18 April 1959.
6. *Ibid.*
7. 'Road Fit For "king" Unpaid For: From Our Own Representative', *The Statesman*, 16 April 1959.
8. '*The God King Finds Safety*', LIFE *magazine*, 25 May 1959.
9. 'Dalai Lama Arrives at Bomdila', P.T.I, *Assam Tribune*, 19 April 1959.
10. *Ibid.*
11. Losel Nyinje Charitable Society & Monyul Social Welfare Association, *The Crossing of the Frontier* (Losel Nyinje Charitable Society, Tawang, 2017), Chapter 7; Interview with Har Mander Singh, 6 September 2015.
12. http://claudearpi.blogspot.co.uk/2014/12/romanticism-and-hostileborders.html, December 2018.
13. http://www.archieve.claudearpi.net/maintenance/uploaded_pics/590418_Tezpur_Statement.pdf, December 2018.
14. Ibid.

15. http://www.archieve.claudearpi.net/maintenance/uploaded_pics/590427_PM_Debate_LS.pdf, December 2018.
16. Ibid.
17. Losel Nyinje Charitable Society & Monyul Social Welfare Association, *The Crossing of the Frontier* (Losel Nyinje Charitable Society, Tawang, 2017), Chapter 6.
18. https://www.indiatoday.in/world/asia/story/tibetan-administrationtibetan-schools-india-159501-2013-04-21, December 2018.

27: Reasons for War

1.   Dr Shashank Joshi, South Asian affairs expert and defence editor at the *Economist*, comments to author, September 2017.
2.   Bruce Riedel, *JFK'S Forgotten Crisis: Tibet, the CIA and the Sino-Indian War* (Brookings Institution, Washington D.C., 2015), p. 111.
3.   Dr Shashank Joshi, in comments to the author, September 2017.
4.   Ibid.
5.   Losel Nyinje Charitable Society & Monyul Social Welfare Association, *The Crossing of the Frontier* (Losel Nyinje Charitable Society, Tawang, 2017), Chapter 7.
6.   Dr Shashank Joshi, in comments to the author, September 2017.
7.   Bruce Riedel, telephone interview with the author, December 2016.
8.   Bruce Riedel, *JFK'S Forgotten Crisis: Tibet, the CIA and the Sino-Indian War* (Brookings Institution, Washington D.C., 2015), p. 91.
9.   Dr Shashank Joshi, in comments to the author, September 2017.
10. Bruce Riedel, *JFK'S Forgotten Crisis: Tibet, the CIA and the Sino-Indian War* (Brookings Institution, Washington D.C., 2015), p. 142.
11. Dr Shashank Joshi, in comments to the author, September 2017.
12. Ibid.
13. Ibid.
14. Bruce Riedel, telephone interview with the author, 7 December 2016.
15. Dr Shashank Joshi, in comments to the author, September 2017.
16. 'What's behind the India-China border stand-off?', https://www.bbc.co.uk/news/world-asia-40478813, July 2017.
17. Ibid.
18. Dr Shashank Joshi, in comments to the author, September 2017.
19. 'What's being the India-China border stand-off?', http://www.bbc.co.uk/news/world-asia-40478813, July 2017.

20. *Ibid.*
21. *Ibid.*
22. 'China claims victory over India in Himalayan border row'; https://www.bbc.co.uk/news/world-asia-41070767, August 2017.
23. BRICS is a group of countries comprising Brazil, Russia, India, China. The group was meeting in Beijing and the Doklam standoff was conveniently resolved just before the summit. It avoided undue awkwardness at the event.
24. 'China claims victory over India in Himalayan border row'; https://www.bbc.co.uk/news/world-asia-41070767, August 2017.
25. The One Belt One Road initiative involves sixty-eight countries, according to CNN, http://edition.cnn.com/2017/05/11/asia/chinaone-belt-one-road-explainer/index.html May 2017.
26. https://www.forbes.com/sites/wadeshepard/2017/06/25/chinanow-has-india-wrapped-up-in-its-belt-and-road/#7664a21c227f, June 2017.
27. Bruce Riedel, *JFK'S Forgotten Crisis: Tibet, the CIA and the Sino-Indian War* (Brookings Institution, Washington D.C., 2015), p. 174.

28: Tibetan Trail

1. Tenzin Choegyal, interview with the author, Dharamsala, May 2015.
2. Ibid.
3. https://www.lionsroar.com/brothers-first/, September 2016.
4. *Ibid.*
5. *Ibid.*
6. Ibid.
7. Tenzin Choegyal, interview with the author, Dharamsala, May 2015.
8. https://www.dalailama.com/the-dalai-lama/biography-and-daily-life/aroutine-day, July 2015.
9. Jampa Phende, interview with the author, Tawang April 2017.
10. Jampa Phende, all quotes from his interview with the author, Tawang Spring, 2017.
11. Arjun Thapa, interview with the author for a news report by the author from Nepal for *The World Tonight,* BBC R4, April 2013.
12. President Jimmy Carter's main legacy work has been to set up Carter Centers around the world, often in developing countries. Nepal in one such center and has its own director.

13. President Jimmy Carter being questioned by the author for a news report by the author from Nepal for *The World Tonight*, BBC R4, April 2013.

14. Arjun Thapa, interview with the author for a news report by the author from Nepal for *The World Tonight*, BBC R4, April 2013.

15. https://audioboom.com/posts/2491868-how-china-s-growingeconomic-influence-in-nepal-affects-the-plight-of-stateless-tibetansthere

16. Arjun Thapa, interview with the author for a news report by the author from Nepal for *The World Tonight*, BBC R4, April 2013.

29: The Tibetan State

1. Mrs Namgyal Lhamo Taklha, interview with the author, Dehradun, November 2017.

2. Har Mander Singh, interview with the author, 21–22 May 2015.

3. Tenzin Choegyal, interview with the author, Kashmir Cottage, May 2015.

4. Tenzin Choegyal, interview with Lisa Katamaya, 1 September 2008, https://www.lionsroar.com/brothers-first/

5. Ibid.

6. Ibid.

7. Ibid.

8. Ibid.

9. https://www.bbc.co.uk/news/magazine-30983402

10. Ibid.

11. https://sinosphere.blogs.nytimes.com/2014/12/18/q-and-a-johnosburg-on-chinas-wealthy-turning-to-spiritualism/?_r=0, December 2018.

12. http://www.bbc.co.uk/news/magazine-30983402, January 2015.

13. Ibid.

14. http://www.reuters.com/article/us-china-politics-vacuum/xijinping-hopes-traditional-faiths-can-fill-moral-void-in-china-sourcesidUSBRE98S0GS20130929, December 2018.

15. Ibid.

16. Ibid.

17. http://in.reuters.com/article/china-tibet-xi-jinping/does-chinas-nextleader-have-a-soft-spot-for-tibet-idINDEE88002I20120901, December 2018.

18. Ibid.

30: Influences

1. Har Mander Singh, interview with the author, 21–22 May 2015.
2. Ibid.
3. Ibid.
4. Losel Nyinje Charitable Society & Monyul Social Welfare Association, *The Crossing of the Frontier* (Losel Nyinje Charitable Society, Tawang, 2017), Chapter 7.
5. Ibid.
6. Har Mander Singh, email interview with the author, June 2017.

ACKNOWLEDGEMENTS

No book of this nature could have been achieved without a great deal of cooperation and support from a host of people.

There are some key figures who have been with me since its inception; one of whom was responsible for getting me to create this book and its offshoots.

Her name is Brenda Elvin. She has been a therapeutic friend and rare print artist for decades and is responsible for helping me to keep this project moving, for structuring the story arc and narrative with patience, logic, coloured paper and markers in her treatment room in west London. Once a week, I would visit her. She would break the story down structurally and dramatically during the manuscript's first draft.

At crisis times in my life, Brenda takes time out to be there for me and support me, and she has done that for decades right into 2019. She says that she supports those she can see helping themselves.

Another loyal person who works quietly in the background for me is my former Lloyd's List editor, James Brewer, who has always edited my book manuscripts, articles and BBC scripts at speed before they go to the commissioning editors whenever I needed him to. After the book was commissioned, he read and edited every chapter before it ever got to the Penguin Random House editor.

One day, director Toral Dixit, whom I did not then know, followed me round Wilkinson's, listening in to me telling a friend about the book. She was the first to try to develop the story for another medium.

Nick Fox is part of the team that manages the Branson Family interests and investments. He has oversight of communications, content and corporate relations. He is responsible for having this book commissioned by Virgin Books India. He had the vision to make sure the story was told in print and the generosity to make it happen. Nick also kindly commissioned the recording of my critical first, main narrative interviews with the Dalai Lama and Har Mander Singh. He gave me that recording and the transcriptions as a gift. I will always be grateful to him for this.

In order to write my manuscript, I needed to cross check the transcription with what had been filmed and over many weeks talented filmmaker, Rahoul Ved Aggarwal, enabled this at his London home studio. Rahoul was commissioned to work with me by Dr Amarjit Singh Khambay and Dr Parvin Kapoor of the Sterling Dental Foundation. He also created various short promo trailers for the story.

Ambassador M.P. Singh, then head of Special Projects and Protocol at the Indian High Commission in London until 2017, was a supportive guide. As Protocol Officer, he interacts with the Dalai Lama and other world leaders. M.P. sent a message to his Dharamsala counterpart before my first visit there.

During the writing of the last two and a half weeks of the full editorial manuscript in April 2018, my sons, Jai and Sukh, spent some time with me while I was staying with the Laven family in Walton upon Thames, Surrey. It was a countryside retreat where I could concentrate on the book, away from the domesticity of my own home in London.

My sons came to me every day. They helped me untangle and rewrite some of the most complex chapters, helping me with technological issues too. May God bless them. They have been faithfully serving me their whole lives; becoming caring men ahead of their time, even as children.

Vicky Kemble helped with regular calls for a while.

Sybren Kramer became my Accountability Coach, Face Timing me nearly every day for a period to help me structure my tasks.

Sophie Cridland was my main support through 2018–19. During these years, I experienced disturbing personal turbulence. Single-handedly, she made sure my work got done by devotedly working with me. The final editorial manuscript would not have been finished if not for Sophie. Her editing and organizing skills are brilliant.

In the book's final two to three months, Matteo, Teodora, Raquel and Niamh came on board.

Sujit Nair, Fellow of the Royal Society of Arts and Chairman of the Europe India Centre for Business and Industry, introduced me to Mike Knowles, then Dean of Sushant School of Design, who introduced me to architect M.N. Ashish Ganju. Mike represented me with Random House India and Ashish was the one who arranged my first interview with the Dalai Lama. After months of waiting for an interview, Ashish asked me to forward my original letter requests on to his special contact, the Dalai Lama's brother, Rinpoche Tenzin Choegyal. Within days, I had been granted an interview date barely a month away with His Holiness the Dalai Lama as well as apologies for the delay.

My cousin, Jeeti Sindhu, and his wife, Harpreet Sindhu, are gracious hosts and support when I and my sons need to stay in New Delhi. Jeeti is a great adviser and technical support for me. Dr Mohinder Singh also provided hospitality at his National Institute of Punjab Studies.

Har Mander Singh was encouraged by his sons, Raj Mander and Harsh Mander. Raj Mander was present at all sittings, answered supplementaries, checked my copy, and dramatically brought the black and white photos to life.

I am grateful to the Dalai Lama for talking to me and for always answering my questions wherever I appeared, whether in Delhi,

Dharmsala or Tawang. I am also grateful to his brother, Rinpoche Tenzin Choegyal, and Tenzin's wife, Mrs Rinchen Khando Choegyal. They were great interviewees, great hosts, and great supports.

Among the Dalai Lama's staff, Tempa Tsering, Representative in Delhi, and Tenzin Taklha, Private Secretary, were helpful. Tempa La always gives me time whenever I meet him. Thubten Samdup, Former Representative of the Dalai Lama for Northern Europe, was encouraging and gave an endorsement. Mrs Namgyal Lhamo, author and sister-in-law to the Dalai Lama, checked and amended relevant chapters too and endorsed the copy.

Thubten Samphel, former Director of Tibet Policy at the International and Information Office, read and corrected the Prologue and first fourteen chapters for the Tibetan side, and Philippa Russell checked the remaining fifteen to thirty. Philippa is not only the respected Construction Manager at the Tibetan Nuns Project, she is also an environmental advocate and managed a rural health centre.

Shashank Joshi, the *Economist*'s defence editor and former Senior Research Fellow at the Royal United Services Institute, graciously read, corrected, and made comments on Chapter 27. He also examined an early chapter for me.

Squadron Leader Amir Khan MSt J, MSc, BA(Hons), Special Engagement Teams (North), supported me all the way through the book, unlocking for me the inner workings of a military mind. Having spent time in theatre with the RAF, he was always available day or night to explain the strategy Har Mander Singh would have deployed and what the mission challenges would have been. Squadron Leader Khan has kindly facilitated location shooting at an RAF base in the UK, and I do hope to be able to record with him one day.

Bruce Riedel, senior fellow in the Saban Center for Middle East Policy at the Brookings Institution, interviewed, was a support and cheerfully checked his chapters too.

When I was going to Dharamsala for the book, Dr Kartar Lalvani gave me special assistance and later asked his Mumbai team to help me through Rohit Shelatkar.

Gurpal Oppal, immigration lawyer, also unhesitatingly supported my trip to Arunachal Pradesh.

Naynesh Desai, Consultant Solicitor at Chan Neill, has been a guardian of the book and multi-media aspects to do with the Dalai Lama project.

Jo Sawicki has been a moral support.

Manoj Nair, founder and CEO of RedGirraffe.com, connected with his batchmates in the Indian Civil Service for my Arunachal visit. They are Suvasish Das IAS, Surabhi Rai IFoS, Dr Abdul Quayum, DCF Indian Forest Service, Pawan Agrahari IAS Forest DFO Officer, Tasso Sira, Adong Moyong Res. Tourism Officer, Arunachal Bhavan.

Dr Quayum was a friendly hub officer for me in Tawang, and he introduced me to the hospitable Lt Col Prerit Rawat, Officer Commanding 117 RCC Mangnam who hosted me at Lumla and in Tawang. Lt Col Rawat also gave me his deputy to work with and arranged part of my family's Dehradun stay through his colleague, Col. Atreya.

My nephew, Commander Tarandeep Bakshi, liaised with Adong Moyong on my behalf.

Captain Pawanexh Kohli is the CEO and Chief Adviser to India's NCCD.

He facilitated my visit to Arunachal, first with Tage Tatung, MD Arunachal Horticultural and Food Processing Board. It was through Pawanexh and Tage that I met Koncho Gyatso, Horticultural Development Officer, who proved invaluable on the ground. Pawanexh also facilitated my panel appearance at the Dehradun Literature Festival at the kind invitation of hosts Mr and Mrs Sanjeev Chopra.

Jabaakhi Borthakur, one of Doordarshan TV's most respected anchors, singlehandedly arranged my helicopter travel to Arunachal by researching the flights, liaising with the hard to reach manager, and also spoke to the District Commissioner in Tawang for me.

The Chief Minister of Arunachal Pradesh, Pema Khandu, welcomed me during my stay and invited me to the opening of a museum dedicated to his late father, Dorjee Khandu, being performed by the Dalai Lama.

Mrs Dorjee Khandu, wife of late Chief Minister Dorjee Khandu, and her daughter, Tenzin Dekey, hosted me for a number of days. The *Asian Voice*'s C.B. Patel and Rupanjana Dutta kindly gave me a sabbatical to write this book.

In New Delhi, Jawed Habib and his manager, Susheil, always help me prepare and recover from research trips.

Anyone who has not been mentioned will, I hope, forgive me for the omission.